DUBLIN
Like a Local

BY THE PEOPLE WHO CALL IT HOME

DUBLIN
Like a Local

BY THE PEOPLE WHO CALL IT HOME

Contents

EAT

DRINK

SHOP

ARTS & CULTURE

meet the locals

NICOLA BRADY

Hailing from Sussex, Nicola has lived in Ireland since 2006 – and in dreamy Dublin from 2016. As a travel writer, she explores the length and breadth of Ireland, eating as much as is humanly possible along the way. When she's not scoping out top foodie spots, she's trawling charity shops and strolling Dublin's Georgian streets.

ÉADAOIN FITZMAURICE

Éadaoin's love affair with Dublin started in 2012, when she moved up for college from Arklow, Co. Wicklow. A social media coordinator by day, Éadaoin spends any spare time she has sampling (and drooling over) the city's tastiest grub, braving the Irish sea with a swim and getting cosy in traditional pubs with her mates – before posting it all on Instagram.

Dublin

WELCOME TO THE CITY

There are two kinds of Dubliner – those who were born here, and those who choose to be here. The common denominator? A fierce feeling of loyalty and pride, as well as a wicked sense of humour. This is a place where everyone you meet wants to stop and chat, whether you're popping to the shop or nipping out for a coffee. It's also a place that's had more than its fair share of hard times, but new ideas abound when times are tough – after all, the 2008 recession kick-started some of the most innovative cafés and bars that still thrive to this day.

If ever there were a city that could charm your socks off, it's Dublin. There's a palpable sense of charisma to the place that ensnares anyone who visits – a cheeky sense of "divilment" that makes you feel like an adventure is always just around the corner. And the city's compact size makes it all the easier to explore, as you amble past Georgian townhouses and Gothic redbrick markets, weaving between shouted conversations in the street and spontaneous calls for a sneaky pint.

In a city so small, it can be hard to spot the decent places amid the tourist traps. But that's where this book comes in. We know the places that Dubliners love, from the brunch spots they'll wait all week for to the underground venues for life-changing gigs. When it comes to the weekend, Dubliners aren't visiting the Guinness Storehouse: they're hopping between the best vintage boutiques and indie galleries and plotting where to get their fix of Korean fried chicken or poitín cocktails.

Whether you're already a Dubliner looking to unearth your city's secrets, or you're keen to discover a side that you won't find in traditional guidebooks, this book will help you to embrace the city with the wild sense of mischief that's woven into its very heart. Enjoy Dublin, but do it the local way.

Liked by the locals

"Dublin may look like a city, but it's got the heart of a village. And that's what I love about it – everything is right at your fingertips, and you never know what the day will bring."

NICOLA BRADY, TRAVEL WRITER

From mass street parties in the summer to festive markets in the winter, there's a cause for celebration with the dawn of each new season in Dublin.

Dublin
THROUGH THE YEAR

SPRING

ST PATRICK'S DAY
After a brittle winter, it's only right that the mother of all parties kicks off spring. This national holiday brings high spirits (well, it's a day off work), and sees locals enjoy the parade, crowd the streets in green hats and mingle with a pint in the pub.

FEELING SPORTY
Spring is sport season, with the Irish rugby team starting its Six Nations campaign and various GAA events in the home of Gaelic sport, Croke Park.

PARK PICNICS
Seduced by the rises in temperature in April, youngsters flock to the city's parks with picnic baskets in tow. They enjoy the longer evenings (known locally as the "grand old stretch"), catching up with friends on the grassy fields.

SUMMER

FESTIVAL FROLICS
Nothing defines Dublin's convivial nature like its summer festival season. Pride sees a riot of colour, Forbidden Fruit puts on the biggest music party, Vodafone Comedy Festival brings the craic and The Big Grill provides tasty BBQ treats.

SEA SWIMS
You're not a proper Dub until you've leapt into the bracing waters of the Irish Sea come summer. Teenagers jump in at the Forty Foot in Sandycove to

celebrate the end of exams while hardy swimmers (some even in the nude) brave Hawk Cliff in Dalkey.

OUTDOOR CINEMAS
Free open-air cinemas spring up across the city as soon as balmy nights hit. Locals spread out on blankets and enjoy classic films with a bite to eat (courtesy of tempting food trucks) in popular Merrion Square.

FLEA MARKETS GALORE
Antique lovers and fashionistas hit the flea markets that begin to pop up at the start of June, from the Dublin Flea on Thomas Street to the sustainable fashion fairs in The Well.

AUTUMN
FIRESIDE PINTS
When the nights draw in and the rain pours, the pubs light their turf fires and locals cosy up by the hearth with a pint.

CULTURAL TOURS
September sees Dubliners head indoors for a dose of culture. Theatre lovers head to both big venues and tiny pop-ups to see new plays courtesy of Dublin Theatre Festival and Fringe, while the curious are drawn to Culture Night for free gigs and literary events.

HALLOWEEN HAPPENINGS
Dubliners go all out for Ireland's most ancient festival. They dress up for themed nights out, enjoy theatrical parades and celebrate with spooky readings at the Bram Stoker Festival.

WINTER
FESTIVE LIGHTS
Light displays mark the start of the Christmas season across the city. Workers walk over illuminated bridges on the way home while families admire the projections covering iconic buildings.

WEEKEND MARKETS
Wrapped-up locals swarm to markets to pick up locally made gifts – high-end at the RDS Irish Design Fair and funky at the Dandelion Christmas Market.

NEW YEAR'S EVE
Dubliners ring in the new year with a knees-up: at the countdown concert, with a singalong in their local boozer or with family and friends at home.

There's an art to being a Dubliner, from the dos and don'ts in the pub to negotiating the city's medieval streets. Here's a breakdown of all you need to know.

Dublin
KNOW-HOW

For a directory of health and safety resources, safe spaces and accessibility information, turn to page 186. For everything else, read on.

EAT

Dubliners rarely eat breakfast out, so it's unusual for cafés to open before 9:30am. As for brunch? They can't get enough of it, and cafés start to buzz from around 11am – if you arrive any later, prepare to wait for a table. Dinner, eaten around 7:30 or 8pm, is the biggest meal of the day and reservations go quickly, so book ahead. Vegan? Mention this when you book (unless, of course, it's a vegan spot).

DRINK

Pub culture is big business. After-work beers are common, but Dubliners tend to save the serious session for after dinner. The culture of a "round" – buying drinks for your group, which each person reciprocates – is an unspoken rule. If you need an extra seat to accommodate your party and see a spare stool, don't just take it – ask the people on that table first.

Last call for bevs is 11:30pm Monday to Thursday, 12:30am on Friday and Saturday, and 11pm on Sundays, always with a half-hour "drinking-up time". Don't expect happy hours (they're illegal in Ireland); do expect some tourist pubs in Temple Bar to sneakily raise prices after 11pm.

SHOP

Shops – particularly boutiques – open a little later, at around 10 or 11am. On Sundays, smaller shops are either closed or only open for the afternoon. Consider supporting the city's time-honoured independent businesses as much as possible (a friendly natter with shop owners is reason enough to). It's worth carrying a tote bag around to avoid the charge for a plastic one.

ARTS & CULTURE

Dublin's larger museums and galleries are, delightfully, free to enter, whatever your age. The exceptions are smaller, private museums, which usually cost around €10. There's rarely a need to book for any museums. Theatre tickets are usually pretty reasonable, particularly in festival season, and it's a very casual scene, so there's no need to dress up.

NIGHTLIFE

Dublin isn't a cheap city to drink in, so unless they've booked a gig or comedy show, most locals have "pre-drinks" at home before heading out around 10pm. The craic usually ends up at the clubs, which tend to open until 3:30am. Thursday, Friday and Saturday are the big nights, with students taking the lead on Wednesdays. Oh, and Dubliners love to get dressed up for a night out.

OUTDOORS

When the sun shines, Dubliners enjoy their picnics in the park or beers by the canal (taking a "bag of cans" to the waterside is a tradition). Though it may not seem the case when you see what some people leave behind, there are fines for littering – €150 on the spot – so don't contribute to it. Be careful around the canals, as the banks aren't protected and the paths are narrow.

Keep in mind

Here are some more tips and tidbits that will help you fit in like a local.

» **Card vs cash** The majority of places accept contactless payments, but it's always worth keeping some cash on you.

» **No smoking** There's a ban on smoking inside public places (bars, cafés, you name it), and a fine for dropping cigarette butts outside.

» **Tip if you'd like** It's polite to tip waiters and table-service bartenders (around 10 per cent), but it's not expected.

» **Stay hydrated** Plenty of cafés and restaurants are happy to refill your water bottle – just ask nicely.

GETTING AROUND

Dublin is made up of a series of tiny neighbourhoods (p14), each with their own distinct character, and its relatively compact size makes it easy to get around. Broadly speaking, the city is divided into the Northside and the Southside, depending on whether you're north or south of the River Liffey, which cuts right through the centre of Dublin. Neighbourhoods and streets are grouped within postal district numbers, such as Dublin 2 (which encompasses the likes of Temple Bar and Grafton Street), and some locals and businesses still refer to these districts when giving directions.

To make your life easier we've provided what3words addresses for each sight in this book, meaning you can quickly pinpoint exactly where you're heading with ease.

On foot

In a city as perfectly small as Dublin, walking is by far the best way to see it in all its glory – and you'll be helping the environment (and avoiding the brutal Dublin traffic) as you stroll. Having said this, Dubliners walk quickly, so don't dither around on the pavement, particularly on narrow streets (of which there are many). If you do need to stop

and check a what3words location, step to the side, out of the way. The pedestrian crossings don't stay on green for very long, so don't dawdle when you're crossing the road, either.

On wheels

Dublin is getting better when it comes to cycling, with over 193 km (120 miles) of lanes that take you from one side to the other in just 30 minutes. Hitting the centre on two wheels can be a little daunting, as drivers aren't the friendliest around cyclists, so stick to the city's bike lanes, be very cautious around buses, never go through a red light (you'll be fined) and always wear a helmet.

Many Dubliners rely on the 24-hour bike-share scheme Dublinbikes. There are 115 docking stations throughout the city, and you'll find a map on the main website. It's a cinch to join up, and a bargain once you have, at €3.50 for one day. You can also buy a three-day subscription for €5 (the first half hour is always free), but only a few terminals enable you to purchase this ticket. You'll need a debit or credit card to register.

Note that the legal drink-drive limit (50 mg of alcohol per 100 ml of blood, equivalent to a small glass of wine or a pint of regular-strength lager) also applies for cyclists. If you're planning a trip to the pub, or you're done for the day, check the bike back in at any station by the close of the allotted time. *www.dublinbikes.ie*

By public transport

If your feet get tired from walking or you require public transport, you can choose from the bus, the Luas (tram) or the DART (rapid transit trains that go along the coast). The easiest way to pay for tickets is with a Leap Visitor Card (you can't yet use contactless), which you can buy online or at the airport. When you board a bus, tell the driver where you're going and tap in; on the Luas or the DART tap in on departure then out when you reach your stop. *www.about.leapcard.ie*

By car or taxi

Dublin's traffic can be exhausting, so only drive if you must. If you want to drive to the coast or mountains, sign up to the car-sharing firm Go Car and rent a car from the fleet parked around the city.

The city's registered cabs are signed up to Free Now, the taxi-hailing app. Dubliners love to moan about it (thanks to its frequent name changes and patchy mapping skills), but it's the easiest way to get a cab in the city. *www.gocar.ie*

Download these

We recommend you download these apps to help you get about the city.

WHAT3WORDS
Your geocoding friend

A what3words address is a simple way to communicate any precise location on earth, using just three words. ///wallet.relate.cherry, for example, is the code for Dublin's iconic café Bewley's. Simply download the free what3words app, type a what3words address into the search bar, and you'll know exactly where to go.

TFI REAL TIME
Your local transport service

The app from Transport for Ireland lays out all your best options for moving around the city, as well as live departures and delay information for each stop. It's a great source for checking when the last train or bus is, too, so you don't miss either.

*Dublin feels more like a collection of little villages,
each neighbourhood with its own distinct vibe.
Here we take a look at some of our favourites.*

Dublin
NEIGHBOURHOODS

Ballsbridge
Tree-lined avenues, grand townhouses and world-class rugby clubs: it's no wonder this quiet suburb has been attracting Dublin's elite since the 19th century. {map 5}

City Centre
When locals refer to "town", they mean this small patch between Grafton and Kildare streets. No one lives here, but everyone and their uncle pass through – mostly students at Trinity College. {map 2}

Creative Quarter
It's in the name, really. This quirky area draws arty locals like moths to a flame with its time-honoured stalls in George's Street Arcade and design boutiques. {map 2}

Docklands
Known as the "Silicon Docks", this tech hub is where Google and Meta headquarters lie. The heartland for media types, it teems with bougie bars and music joints. {map 5}

Drumcondra
Cheap eats, low-key pubs and a lively vibe – especially when matches play at Croke Park – are all that's needed to tempt young professionals and students to put down roots in this up-and-coming area. {map 3}

Dún Laoghaire
When families and couples want to escape the centre, they retreat to this seaside town. Aside from its buzzing pier, it's also famed for its lush park and adjoining market – the perfect combo for scenic picnics. {map 6}

Glasnevin
Dominated by the cemetery and Botanic Gardens, this residential area is as quiet as they come, so it's easy to see why families and senior citizens call it home. {map 6}

Howth
Sorry, Dún Laoghaire: you've got competition. This cutesy fishing village is loved for its hiking trails, market and Dublin's – heck, even Ireland's – best seafood joints. {map 6}

The Liberties
Old meets new here, where breweries and distilleries hark back to a centre of industry

(Guinness Storehouse, we're looking at you) and indie cafés line medieval streets. Historic yet innovative, the area is a taste of characterful and diverse Dublin. {map 4}

Merrion Square

Oscar Wilde once lived here, so it's pretty fancy. Based around the gardens of the same name, this small area is lined with Georgian houses, chichi restaurants and elite museums. Oh, and expect chic locals to match. {map 5}

North City

Literally meaning north of the Liffey, North City has a rep for being a little rough around the edges. But no one cares when they're watching a top-notch theatre show or folk band play in this lively district. {map 3}

Phibsborough

Thanks to youngsters making the most of cheaper rents, Phibsborough is on the up. Trendy and vibrant, it's awash with arty brunch spots and indie bookstores, but its real edge is having a community spirit like no other. {map 3}

Portobello

It's okay to boast if you live here – everyone wants to. Close to the centre yet with a village vibe, Portobello is loved for its top foodie spots and canal – the place to be on a balmy night. {map 4}

Ranelagh

Move over, Ballsbridge – Ranelagh is Dublin's new exclusive address. Largely home to the high-earning (it's a spenny place to be), Ranelagh is an area of yoga studios, health stores and – surprisingly – fab street art. {map 5}

Rathmines

Filled with Dublin's young professionals thanks to its easy access to the centre, Rathmines has everything youngsters want: buzzy pubs, hip charity shops, cool art galleries. {map 5}

Sandymount

You can hardly move for pushchairs in this cute village by the sea, where families spend days on the beach and kids play on the little green at its centre. {map 6}

Smithfield

Formerly a warehouse district, Smithfield has seen a revival of late thanks to a thriving arts scene. There's always something on: an indie film, a crafts market, a buzzy street festival. {map 3}

St Stephen's Green

This grand old park is so beloved by Dubliners, it's basically a neighbourhood. Flanked with cute shops and restaurants, it draws crowds on sunny days. {map 2}

Stoneybatter

Once run-down, this area has seen gentrification of late, but has sworn in loyal (read: hipster) locals as a result. If you meet a bearded Dub who loves craft beer, rest assured he lives in this free-spirited district. {map 3}

Temple Bar

No proper Dubliner would be seen dead in the touristy pubs here, but it's not all rowdy nightlife. Tempting locals to brave Dublin's Times Square are top vintage stores and galleries. {map 1}

Dublin
ON THE MAP

*Whether you're looking for your
new favourite spot or want to check
out what each part of Dublin has
to offer, our maps – along with
handy map references throughout
the book – have you covered.*

6

BLANCHARDSTOWN

CASTLEKNOCK

Liffey

PALMERSTON

Phoeni
Park

BALLYFERMOT

CLONDALKIN

NEWCASTLE

TALLAGHT

RATHCOOLE

KILL

0 kilometres   3

0 miles   3

NORTH
CITY

ORMOND QUAY LOWER

ORMOND QUAY UPPER

ORMOND QUAY

Grattan
Bridge

River Liffey

Millennium
Bridge

QUAY

WELLINGTON

Temple Bar Gallery
+ Studios

The Workman's Club

ESSEX QUAY

Dollard Market

DiFontaine's
Pizzeria

ESSEX ST EAST

TEMPLE BAR

Indigo & Cloth

Smock Alley Theatre

Scout

ESSEX STREET WEST

Gutter
Bookshop

Piglet

Project Arts Centre

The New Theatre

Zaytoon

Street 66

PARLIAMENT ST

Photo
Museum Ireland

Temple Bar
Book Market

Nine
Crow

Irish Film Institute

EUSTACE ST

TEMPLE LANE SOUTH

Olympia
Theatre

DAME STREET

Spar

Dublin
City Hall

LORD EDWARD STREET

FISHAMBLE STREET

DAME LANE

The George

Izakaya
Baseme

Bull and Castle

Christ Church
Cathedral

WERBURGH STREET

Dublin
Castle

Dubh Linn
Garden

Pi Pizza

SOUTH GREAT GEORGE'S STREET

Ukiyo

Chester Beatty Library

STEPHEN STREET UPPER

STEPHEN STREET LOWER

Chimac

Uno Mas

AUNGIER STREET

GOLDEN LANE

0 metres   100
0 yards   100

MAP 1

Ha'penny
Bridge

1

EMPLE
BAR
a Vintage

Vintage
Cocktail Club

cy's
unge

Seafood   Fresh
Temple Bar

RAL BANK
PLAZA
DAME   STREET

AME LANE
he Comedy Crunch

Fallon & Byrne

CREATIVE
QUARTER

ING ST SOUTH

E EAT

Bull and Castle *(p36)*
Chimac *(p47)*
Pi Pizza *(p45)*
The Seafood Café *(p48)*
Uno Mas *(p43)*

D DRINK

Piglet *(p67)*
Street 66 *(p60)*
Vintage Cocktail Club *(p62)*

S SHOP

Fallon & Byrne *(p94)*
Fresh Temple Bar *(p84)*
Gutter Bookshop *(p100)*
Indigo & Cloth *(p89)*
Lucy's Lounge *(p85)*
Nine Crows *(p84)*
Scout *(p97)*
Temple Bar Book Market *(p101)*
Tola Vintage *(p85)*

A ARTS & CULTURE

Chester Beatty Library *(p114)*
Christ Church Cathedral *(p109)*
Photo Museum Ireland *(p119)*

Irish Film Institute *(p124)*
The New Theatre *(p120)*
Olympia Theatre *(p120)*
Project Arts Centre *(p129)*
Smock Alley Theatre *(p123)*
Temple Bar Gallery +
    Studios *(p118)*

N NIGHTLIFE

The Comedy Crunch *(p144)*
DiFontaine's Pizzeria *(p152)*
Dollard Market *(p153)*
The George *(p151)*
Izakaya Basement *(p137)*
Spar *(p155)*
Ukiyo *(p149)*
The Workman's Club *(p143)*
Zaytoon *(p154)*

O OUTDOORS

Ha'penny Bridge *(p179)*

SUFFOLK STREET

S Avoca

GREAT GEORGE'S ST

EXCHEQUER STREET **A**

Irish Design Shop **S**

Dublin Comedy Improv **N**

WICKLOW STREET

Tapped **D**

Hang Tough Contemporary
Kaph **D** **S** Industry & Co

Siopaella **S**

N Mother

Loose Canon Cheese & Wine **D**

SOUTH

Om Diva **S**

S Costume

Farrier and Draper **D**

STREET SOUTH

Fresh Cuts **S**

Grogan's **D** **S** Chupi
N **S** Article
Pygmalion

STREET

Asia Market **S**

Ulysses Rare Books **S**

Hogans **D**

D

The Bar with No Name

Drury **D** Buildings

WILLIAM STREET

CLARENDON STREET

D

STREET

The Long Hall

Sass Mouth
A Dames Film **D** Clement
A Club **D** & Pekoe

Bunsen **E**

Sheridans Cheesemonger

Amy Austin **D**

Brooks Private Cinema

GRAFTON STREET

Kehoe's **D**

S

CREATIVE QUARTER

S A Store is Born

Maneki **●**

STREET

E Glas

CHATHAM STREET

CITY CENTRE

DRURY STREET

AUNGIER STREET

KING STREET SOUTH

Peruke & Periwig **D**

9 Below **D**

MERCER STREET LOWER

ST STEPHEN'S GREEN NORTH

The Little Museum of Dublin

D The Swan Bar

YORK STREET

ST STEPHEN'S GREEN WEST

YORK STREET

O St Stephen's Green

D Network

St Stephen's Green

0 metres   100
0 yards   100

MAP 2

Trinity College

2

Douglas Hyde Ⓐ

NASSAU STREET

● Hodges Figgis

eatherblade

Ⓔ EAT

Bunsen *(p46)*
Featherblade *(p41)*
Glas *(p40)*

Ⓓ DRINK

9 Below *(p76)*
Amy Austin *(p66)*
The Bar With No Name *(p61)*
Clement & Pekoe *(p75)*
Drury Buildings *(p69)*
Farrier and Draper *(p78)*
Grogan's *(p71)*
Hogans *(p59)*
Kaph *(p75)*
Kehoe's *(p56)*
The Long Hall *(p56)*
Loose Canon
    Cheese & Wine *(p65)*
Network *(p73)*
Peruke & Periwig *(p62)*
The Swan Bar *(p59)*
Tapped *(p78)*

Ⓢ SHOP

Asia Market *(p94)*
Article *(p96)*
Avoca *(p99)*
Chupi *(p96)*

Costume *(p90)*
Fresh Cuts *(p88)*
Hodges Figgis *(p102)*
Industry & Co *(p99)*
Irish Design Shop *(p98)*
Om Diva *(p90)*
Sheridans Cheesemongers *(p94)*
Siopaella *(p86)*
A Store is Born *(p86)*
Ulysses Rare Books *(p102)*

Ⓐ ARTS & CULTURE

Brooks Private Cinema *(p127)*
Douglas Hyde *(p116)*
Hang Tough Contemporary *(p118)*
The Little Museum
    of Dublin *(p112)*
Sass Mouth Dames Film Club *(p126)*

Ⓝ NIGHTLIFE

Dublin Comedy Improv *(p146)*
Maneki *(p148)*
Mother *(p139)*
Pygmalion *(p139)*

Ⓞ OUTDOORS

St Stephen's Green *(p160)*

0 metres 300
0 yards 300

Royal Canal

WHITWORTH ROAD

PHIBSBOROUGH ROAD

CABRA ROAD

E Two Boys Brew

NORTH CIRCULAR ROAD

PHIBSBOROUGH

NORTH CIRCULAR ROAD

PHIBSBOROUGH ROAD

DORSET STREET LO

O Blessington Street Basin

Chapter One **E**
Irish Writers' Centre
The Hugh Lane **A**

GRANGEGORMAN

GRANGEGORMAN LOWER

CONSTITUTION HILL

King's Inns Park

PARNELL SQUARE

14 Henrietta **A**
Street

BOLTON STREET

PARNELL STREET

MANOR ST STONEYBATTER

D L. Mulligan Grocer

STONEY-BATTER

The Cobblestone **A**

NORTH KING STREET

Cineworld **A** **N** Woolshed Baa and Grill

NORTH CITY

Namaste **N** India

BLACKHALL PLACE

QUEEN ST

SMITHFIELD

Lilliput **S** Stores

Bar 1661 **D**

D The Virgin Mary MARY STRE

Secret **A** Street Tours

Light House **A** Cinema

N Marrakesh

Arran Street East **S**

MARY'S LANE

CAPEL STREET

UPPER ABBEY ST

Wig

Mob Theatre **S**

The Grand **N** Social

Token **E** **D** Proper Order

CHURCH STREET

Fish Shop **E**

SMITHFIELD

CHANCERY STREET

Brother **E** Hubbard

N Pantibar

S
The Wir Stair

Mellows Bridge

ARRAN QUAY

Liffey

ORMOND QUAY

Grattan Bridge

TEMPL BAR

Father Mathew Bridge

Mountjoy
Square

E 147 Deli

he Gate

A Savoy Cinema

O'CONNELL ST UPPER

MARLBOROUGH STREET

O'CONNELL ST LOWER

The
Academy

O
River
Liffey

ffey

PDINER ST UPPER

E EAT

147 Deli (p47)
Brother Hubbard (p35)
Chapter One (p40)
Fish Shop (p49)
Token (p44)
Two Boys Brew (p32)

D DRINK

Bar 1661 (p62)
L. Mulligan Grocer (p78)
Proper Order (p75)
The Virgin Mary (p60)

S SHOP

Arran Street East (p98)
Lilliput Stores (p92)
The Winding Stair (p103)

A ARTS & CULTURE

14 Henrietta Street (p115)
Cineworld (p125)
The Cobblestone (p129)
The Gate (p123)
The Hugh Lane (p119)
Irish Writers' Centre (p128)
Light House Cinema (p125)
Savoy Cinema (p126)
Secret Street Tours (p108)

N NIGHTLIFE

The Academy (p142)
The Grand Social (p140)
Marrakesh (p149)
Mob Theatre (p145)
Namaste India (p152)
Pantibar (p137)
Wigwam (p151)
Woolshed Baa and Grill (p148)

O OUTDOORS

Blessington Street Basin (p169)
River Liffey (p170)

River Liffey
Mellows Bridge
ARRAN QUAY
USHER'S QUAY
Father Mathew Bridge
ORMOND QUAY UPPER
River Li
ESSEX QUAY

DAME STREET

BRIDGEFOOT STREET

THOMAS STREET
HIGH STREET
Christ Church Cathedral
Dublin Castle

Vicar Street **N** **E** Variety Jones

PATRICK STREET

St Patrick's Park

MARROWBONE LANE

Marrowbone Books **S**
LIBERTIES
Two Pups Coffee **E** **S**
Space Out Sister **O** St Patrick's Cathedral
A Marsh's Library
Fallons **D**
KEVIN STREET LOWER

CORK STREET

NEW STREET SOUTH

Aloft Dublin City Open Terrace **O**
Opie

Cherry Comedy **N**

DONORE AVENUE

The Fumbally **E**
Whel
McGuinness Traditional Take Awa

The Cake Café **E**
Last Booksho

CLANBRASSIL STREET LOWER

The Wine Pair **D**
PORTOBELL

Alma **E** STREET

57 The Headline **E**
HARRINGTON

Clanbrassil House **E**
CLANBRASSIL ST UPPER

Brindle Coffee & Wine **D**

SOUTH CIRCULAR ROAD

Irish Jewish Museum **A**

Grand Canal, Portobello

Locks Restaurant **E**

Grand Canal
PARNELL ROAD
GROVE ROAD

0 metres 300
0 yards 300

MAP 4

Millennium
Bridge

TEMPLE
BAR

4

CREATIVE
QUARTER

St Stephen's
Green -

IFFE ST

N Dicey's Garden
Anseo Comedy Club
Anseo
Listons Food Store

Pickle

Iveagh
Gardens

Mad Egg

HARCOURT   ROAD

E EAT

57 The Headline *(p38)*
Alma *(p33)*
The Cake Café *(p34)*
Clanbrassil House *(p41)*
The Fumbally *(p34)*
Locks Restaurant *(p42)*
Mad Egg *(p45)*
Pickle *(p43)*
Two Pups Coffee *(p32)*
Variety Jones *(p43)*

D DRINK

Brindle Coffee & Wine *(p65)*
Fallons *(p57)*
The Wine Pair *(p66)*

S SHOP

Last Bookshop *(p101)*
Listons Food Store *(p92)*
Marrowbone Books *(p100)*
Space Out Sister *(p91)*

A ARTS & CULTURE

Irish Jewish Museum *(p113)*
Marsh's Library *(p111)*

N NIGHTLIFE

Anseo *(p142)*
Anseo Comedy Club *(p146)*
Cherry Comedy *(p146)*
Dicey's Garden *(p136)*
Opium *(p139)*
McGuinness Traditional
    Take Away *(p155)*
Vicar Street *(p142)*
Whelan's *(p141)*

O OUTDOORS

Aloft Dublin City Open
    Terrace *(p178)*
Grand Canal, Portobello *(p169)*
St Patrick's Cathedral *(p176)*

MAP 5

5

E EAT

Angelina's *(p33)*

The Butcher Grill *(p36)*

The Exchequer *(p38)*

The Old Spot *(p37)*

Meltdown *(p46)*

Póg *(p35)*

D DRINK

3fe *(p72)*

Library Street *(p66)*

The Barge *(p68)*

Blackbird *(p71)*

Ely Wine Bar *(p67)*

The Horseshoe Bar *(p77)*

House *(p71)*

The Palace Bar *(p57)*

Pavilion Bar *(p69)*

Searsons *(p76)*

Toners *(p68)*

Two Fifty Square *(p73)*

S SHOP

April and the Bear *(p97)*

Bow & Pearl *(p89)*

The Company of Books *(p103)*

Morton's *(p93)*

A ARTS & CULTURE

Abbey Theatre *(p121)*

Atelier Now *(p117)*

EPIC The Irish
Emigration Museum *(p108)*

The Lir *(p123)*

Museum of Literature
Ireland *(p114)*

National Gallery of Ireland *(p117)*

National Museum of Ireland –
Archaeology *(p113)*

National Museum of Ireland –
Natural History *(p115)*

Omniplex *(p127)*

Stella Cinema *(p124)*

Sweny's Pharmacy *(p130)*

The Tara Building *(p130)*

Windmill Lane Recording
Studios *(p112)*

N NIGHTLIFE

Laughter Lounge *(p144)*

Ruby Sessions *(p143)*

The Sugar Club *(p140)*

Xico *(p136)*

O OUTDOORS

Cycle the Docklands *(p183)*

Dartmouth Square Park *(p161)*

Grand Canal, Docklands *(p170)*

Iveagh Gardens *(p160)*

Kayaking on the River Liffey *(p183)*

Merrion Square Park *(p163)*

Samuel Beckett Bridge *(p177)*

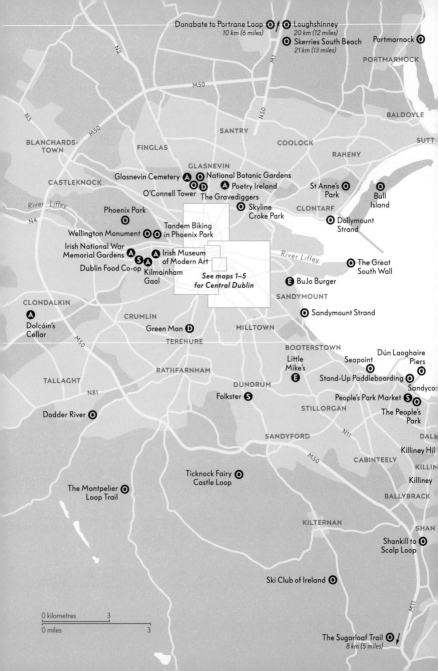

Donabate to Portrane Loop ⊙ ⁄ ⊙ Loughshinney
10 km (6 miles)

⊙ Skerries South Beach
21 km (13 miles)

Portmarnock ⊙

PORTMARNOCK

BALDOYLE

SUTT

N2

M50

N50

M1

SANTRY

COOLOCK

RAHENY

BLANCHARDS-
TOWN

N3

M50

FINGLAS

CASTLEKNOCK

GLASNEVIN

Glasnevin Cemetery Ⓐ ⊙ National Botanic Gardens
⊙Ⓓ Ⓐ Poetry Ireland
O'Connell Tower Ⓐ The Gravediggers

St Anne's ⊙
Park

Bull
⊙ Island

River Liffey

N4

Phoenix Park
⊙
Wellington Monument ⊙⊙ Tandem Biking
in Phoenix Park

⊙ Skyline
Croke Park

CLONTARF

⊙ Dollymount
Strand

Irish National War Ⓐ Ⓐ Irish Museum
Memorial Gardens Ⓢ of Modern Art
Dublin Food Co-op Ⓐ Kilmainham
Gaol

River Liffey

⊙ The Great
South Wall

*See maps 1–5
for Central Dublin*

Ⓔ BuJo Burger

SANDYMOUNT

CLONDALKIN

Ⓐ
Dolcáin's
Cellar

CRUMLIN

⊙ Sandymount Strand

M50

Green Man Ⓓ

MILLTOWN

TERENURE

BOOTERSTOWN

Dún Laoghaire
Seapoint Piers ⊙

DUNDRUM

Little
Mike's
Ⓔ

⊙
Stand-Up Paddleboarding ⊙

TALLAGHT

N81

RATHFARNHAM

Sandyco

Folkster Ⓢ

People's Park Market Ⓢ⊙

Dodder River ⊙

STILLORGAN

The People's
Park

SANDYFORD

SANDYFORD

N11

DALK

Killiney Hil

CABINTEELY

KILLIN

M50

Killiney

Ticknock Fairy ⊙
Castle Loop

BALLYBRACK

The Montpelier ⊙
Loop Trail

KILTERNAN

SHAN

Shankill to ⊙
Scalp Loop

Ski Club of Ireland ⊙

M11

The Sugarloaf Trail ⊙ ⁄
8 km (5 miles)

0 kilometres   3

0 miles   3

MAP 6

6

Octopussy's E, King Sitric E, Beshoff's the Market E, Howth Cliff Path O
HOWTH

Dublin Bay

e Dalkey
ck Kayaking to O Dalkey Island
Rock climbing in Dalkey Quarry

E EAT
Beshoff's the Market *(p50)*
BuJo Burger *(p44)*
The Dalkey Duck *(p38)*
King Sitric *(p50)*
Little Mike's *(p50)*
Octopussy's *(p49)*

D DRINK
The Gravediggers *(p59)*
Green Man *(p64)*

S SHOP
Dublin Food Co-op *(p95)*
Folkster *(p90)*
People's Park Market *(p93)*

A ARTS & CULTURE
Dolcáin's Cellar *(p128)*
Glasnevin Cemetery *(p111)*
Irish Museum of Modern Art *(p116)*
Irish National War Memorial Gardens *(p109)*
Kilmainham Gaol *(p111)*
Poetry Ireland *(p130)*

O OUTDOORS
Bray to Greystones Cliff Walk *(p174)*
Bull Island *(p166)*
Dodder River *(p171)*
Dollymount Strand *(p171)*
Donabate to Portrane Loop *(p173)*
Dún Laoghaire Piers *(p168)*
The Great South Wall *(p168)*
Howth Cliff Path *(p172)*
Kayaking to Dalkey Island *(p180)*
Killiney *(p166)*
Killiney Hill *(p174)*
Loughshinny *(p165)*
The Montpelier Loop Trail *(p175)*
National Botanic Gardens *(p161)*
O'Connell Tower *(p177)*
The People's Park *(p162)*
Phoenix Park *(p162)*
Portmarnock *(p164)*
Rock climbing in Dalkey Quarry *(p180)*
Sandycove *(p165)*
Sandymount Strand *(p164)*
Seapoint *(p166)*
Shankill to Scalp Loop *(p173)*
Skerries South Beach *(p167)*
Ski Club of Ireland *(p181)*
Skyline Croke Park *(p176)*
Stand-Up Paddleboarding *(p183)*
St Anne's Park *(p163)*
The Sugarloaf Trail *(p175)*
Tandem Biking in Pheonix Park *(p181)*
Ticknock Fairy Castle Loop *(p172)*
Wellington Monument *(p179)*

AY
O Bray to Greystones Cliff Walk

EAT

Nothing brings Dubliners together quite like eating. Food is served with a dose of fun – whether it's scoffing chips before the seagulls get 'em or a boisterous group meal in the pub.

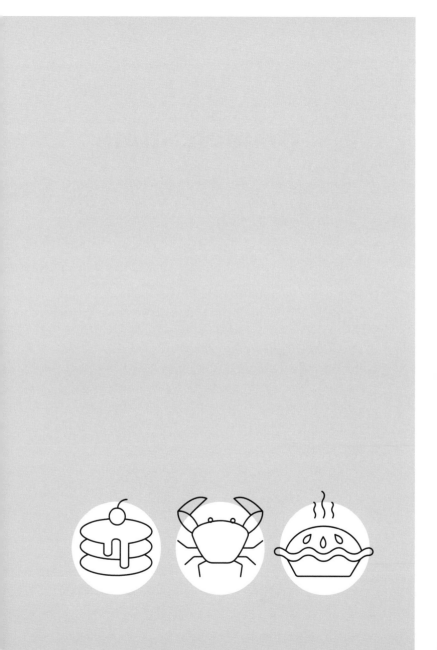

Brunch Spots

This isn't just a meal. Brunch in Dublin is the social highlight of any weekend, where friends gather over stacks of pancakes and skillets of bubbling shakshuka to catch up on all the week's gossip.

TWO BOYS BREW

Map 3; 375 N Circular Road, Phibsborough; ///aware.firms.ranch;
www.twoboysbrew.ie

Whatever you're in the mood for, you'll find it at this ever-bustling spot. Fancy something light? The coconut granola will hit the spot. Sweet tooth? Go for the ricotta hotcakes with blueberries and vanilla roasted strawberries. Absolutely ravenous? Tackle the chicken thigh burger served with zingy slaw. You'll just have to keep returning to try it all.

TWO PUPS COFFEE

Map 4; 74 Francis Street, Liberties; ///valve.appeal.bigger;
www.twopupscoffee.com

With its Bowie-esque lightning bolt on the door and constant gaggle of dogs at the entrance, Two Pups is an easy place to spot (the ever-lively queue outside helps, too). Inside, it's a little Tardis of loveliness serving up hangover cures for everyone who calls the

Get here before noon if you can. Weekend tables are like gold dust, and there are no reservations.

Liberties neighbourhood home. As gregarious groups share stories over slabs of sourdough, intimate twosomes snag a quiet seat in the back.

ANGELINA'S

Map 5; 55 Percy Place, Ballsbridge; ///format.defend.gravy; www.angelinas.ie

When Saturday rolls around, you'll find dressed-up Dubliners huddled together on Angelina's burgundy leather booths or soaking up the canalside vibes on the terrace (depending on the weather). Here, they share side orders of parmesan fries and clink their Bellinis with gusto. The weekend-only brunch menu is fairly classic – think eggs Benedict and avo with everything – but there are some cool twists, like the brunch pizza topped with black pudding and egg yolk.

» Don't leave without ordering a Bloody Mary – the extra kick you're tasting is a shot of poitín, otherwise known as Irish moonshine.

ALMA

Map 4; 12 S Circular Road, Portobello; ///invest.chill.plant; www.alma.ie

This teeny tiny Argentinian joint has a fiercely loyal fan base among its Portobello locals. The menu may be small, but it packs a punch, filled with drool-worthy dishes you'll be dreaming of long after you've licked your plate clean. If you're spoiled for choice, stick with what the trendy regulars order – the signature pancakes drenched in *dulce de leche* and dollops of brandy-spiked mascarpone.

THE FUMBALLY

Map 4; 8 Fumbally Lane, Liberties; ///banana.encounter.surely;
www.thefumbally.ie

Head here during the week and you'll find many a freelancer typing furiously on one of the huge communal tables. But at the weekend, it's all about boisterous catch-ups with groups of friends, who order plates laden with falafel, pulled porchetta and, of course, avocado toast. The homemade fermented sodas are as delicious as they are wholesome (with the addition of being a great hangover cure).

THE CAKE CAFÉ

Map 4; 8 Pleasants Place, Portobello; ///trio.formal.whips;
www.thecakecafe.ie

Tucked behind the Last Bookshop (p101), this cosy oasis is the favourite haunt of Sunday brunchers making their lazy way down Camden Street. Settle into one of the outdoor patio tables and you're instantly transported to the countryside, with towering plants

Try it!
MAKE A CAKE

If the sight of the photogenic desserts on the counter leave you a little jealous, take one of The Cake Café's monthly baking lessons (€60) to learn how to make cakes, cookies and bread. You'll leave laden down with treats for your own sweet brunch.

framing the pretty garden furniture that's waiting to be lounged upon. The brunch menu is filled with classics with a twist: choose a portion of eggs topped with spicy peanut *rayu* (chilli oil), leaving room for a slice of heavenly signature cake.

BROTHER HUBBARD

Map 3; 153 Capel Street, North City; ///scare.risen.pitch; www.brotherhubbard.ie

One of the few places in Dublin serving brunch every day, Brother Hubbard is an ever-bustling spot doling out dishes with a Middle Eastern flavour – think eggs poached in smoked aubergine sauce and halloumi sprinkled with homemade *zhoug* (spicy coriander sauce) and dukkah. The dining space itself is huge, so you can get a gang together on one of the big tables or tuck yourself into a corner with a fiddle leaf fig tree and some *romesco bravas* potatoes for company.

PÓG

Map 5; Trinity Plaza, Tara Street, City Centre; ///logic.duke.neck; www.pog.ie

All of the tables at Póg seem to be filled with groups of girlfriends who reach for their phones as soon as the fluffy pancakes arrive from the kitchen, ready to snap away. No one can blame them: with a list of toppings as long as your arm, these photogenic stacks bring all your pancake fantasies to life (and taste as good as they look).

» Don't leave without trying the pink beet chai, which is both utterly delicious and pretty enough to post on social media.

Sunday Roasts

Though practically an institution, not a lot of Dublin pubs serve Sunday roasts (it's usually more of a family affair at home). The ones that do, though, know how to replicate that homely vibe with precision.

BULL AND CASTLE

Map 1; 5–7 Lord Edward Street, Liberties; ///hers.chat.stuck; www.fxbuckley.ie

It's a bold Dubliner who claims this spot serves up roasts better than their mammy, but it's a statement many regulars stand by. The meat at this gastropub is top-notch, which is to be expected since the place is owned by a Dublin family butcher. Beef is your only option but it's oh so good, served nice and pink with crispy roast potatoes, buttery greens and sticky roast garlic (and a pint, if you wish).

THE BUTCHER GRILL

Map 5; 92 Ranelagh Road, Ranelagh; ///singer.pints.chase; www.thebutchergrill.ie

A killer steakhouse during the week, come the weekend this place is the king of roast dinners. Wooden platters emerge from the kitchen piled high with slivers of rare roast beef and towering Yorkshire puds

After your meal, head over to Smyths of Ranelagh, a cosy pub where you can wait out your meat sweats.

alongside devilish sides like cauliflower cheese. The space is teeny tiny and often booked out, so plan ahead and save it for those long-awaited BFF catch-ups.

LOCKS RESTAURANT

Map 4; 1 Windsor Terrace, Portobello; ///hits.match.fingernails; www.locksrestaurant.ie

Set on a pretty, tree-lined corner of Portobello, this canalside restaurant is where Dublin's top chefs come to eat on their days off. Make a booking on a Sunday for Locks' roast, which features soft-as-butter beef ribs and wild rabbit with charred miso broccoli. There's a wonderfully languid feeling about the place, with diners taking their time over their mains, dithering over the cheese trolley and ordering one last glass of wine for the road.

THE OLD SPOT

Map 5; 14 Bath Avenue, Sandymount; ///eggs.matter.notice; www.theoldspot.ie

With a classic gastropub feel that oozes a homely atmosphere, this is the perfect setting for a dreamy Sunday lunch with a gaggle of friends. The two roast options are generally free-range chicken or dry-aged beef, and come served with duck fat roasties, cauliflower cheese and a heavenly red wine gravy that keeps locals coming back.

» Don't leave without trying the gorgeous summer greens risotto, if you're after something different on your fourth visit of the month.

57 THE HEADLINE

Map 4; 56–7 Clanbrassil Street Lower, Liberties;
///tens.wisely.tiny; www.57theheadline.com

Close your eyes and picture the perfect Sunday: it's in a place just like this. With cosy armchairs, stacks of papers and a killer roast, this pub is the dream spot for a chilled-out afternoon. They use the best aged beef, but will whip up a vegan alternative if you ask nicely.

THE EXCHEQUER

Map 5; 19 Ranelagh Road, Ranelagh; ///waddled.body.chest;
www.theexchequerwinebar.ie

There's a real family vibe to the proceedings at this sleek wine bar. Perfect for big feasts, each roast serves four people, emerging from the kitchen carved on a platter, with delicious sides and a bottle of wine to boot. It requires a bit of forward planning, as you need to place your order by the Friday before.

THE DALKEY DUCK

Map 6; Castle Street, Dalkey; ///pitcher.spoils.ripe; www.thedalkeyduck.ie

If it's drizzly outside, the cosy fireside tables at The Dalkey Duck are the place to be so get there at opening to snag the toastiest spot. The food is equally comforting: roast beef, lamb shank or half a chicken, accompanied by fluffy Yorkshire puds, lashings of gravy and, of course, a creamy pint of Guiness.

>> **Don't leave without** nipping over the road to Bel Gelato for a scoop of sour cherry ice cream – it's the perfect post-roast dessert.

Liked by the locals

"My favourite day of the week is Sunday. We started serving roast dinners four years ago and thought it was something we would have to build a following for, but good news travels fast!"

MÁIRE NI MHAOLIE, OWNER OF 57 THE HEADLINE

Special Occasion

Dubliners are always after an excuse to celebrate, but special means something different to us all. Whether it's a rowdy bargain birthday lunch or an anniversary in a romantic hideaway, the city caters to every taste.

GLAS

**Map 2; 16 Chatham Street, Creative Quarter; ///traps.woven.ages;
www.glasrestaurant.ie**

There are a good few vegetarian restaurants dotted around the city, but Glas is Dubliners' meat-free spot of choice when their anniversaries roll round. This gorgeously styled space with palm fronds, sexy lighting and a vaguely art deco vibe makes for a dreamy date spot where couples can't help but make eyes at each other over dark chocolate mousse.

CHAPTER ONE

**Map 3; 18 Parnell Square, Rotunda; ///wide.fence.drape;
www.chapteronerestaurant.com**

The height of double Michelin-starred decadence, Chapter One is often dubbed the best restaurant in the city, but it's far from stuffy. The wait staff crack jokes as they set your Irish coffee alight or bring

Chapter One's multi-course lunch menu is (slightly) more wallet friendly, at €75 per person.

out extra bread so that your hungry party can wipe their plates clean. When the dishes are this good (and the prices this high) you'll want to savour every morsel.

CLANBRASSIL HOUSE

Map 4; 6 Clanbrassil Street Upper, Liberties; ///speeds.slides.vibes; www.clanbrassilhouse.com

This is the kind of neighbourhood bistro that everyone wants at the end of their road. Inventive chefs cook up a storm in a tiny kitchen, where much of the food is charred over smouldering charcoal. Opt for the family-style menu, and mismatched china plates will keep coming from the kitchen, filled with eye-poppingly good delights to share with your hungry party.

>> Don't leave without trying the light-as-air fermented potato bread, slathered in tangy cultured butter.

FEATHERBLADE

Map 2; 51b Dawson Street, St Stephens Green; ///plot.silks.weep; www.featherblade.ie

Featherblade isn't your traditional steakhouse. A bustling, sultry spot with plump cushions, it has a welcoming vibe that makes it perfect for marking a special occasion, while the short and sweet menu cuts down on dithering time. They use more unusual cuts of beef (which means better prices) cooked over the coals to perfection, with side dishes like beef dripping chips and creamy mac 'n' cheese.

Solo, Pair, Crowd

Whether you're after a quick bite on your own or a celebratory meal with family, there's a place for you.

FLYING SOLO
No decisions necessary
Have you ever wanted to look at a menu and announce loudly "I'll take it all!" At Lucky Tortoise do just that: the "All In" dim sum menu is a steal at €28.

IN A PAIR
Spot of romance
The tiny bistro Grano in Stoneybatter is the closest thing to Italy you'll find on these shores. The owner's mamma regularly flies over from Calabria to handroll the pasta. Share the creamy tiramisu with your BFF or date.

FOR A CROWD
Order up a storm
Incessant chatter and the clink of cocktail glasses hit you as soon as you enter Kinara. There's a real good-time vibe about this Ranelagh restaurant, which serves up some of the city's finest Pakistani food.

PICKLE

Map 4; 43 Camden Street Lower, Portobello; ///advice.minds.with;
www.picklerestaurant.com

Ask any Dubliner where to find the best Indian food and they'll send you here. Pickle specializes in dishes that are a little different, like guinea fowl korma and wild boar vindaloo. It's a date night staple, where romance blossoms at moodily lit tables laden down with incredibly good curries.

UNO MAS

Map 1; 6 Aungier Street, Creative Quarter; ///sugars.mixer.look;
www.unomas.ie

Doling out a modern fusion of Spanish and Irish tapas, this spot sent Dublin foodies into a frenzy when it opened. It attracts those seeking a special date night, where candlelit tables create an alluring atmosphere for sharing elegantly plated, top-notch food.
» Don't leave without ordering the hearty, salt-aged Delmonico beef for your main, served with Béarnaise sauce.

VARIETY JONES

Map 4; 78 Thomas Street, Liberties; ///found.switch.town;
www.varietyjones.ie

This punk restaurant attracts cool diners to match. It's tiny, laidback and feels like dining at a friend's house: almost all of the six courses are chosen for you by the chef. The menu is pretty meat heavy, and it's all cooked on the hearth for a smoky flavour.

Comfort Food

The perfect antidote to Dublin's long, cold winters, comfort food is all about bringing gangs of hungry mates together over towering dishes that are delightfully messy and purely indulgent.

BUJO BURGER

Map 6; 6A Sandymount Green, Sandymount; ///colleague.invent.golf; www.bujo.ie

When you've got a burger craving that just won't quit, this joint out by the sea is the answer. BuJo is always abuzz with groups of friends trying to nab the best booth seats from which to tuck into succulent grass-fed beef patties, dive into gooey milkshakes and wipe melted Irish cheese from their chins. Veggies aren't forgotten, though, with tasty Beyond Meat burgers on the menu.

TOKEN

Map 3; 72–4 Queen Street, Smithfield; ///misty.rocks.gravel; www.tokendublin.ie

This buzzing arcade bar has it all – towering plates of high-end fast food with a backdrop of loud music, laughter and vintage pinball machines. Best of all, it's vegan friendly, and the "big macs" are

If you're hooked on the games, opt for the €35 meal deal for a main, side, booze and game tokens.

tasty enough to convert any carnivore. You'll order way too much, but part of the fun is to keep dipping into the sharing plates between rounds of Pac Man.

PI PIZZA

Map 1; 73–83 S Great George's Street, City Centre; ///safe.lines.things; www.pipizzas.ie

There's almost always a queue at Pi, but this is pizza that's well worth a wait. Give them your number, pop over to Hogans (p59) for a pint, and start getting excited about these perfectly charred pizzas. The circular booths are the prime seat for friends, who talk over each other animatedly as they share slices, but the high stools are great for those tucking in on their own.

» **Don't leave without** trying the vanilla ice cream doused in olive oil and sea salt. There's nothing vanilla about that.

MAD EGG

Map 4; 2–3 Charlotte Way, Camden Street Lower, Portobello; ///reveal.rival.daring; www.madegg.ie

The sight of the alluring neon egg sign here means you're in for a good feed. Dreamily tender fried chicken stuffed into burgers slathered with honey butter, candied bacon and hot sauce keep addicted fans coming back, but it's the cheesecake that really gets the heart racing. It's served plain so you can drizzle it with whatever you fancy, like Oreo crumbs or smashed Maltesers. How artfully you do it is up to you.

BUNSEN

Map 2; 36 Wexford Street, Portobello; ///curl.calm.orange; www.bunsen.ie

You'll struggle to find a Dubliner who hasn't tried a burger from this chain and isn't obsessed as a result. Simplicity pays off at this popular spot: choose between a burger or cheeseburger (the patties of which are ground up fresh each morning), single or double, and three kinds of fries, but that's it. Order it medium for the juiciest bite and prepare to get messy – this isn't the place for a first date.

MELTDOWN

Map 5, 15 Montague Street, St Stephen's Green, ///clubs.roses.dusty
www.meltdown.ie

Dublin is a city that loves its cheese toasties, so locals had somewhat of a meltdown when this spot opened. Tucked away on a little lane just off Harcourt Street, Meltdown attracts staunch fans who come by weekly as well as those who gratefully stumble upon it while

Shh!

Take a walk around Dublin, and you'll soon notice that this city is obsessed with doughnuts. But while many places sell giant, candy topped concoctions, you'll find the real deal in a tiny kiosk on O'Connell Street *(www.therollingdonut.ie)*, where tiny doughnuts have been made fresh since 1978. Just follow the scent of warm cinnamon sugar in the air, and order a batch to eat while sitting by the River Liffey. Bliss.

walking the cobblestone streets. Once you're here, though, you'll want to shout about it – if you can come up for air between those heart-warming bites of cheesy goodness, that is.

# CHIMAC
Map 1; 76 Aungier Street, Creative Quarter; ///treat.minus.wins; www.chimac.ie

When it comes to pure indulgence, you can't beat this Korean fried chicken joint. Expect hungry youngsters tucking into burgers dripping in Ssamjang and BBQ sauce, sticky bacon glazed in sriracha, and loaded fries with gooey kimchi cheese. There's always a bustling, party vibe, thanks in no small part to the enamel mugs filled with potent frosé that's so good, you can't help but order refills.

» Don't leave without trying the fried chicken "nuggs" drenched in a spicy sriracha caramel sauce.

# 147 DELI
Map 3; 147 Parnell Street, Rotunda; ///actor.warm.pumps; 01 872 8481

It might look like a run-of-the-mill deli, but don't be fooled. This is where you'll find Dublin's most satisfying sandwiches, perfect for curing any wine-induced headaches from the night before. The regular menu is solid, but it's the rotating weekly special that tempts the lunchtime work crowd to queue for half of their precious break. A prime example? The Dublin Dip, with rare reverse-seared beef layered with melted Gruyère cheese, charred onions and wild garlic, squashed between sourdough and served with a red wine gravy for dunking. Perfection.

Seafood Spots

Thanks to pristine waters and plentiful fishing villages, Irish seafood is some of the best in the world. And as Dublin is right on the coast, it can all be on your plate in a matter of hours.

THE SEAFOOD CAFÉ

**Map 1; 11 Sprangers Yard, Fownes Street Upper, Temple Bar;
///dull.ship.rotate; www.klaw.ie**

This relaxed restaurant is the closest thing you can get to a seafood shack in the middle of the bustling city. The lobster rolls are the stuff of legend, with thick chunks of the crustacean squished between pillowy soft, buttery brioche buns alongside a pile of crispy fries; add a chilled glass of white (or a Bloody Mary, served spicy with a whole oyster on the side) and you'll be transported to the seaside in seconds.

FISH SHOP

**Map 3; 76 Benburb Street, Smithfield; ///alive.factor.sorters;
www.fish-shop.ie**

There are plenty of places in Dublin to get killer fish and chips (and plenty of duds, too), but this is on a whole other level. The menu is scrawled each day on a blackboard, so you might have pollock or haddock, but rest assured the fish is always zingily fresh and shrouded in the perfect crisp batter that cracks open when you tap it with a fork. There's also a great choice of natural wines to wash it down with.

» **Don't leave without** asking the bartender to pair you with the perfect wine to complement your dish. The menu is filled with names you won't understand, but there's no snootiness here.

OCTOPUSSY'S
Map 6; West Pier, Howth; ///oversaw.eaten.scheduling;
www.octopussy.ie

The menu might call it seafood tapas, but Octopussy's portions are so big that you'll be stuffed after one. Think piled-high bowls of mussels, heaped servings of paella and rings-upon-rings of calamari, all served up with thick wedges of lemon and doorstop slices of treacly soda bread. Tuck into the feast while watching the fishers (and one friendly seal) at work in Howth Harbour.

Shh!

You'll have to be in the right place at the right time to catch The Salty Buoy food truck (www.saltybuoy.ie). This repurposed Citroën H van moves to a different location each week, selling chef Niall Sabongi's best seafood dishes from a hatch. Dripping with bright green herby garlic butter, the hake kiev is legendary. Usual stops include Harold's Cross and The Digital Hub on Thomas Street.

LITTLE MIKE'S

Map 6; 63 Deerpark Road, Mount Merrion, Blackrock;
///angel.sparks.asset; www.michaels.ie

There's nothing little about the seafood platters at this neighbourhood favourite. Meaty lobster, giant prawns and crab claws the size of your fist are all drowned in excessive amounts of lemon butter – it's so good, you'll want to weep. Nab one of the counter stools by the kitchen to watch the owner and local legend Gaz work his magic.

BESHOFF'S THE MARKET

Map 6; 17–18 West Pier, Howth; ///fruitful.ambivalent.preparation;
www.beshoffs.ie

As great as the city's restaurants are, you can't beat eating seafood with the scent of the sea in the air and the sound of water lapping nearby. At this fishmonger set on the pier, the catch of the day is flung up and cooked immediately. You can't get fresher than that.

KING SITRIC

Map 6; East Pier, Howth; ///upstarts.tenants.rigid; www.kingsitric.ie

Handily located right by the start (and end) of the Howth Cliff Path *(p172)*, this is the perfect place to wrap up a seaside hike. What better way to perk up aching legs than with a platter of Dublin Bay prawns, crab claws and lobster dripping in garlic butter?

» Don't leave without popping into Ye Olde Hurdy Gurdy Museum of Vintage Radio. Set in the Martello tower, just behind King Sitric, this quirky museum has everything from gramophones to stamps.

Liked by the locals

"There's something very special about Dublin seafood. A few oysters and a savage pint of Guinness is up there with a perfectly poached lobster and a fine wine."

GAZ SMITH, OWNER OF LITTLE MIKE'S

Dinner at
TERRA MADRE

Finish the day at this truly authentic Italian joint, where life-changing pasta is served alongside bucketfuls of charm, courtesy of the owner, Marco.

O'CONNELL ST LOWER

NORTH CITY

BACHELORS WALK **4**

Ha'penny Bridge

WELLINGTON QUAY

Liffey

TEMPLE BAR

EUSTACE ST

DAME ST

Mooch around
FALLON & BYRNE

Any local will tell you this is the best grocery store in town. Stock up on Irish seaweed salt, truffle powder and spicy Dublin peanut butter.

SOUTH GREAT GEORGE'S ST

*Red-bricked **George's Street Arcade** is Europe's oldest covered market, and has been home to the best (and quirkiest) traders since 1881.*

3 EXCHEQUER STREET

DRURY ST

CREATIVE QUARTER

GRAFTON STREET

DAWSO

PATRICK STREET

STEPHEN ST LOWER

Lunch at
ASSASSINATION CUSTARD

Get cosy at this two-table only, husband-and-wife-run café. The menu changes daily, based on what the owners want to cook.

AUNGIER STREET

MERCER STREET

CITY CENTR

St Stephen's Green

KEVIN ST UPPER **1**

NEW STREET SOUTH

KEVIN ST LOWER

CUFFE STREET

2

LONG LANE   CAMDEN ROW

WEXFORD ST

Learn some skills at
THE FUMBALLY STABLES

Swing by this cultural centre to see if a food market or pop-up event is on, or enjoy a pre-booked sourdough class.

CAMDEN STREET LOWER

An afternoon of
Dublin's finest food

A day of dining in Dublin is always one well spent. Food culture here is pure comfort, where cosy spots transport you to your grandparents' dining room and tempt even the least culinary locals to rustle up the ingredients and hone the skills needed to recreate those hearty plates at home. It may be surprising that some of the city's best community- and family-run spots lie in the epicentre of the tourist tracks, but if you look hard enough, you'll find places that champion the finest organic produce, and generations of cooks and producers that love a chat. There's simply no excuse for a bad meal in the centre.

1. Assassination Custard
19A Kevin Street Lower,
Portobello; 087 997 1513
///bucket.invest.desk

2. The Fumbally Stables
Fumbally Lane, Liberties;
www.thefumballystables.ie
///films.cats.shack

3. Fallon & Byrne
11–17 Exchequer Street,
Creative Quarter;

www.fallonandbyrne.com
///slang.ideas.dates

4. Terra Madre
13A Bachelors Walk;
www.terramadre.ie
///scared.apple.shut

George's Street Arcade
///trial.judges.stop

DRINK

Humble pubs, bars and cafés are extensions of the family home in Dublin, where time is spent catching up over a latte or bantering with a beer in hand.

Proper Pubs

Dubliners love a pint, so it's no surprise that the humble pub is the beating heart of their social lives. It's about more than the booze, though, with cheerful vibes, charming regulars and cosy little nooks.

THE LONG HALL

Map 2; 51 S Great George's Street, Creative Quarter;
///acute.pretty.fiend; 01 475 1590

This old-fashioned boozer tops the list of favourite pubs for many a Dubliner. When you enter, it feels like you're walking back in time – after all, the interior has barely changed since 1881, and it's been around longer still. There's plenty of carved wood, an ornate ceiling and happy punters filling the red stools. Best of all, the bartenders do table service when it's busy, so you can stay firmly in your seat.

KEHOE'S

Map 2; 9 Anne Street S, City Centre;
///dirt.inspector.bother; www.kehoesdublin.ie

If all that shopping on Grafton Street leaves you thirsty, this spot just off the busy road has you covered. Kehoe's feels like an extension of your living room, letting you nip in and hide from the world for an

Get here early to snag the "snug", an enclosed room unique to Irish pubs and the coveted seat for a gossip.

hour. On a sunny day, you'll know you've found the right spot when you see crowds pouring out onto the pavement to soak up the rays while sipping on a pale ale.

FALLONS

Map 4; 129 The Coombe, Liberties; ///army.refers.cards; 01 454 2801

This tiny pub is one of the oldest in the city, in the historic whiskey-distilling district of the Liberties. The floor is slanting and crooked, the seats are well worn, and the pot-bellied stove in the corner keeps everything nice and toasty. Oh, and speaking of toasties – ask nicely, and the barman will whip you up a classic grilled cheese and ham sandwich if it's a quiet afternoon. Perfect with a classically Irish pint of Guinness.

THE PALACE BAR

Map 5; 21 Fleet Street, Temple Bar; ///double.chin.marked;
www.thepalacebardublin.com

A dark and sultry interior, a trusted cohort of regulars and an excellent selection of whiskey behind the bar make this the only pub worth visiting in Temple Bar. In fairness, it's right on the edge of the tourist strip, so there's no hint of the paddwhackery that goes on further down the road. In short? A classic Dublin pub where you can be sure of a great pint and even better craic.

» Don't leave without trying a dram of their very own whiskey. There's a variety of blends on offer, but the 14-year-old single malt is class.

Solo, Pair, Crowd

The classic Dublin pub isn't the only kind of boozer you'll find in the city. There's a lot more variety than you might expect, whatever you're after.

FLYING SOLO
A friendly natter

It's easy to get chatting to the bartender and neighbouring punters at The Dawson Lounge, seeing as it's the smallest pub in Dublin. Unfussy, cosy and welcoming, it's as old-school as they come.

IN A PAIR
Food truck central

The Bernard Shaw is a great pub for a date because, if that one drink looks like dinner, you can just pop out to the street food trucks in its courtyard.

FOR A CROWD
Play a game

Feeling competitive? The Back Page is fantastic for boozy games with your mates, with ping pong tables, darts, snooker and video games to choose from.

THE SWAN BAR

**Map 2; 2 Aungier Street, Creative Quarter; ///dairy.transit.spend;
www.theswanbar.com**

There's something about The Swan that makes it a great midweek
pub, where you can pop in after work for a quiet one. That's most
probably helped by the chilled-out, cosy vibe – the turf fire is always
smouldering, so it's especially perfect on a drizzly evening. Nod
hello to the regulars propping up the bar, grab a drink and settle in.

HOGANS

**Map 2; 59 S Great George's Street, Creative Quarter;
///player.bought.tender; 01 677 5904**

There's a magnetic feel to this spot, where you can meet someone
for a swift one before dinner and realize that hours have passed and
you haven't left. With a modern feel that still retains the classic vibe,
Hogans caters to both old-timers seeking a cosy spot to read the
newspaper and good-timers people-watching from pavement tables.

THE GRAVEDIGGERS

Map 6; 1 Prospect Square, Glasnevin; ///dared.mobile.class; 087 296 3713

Right next to Glasnevin Cemetery (hence the name), this is a Dublin
institution. It was always said that the gravediggers used to be
passed pints of stout through a hatch between the two buildings,
but nowadays the friendly bartenders stick to the regular methods.

» Don't leave without trying a bowl of coddle, the traditional Dublin
stew made with sausages and bacon. It's the kind your mammy makes.

Cocktail Joints

The city's cocktail scene has never been hotter, thanks to creative mixologists who are stirring things up – literally. Tempting locals to forgo a Guinness pint are fruity concoctions and laidback lounges to sip them in.

STREET 66

Map 1; 33–4 Parliament Street, Temple Bar;
///skins.store.navy; www.street66.bar

There's always a party at this beloved gay bar, where cocktails come at a price that won't make you wince come morning and convivial regulars are always propping up the bar. Some argue that it's at its most charismatic in the day: punters arrive with their dogs, who patiently provide therapy-worthy belly rubs while you sip whiskey sours and have a proper natter.

THE VIRGIN MARY

Map 3; 54 Capel Street, North City; ///dots.lives.healers;
www.thevirginmarybar.com

Sure, Dubliners have a reputation for loving a drink, but the trend for alcohol-free alternatives has been skyrocketing over the last year, driven by health-conscious millennials. The top-notch cocktails, made using spices, shrubs and bitters, are far from the cheap and tacky mocktails of yesteryear. There's a lovely relaxed atmosphere in the stylish space, where patrons of all ages drop in for a couple and prove that craic doesn't always need to go hand in hand with booze.

» **Don't leave without** trying the spicy Virgin Mary, with handpressed tomato juice and a smack of pickle on the after note.

THE BAR WITH NO NAME

Map 2; 3 Fade Street, Creative Quarter;
///swept.zealous.couch; www.noname.bar

This so-called "secret bar" is far from a secret among hip young Dubliners, all of whom know that the little wooden snail sign means the fun is just getting started. Set above Hogans pub *(p59)*, this spacious and airy joint has a house party vibe to it, complete with a great little outdoor patio and a killer selection of cocktails – the gin basil smash is like summer in a glass. Get there early in the evening to sink into one of the leather chesterfield couches and let the chaotic chatter and spirited laughter commence.

Try it!
MASTER THE MIXING

Shaken or stirred? It's up to you to decide in a cocktail-making class at The Little Pig *(www.thelittlepig.ie)*, a plush speakeasy. You'll learn flavour profiles and the best combinations, then create the winning mix.

VINTAGE COCKTAIL CLUB

Map 1; 15 Crown Alley, Temple Bar; ///shelf.ending.solved;
www.vintagecocktailclub.com

This discreet 1920s-style speakeasy has stood the test of time, no doubt thanks to its exceptional cocktails at modest prices. Ring the doorbell and you'll be ushured into a fabulous granny-chic space, where friendly staff help you figure out exactly what you're in the mood for. (It's usually one of their own favourites.)

PERUKE & PERIWIG

Map 2; 31 Dawson Street, St Stephen's Green;
///steer.hooked.clay; www.peruke.ie

There's a deliciously dark and sexy mood in this renowned spot, with tiny rooms covered in crushed velvet and deep couches seating a well-dressed clientele. You can sneak in here for one and emerge blinking into the street lights a few hours later after discovering ingredients you never knew existed and spirits you didn't know you liked.

» Don't leave without trying a Pass the Dutchie margarita, made with sage-infused tequila and Cointreau blended with Earl Grey.

BAR 1661

Map 3; 1–5 Green Street, North City; ///claims.tall.foil; www.bar1661.ie

Irish poitín (or moonshine) was not only illegal for many years, but so potent it could knock your head off. Nowadays the spirit is legal, more subdued and the hot order of choice in Dublin and this dedicated bar, where cool mixologists use it as their star component.

Liked by the locals

"We've had the Wee Dram cocktail on our menu since we opened. We use Bushmills ten-year-old as the base, enhance the flavour of the whiskey with port, apple and pear, and finish with a pimento dram mist and orange oils. It's a beaut."

GARETH LAMBE, MANAGER AT VINTAGE COCKTAIL CLUB

Wine Bars

There's been something of a wine renaissance of late, with niche gems run by friendly experts popping up across town. When friends plan an overdue catch-up, these classy bars are their hangout of choice.

GREEN MAN

Map 6; 3 Terenure Road N, Terenure;
///soon.drip.stared; www.greenmanwines.ie

Part shop, part bar, this is a paradise for oenophiles. You'll likely rub shoulders with connoisseurs who stroke their chins as they ponder the bottle-lined shelves, but it's an unpretentious affair. For those who aren't experts, get chatting to the staff – their knowledge is second to none, and they specialize in artisanal, natural and

Try it!
WINE TASTING

If you're hoping to learn more about wine, look out for tastings in Green Man, often led by vineyard owners and growers. The stories are fascinating, the wine is gorgeous and the atmosphere is laidback.

biodynamic wines (or, wine made with minimal intervention on a small scale). Don't believe the rumour that natural wines don't give you a hangover — the little nibbles might help to prevent that.

BRINDLE COFFEE & WINE
Map 4; 34 Lennox Street, Portobello; ///rather.singer.drill; www.brindlecoffeewine.com

Full of charming Georgian houses and pretty cafés, Portobello is one of the cutest neighbourhoods in the city. And when First Draft shifted from being just a coffee shop to also serving wine in the evenings, the area got all the cuter. As day turns into night, the coffee mugs are swapped out for wine glasses, when Portobello locals fill the benches and deck chairs for their animated catch-ups.

LOOSE CANON CHEESE & WINE
Map 2; 29 Drury Street, Creative Quarter; ///games.cove.player; www.loosecanon.ie

There's something quintessentially European about this tiny wine and cheese shop, set underneath the Gothic red brick spires of George's Street Arcade. There are only a couple of stools, so most stand by the window, catching up over a glass of natural wine, watching the shoppers pass by and nibbling on charcuterie and cheese boards. If it's a nice day, there's a rush to nab the small bench outside to catch some rays.

» **Don't leave without** trying one of the obscenely good toasties, dripping with artisan cheese. Hands down the best in Dublin.

LIBRARY STREET

Map 5; 101 Setanta Place, City Centre; ///regard.brave.wooden;
www.librarystreet.ie

At this hip wine bar/restaurant hybrid, you won't go thirsty or hungry, with loads of grape varieties available by the glass and unbelievably good small plates to match. It's easier to get a seat at 5pm, so plan to arrive by then before the chic masses descend from their offices to drink the place dry.

» Don't leave without pairing your glass of wine with the crispy mushroom-stuffed chicken wing, served on a bed of tarragon mayo.

THE WINE PAIR

Map 4; 79 Clanbrassil Street Lower, Liberties;
///cheat.answer.clap; www.thewinepairdublin.com

Not only can you get some fantastic wines on tap at this friendly bar, you can also buy a refillable bottle to take away – handy if you're in the area for a few days. As the name suggests, you need good wine fodder, so order a plate of Irish cheese creations to go with a fruity glass of red and you'll be "happy out", as Dubliners say.

AMY AUSTIN

Map 2; Unit 1, Drury Street, Creative Quarter;
///credit.chop.ranked; www.amyaustin.ie

Nothing says hipster like a wine bar set inside a car park. The kind of buzzy, gregarious spot that Dublin never knew it needed epitomizes industrial chic, attracting a vibrant crowd that oozes the same level of

Head here on a Monday for 25 per cent off wine (the perfect time to try out a vintage).

cool. Whether you're bopping to the upbeat tunes, debating which wine on tap to try next or petting a pug (yep, it's dog friendly), a fun time is guaranteed.

PIGLET

Map 1; Cow's Lane, Temple Bar; ///wished.pass.walks; www.pigletwinebar.ie

Those in the know whisper in hushed tones about Piglet for fear it will make its way into the plans of chatterbox crowds. On a sweet little lane on the furthest (calmest) edge of Temple Bar, this under-the-radar wine bar is a staple for those looking to enjoy a tipple on their own and unwind. You'll often find people sipping a glass as they watch the city go by, particularly straight after work. The menu of wines is split up into "usual" and "weird", so let the day you've had steer you a direction.

ELY WINE BAR

Map 5; Ely Place, St Stephen's Green; ///fired.amused.slot;
www.elywinebar.ie

With that traditional, almost Manhattan feel thanks to high stools at the bar and sexy little booths, it's no wonder this is one of the more established wine bars in the city. Ely runs as a full restaurant as well, so you can stick around for dinner and enjoy the dreamy, lengthy wine list for longer. You'll also find one of the best selections of natural cava and champagnes, so if you have something to celebrate, this is the place to go for some bubbles.

Alfresco Tipples

As soon as the sun peeks through the clouds, Dubliners are straight out of the pub doors and into the fresh air with their pints. Nothing beats the buzz of outdoor terraces and courtyards on summer days.

THE BARGE

Map 5; 42 Charlemont Street, Ranelagh;
///result.grit.pans; www.thebarge.ie

When the sun shines in Dublin, it seems the whole city flocks to this canalside institution. There's a festival buzz to the atmosphere here, where all manner of crowds rub shoulders as they snake their way in and out of the bar, careful not to spill a drop of precious beer. Don't expect to leave early: you're staying for the night with the rest of them (though you can head inside for a bite to eat once the sun sets).

TONERS

Map 5; 139 Baggot Street Lower, Merrion Square;
///fallen.joke.random; www.tonerspub.ie

One of Dublin's most beloved pubs, Toners is the kind of place that works for whatever mood you're in: a quiet pint in the afternoon, a rowdy Saturday night or, best of all, some chilled drinks in the

Enjoy the atmosphere of a match day and visit when a Gaelic football game is shown on the big screens.

sunshine in the big outdoor yard. It gets the sun pretty much all day, but there are heaters as well if the Dublin elements aren't playing ball.

PAVILION BAR

**Map 5; College Green, Trinity College Dublin, City Centre;
///cabin.decide.vibrate; www.pavilionbar.ie**

This might be on the Trinity College campus, but it's not only open to students. Locals of all dispositions flock to the Pav, as it's known to its regulars, for a prime bit of city centre real estate. It's right on the sports field, making it the perfect spot to laze around among students who come to chill out with a beer or catch up on some reading with a G&T.

DRURY BUILDINGS

**Map 2; 55 Drury Street, Creative Quarter; ///mixed.noses.visit;
www.drurybuildings.com**

While tourists stop at the abstract mural sneaking up the exterior, those in the know step inside the Drury Buildings, making their way to the cute terrace garden that lies out the back. As well-designed as any interior space, with stylish seating, artwork and plenty of greenery, this is for alfresco drinking in utter style. The cocktails are addictive, the menu of nibbly bites (think sliders, croquettes and gambas) always hits the spot and there's a DJ at weekends to boot.

» Don't leave without trying the Rosolio Spritz. Made with bergamot and elderflower, it's like summer in a glass.

Liked by the locals

"Blackbird is a great spot to idle away a few hours in the sun as you work your way through its impressive menu of locally brewed beers – and the pizza and board games certainly don't hurt either!"

JOHN BALFE, RATHMINES RESIDENT
AND JOURNALIST

BLACKBIRD

Map 5; 82–4 Rathmines Road Lower, Rathmines;
///judges.grabs.latter; www.blackbirdrathmines.com

It's a safe bet that anyone who lives in Rathmines has been on a first date here. This uber-cool pub attracts couples like a magnet, who flock to the side patio with its retractable roof and fairy lights on a nice day. There are stacks of board games up on the bar, too, so you can flirt over Connect 4 as you sip on your craft beer.

GROGAN'S

Map 2; 15 William Street S, Creative Quarter;
///deep.ocean.tone; www.groganspub.ie

Rest assured that if it's sunny, you'll be fighting for an outdoor table here. Smack bang in the city centre, these seats are the hottest in town for people-watching. It's the characters you'll see who'll shape a visit, from buskers strumming a guitar to backpackers ambling through. **» Don't leave without** trying the famous Grogan's toastie, with a huge dollop of mustard on the side. Pure soakage.

HOUSE

Map 5; 27 Leeson Street Lower, St Stephen's Green;
///gravy.create.pretty; www.housedublin.ie

The sheltered garden at the back of these two Georgian townhouses is the ultimate in alfresco luxury, with wicker chairs, woollen blankets and an outdoor bar. On sunny days, ice buckets and prosecco dot every table of those who've come dressed to impress.

Coffee Shops

Dubliners will tell you that a day without coffee is simply unthinkable. Lucky for locals, Dublin's coffee scene is thriving with cool cafés where instant brews are a thing of the past.

3FE

Map 5; 32 Grand Canal Street Lower, Docklands;
///losses.ramp.editor; www.3fe.com

The guys behind 3fe are generally considered to be the coffee aficionados of Dublin. You'll find 3fe beans in plenty of cafés all over the city, but nothing beats sipping a smooth espresso (3fe stands for Third Floor Espresso, after all) in the company's original outpost in the Docklands. The working crowd at the nearby tech offices and

Try it!
BREW A CUP

Keen to know how they make latte art?
Want to improve your at-home macchiatos?
Take a fun one-day workshop with
The Dublin Barista School
(www.dublinbaristaschool.ie).

the freelancers who set up stations here back this up, starting their day off the right way by sipping on a rich coffee between bites of a warm, custardy Danish pastry out on the pavement.

NETWORK

Map 2; 39 Aungier Street, Creative Quarter; ///treat.woes.bells; www.networkcafe.ie

Everything is taken care of with a great deal of earnestness at this stylish spot, which would feel intimidating were the staff not so damn nice. There's no barista snobbery, and they'll happily chat to you about coffee for hours, especially if you're a novice. This is the kind of place with scales, glass beakers and precise latte art at play, but it's also where you can have lengthy chats, catch up on emails on a quiet weekday morning and even pet a visiting dog or two.

TWO FIFTY SQUARE

Map 5; 10 Williams Park, Rathmines; ///baked.parks.broke; www.twofiftysquare.com

Rathmines can feel a little hectic at the best of times, but this airy, light-filled space is far enough away from the main drag to feel like a little reprieve from it all. It's rarely crowded, so real coffee connoisseurs (including the odd sports star) welcome a moment of zen to indulge in a Vietnamese iced coffee or a macchiato.

» Don't leave without grabbing a bite to eat. The brunch menu, featuring hearty dishes like the Big Breakfast Brioche, is an ode to the weekend and served all week long.

Solo, Pair, Crowd

You'll find a coffee shop on practically every street in Dublin, but they don't all cater to your party needs so acutely as these.

FLYING SOLO
Scandi vibes
Found right by tranquil St Patrick's Cathedral, Søren & Son is the perfect place to grab a coffee (or turmeric latte) and read your book in peace.

IN A PAIR
Happy and you know it
Grab a hot drink from Happy Out, a container coffee stall, to accompany you on a stroll along Bull Island (p166). It may be the only place you can get a drink on this beach, but it's also the only place you need.

FOR A CROWD
Sip and socialize
Gather the gang at one of the long wooden tables in Smithfield's Urbanity, a small batch roastery serving excellent coffee with industrial chic vibes.

CLEMENT & PEKOE

Map 2; 50 William Street S, Creative Quarter;
///spill.plates.rating; www.clementandpekoe.com

Visit this rustic coffee house often enough and you'll recognize the
trendy regulars, installed on one of the benches out at the front as
daytime drip blends turn into evening wind-down cuppas. Sure,
there are heaps of cosy tables inside, but if you want to watch who's
coming and going on William Street, these are the seats you need.

PROPER ORDER

Map 3; 7 Haymarket, Smithfield; ///twigs.cheeks.fled;
www.properordercoffeeco.com

Proper Order's baristas take their coffee seriously, using specially
sourced beans, and all manner of gizmos and gadgets to make the
perfect brew. They also seem to know all their regulars by name,
whether they're popping in for a bag of beans or a house drip.

» Don't leave without checking out the fantastic street art pieces that
splash the side of the buildings just around the corner on Burgess Lane.

KAPH

Map 2; 31 Drury Street, Creative Quarter; ///prices.bath.count; www.kaph.ie

When the entrance level bustles with parents and office workers
seeking a caffeine fix, those with inside knowledge take their flat
whites and cupcakes to the oft-forgotten second floor for a moment
of calm. It's the perfect spot to hide out for the afternoon, whether
you need to check your emails or simply indulge in a good book.

Whiskey Dens

Think of Irish whiskey and you're probably picturing an older generation sipping the stuff neat. Think again. With mixologists jazzing up the spirit in stylish bars, it's now all anyone wants to drink.

9 BELOW

Map 2; 9 St Stephen's Green; ///candle.slug.lame; www.9below.ie

When this sultry bar opened, it quickly gained a reputation for one thing: the most expensive whiskey in the city, a glass of which would set you back a whopping €1,200. Luckily, there's a huge selection of whiskeys on offer here that are nowhere near that price, which is why the sleek suited and well-dressed make their way to 9 Below when they want to make like Don Draper and sip an excellent whiskey in style (without sacrificing next month's rent).

SEARSONS

Map 5; 42–4 Baggot Street Upper, Ballsbridge;
///factor.crash.asks; www.searsonsbar.ie

The whiskey bar in this pub has some seriously rare blends displayed. Let's just say, this isn't a cabinet you want to bump into for fear of smashing the precious bottles. As well as all the classics (Bushmills,

Jameson, Tullamore Dew), it showcases cool young Irish distilleries (Roe & Co, Teeling, Slane). As rowdy chants filter through from the garden on match days, you can sip your way through an Irish tasting platter with a feeling of sophistication away from the hubbub.

THE HORSESHOE BAR
Map 5; 27 St Stephen's Green; ///crazy.ridge.data; www.theshelbourne.com

There's something about this bar that transports you back to another era. If you close your eyes, you can almost smell the cigar smoke from years gone by. It's been tucked into the back of the historic Shelbourne Hotel for the past 60 years (with a few revamps, mind), so rest assured the red walls of this moody place will have as many stories to tell as your grandpa. And with red leather banquettes all within earshot of one another, it remains the place to come for a healthy dash of gossip alongside an old-fashioned.

» **Don't leave without** trying a premium whiskey flight, which lets you explore four whiskeys from each province of Ireland. Cheers to that!

Try it!
GET IN THE SPIRIT

Roe & Co (www.roeandcowhiskey.com), right in the heart of the traditional whiskey-distilling district, is an incredible spot to experience immersive tastings. There's even a cocktail-making workshop.

L. MULLIGAN GROCER

Map 3; 18 Stoneybatter; ///swift.agenda.oven; www.lmulligangrocer.com

Part gastropub, part old boozer, L. Mulligan Grocer is the lynchpin of Stoneybatter life. The delicious pub grub always tempts groups of friends and families, but the staggering array of rare whiskeys keep old-timers coming back. As a finishing touch, the famous L. Mulligan Grocer Scotch eggs go surprisingly well with a glass of their finest spirit.

FARRIER AND DRAPER

Map 2; 59 William Street S, Powerscourt Centre, Creative Quarter; ///hugs.areas.scarf; www.farrieranddraper.ie

Plush velvet armchairs, vintage-style paintings and emerald coloured walls give a gorgeous boudoir feel to this snug place. It's a stylish spot where couples canoodle by the open fire during the week and groups of girlfriends settle in for whiskey cocktails at the weekend.

» **Don't leave without** trying the Spice Bag Margarita, a nod to Dublin's beloved takeaway dish, made with chili-infused tequila.

TAPPED

Map 2; 47 Nassau Street, City Centre; ///deflection.patio.serves; www.tappeddublin.com

This cavernous, industrial-chic bar may look like a craft beer hangout but it's actually a paradise for whiskey fans, run by the Dingle Distillery. Behind the giant concrete bar, the walls are lined with the distillery's own bottles (as well as a few guest stars), which are poured out on the rocks or mixed into cocktails.

Liked by the locals

"L. Mulligan Grocer co-owner Seáneen always has a varied selection of whiskeys behind the bar and she's spot on with pairing suggestions, such as the divine Bushmills 16-year-old with dark Valrhona chocolate – a whiskey lover's taste sensation."

SONIA HARRIS POPE, WHISKEY AFICIONADO AND PR

0 metres 250
0 yards 250

Perk yourself up
VICE COFF

There's Irish Coffee, t
there's Vice Irish Cof
Order this award-win
brew, which is made
small batch whiskey, cre
and the very best espre

CAPEL STREET

UPPER ABBEY ST

Shake it up at
JAMESON DISTILLERY

Neat whiskey not for you? Take a cocktail-making class at this iconic distillery, where you'll learn how to whizz up a mean old-fashioned.

3

SMITHFIELD

HAMMOND LANE

CHANCERY STREET

Mellows
Bridge

ARRAN QUAY

USHER'S QUAY

BRIDGEFOOT STREET

Father Mathew
Bridge

River Liffey

TEMPLE
BAR

DAME STREET

BRIDGE ST LOWER

HIGH STREET

SOUTH GREAT GEORGE'S ST

THOMAS COURT

PATRICK STREET

*A river of ignited whiskey
swept through the*
Liberties *in 1875, when
the Dublin Whiskey Fire
caused barrels to burst in
a nearby storehouse.*

CREATI
QUART

BULL
ALLEY ST

GOLDEN LANE

PIMLICO

AUNGIER ST

THE
LIBERTIES

NEW ROW SOUTH

4

KEVIN ST UPPER

CUFFE ST

Snoop around at
TEELING DISTILLERY

The Teeling family have been in business for centuries. On a tour at this new working distillery, you'll learn how their whiskey is made.

NORTH CITY

A Victorian-era boozer, **Bowes Lounge Bar** *used to host the Irish Whiskey Society – an appreciation group that was founded in this pub.*

WESTMORELAND ST

1 **Swot up at the IRISH WHISKEY MUSEUM**
Sip whiskey from a range of different distilleries as you're led on a guided tour through the origins of the Irish spirit.

STREET

CITY CENTRE

Stephen's Green

An afternoon on
the whiskey trail

Whiskey is woven into the very fabric of Ireland's history – in fact, the word "whiskey" comes from the Irish *uisce beatha*, which literally means "water of life". And it was the lifeblood of the capital in the 1800s, when Dublin was a hotbed of distilleries. Though a period of decline in the last century damaged the industry (and dozens of those distilleries), Dubliners have found their way back to the spirit. Yes, the whiskey scene may now be all about hot new cocktails in sexy bars, but you can't sip the stuff without toasting its legacy.

1. Irish Whiskey Museum
119 Grafton Street, City Centre; www.irishwhiskey museum.ie
///gossip.pilots.badge

2. Vice Coffee
54 Middle Abbey Street, North City; www.vicecoffeeinc.com
///wires.wins.gold

3. Jameson Distillery
Bow Street, Smithfield; www.jamesonwhiskey.com
///popped.orbit.hangs

4. Teeling Distillery
13–17 Newmarket, Liberties www.teelingwhiskey.com
///third.hats.riders

Bowes Lounge Bar
///issue.rescue.mouth

SHOP

Forget fast fashion and generic high street stores: Dubliners love nothing more than scouting vintage gems, celebrating local designers and indulging in organic produce.

Vintage Gems

Never ones to follow the crowd, thrifty Dubliners embrace decades-old vintage stores over fast fashion on the high street. The best stores lie in the city centre, and are the go-to stop for one-of-a-kind pieces.

FRESH TEMPLE BAR

Map 1; 1 Crown Alley, Temple Bar; ///stages.items.indeed; www.freshtemplebar.com

Everywhere you go in Dublin, you'll see 20-somethings embracing the 1990s look, with bucket hats, oversized denim and crop tops aplenty. They pick it all up at this trendy spot, where reworked items sit next to original, untouched vintage and first-rate accessories. If you're ever attending a festival in Ireland, you're almost guaranteed to see a chain belt or bum bag from this popular store.

NINE CROWS

Map 1; 22 Temple Lane S, Temple Bar; ///bets.amount.transmitted; www.shopninecrows.com

If you're nursing even a hint of a headache, this isn't the place to be. Every inch is covered in bright neon colours, from abstract shapes on the walls to tie-dye T-shirts. A wonderfully eclectic crowd flock here

Tour the charity shops along Georges Street after to find treasures at Oxfam, Vincent's and Enable Ireland. to dig out some bargains, so expect hipsters poring over pre-loved sportswear and eccentric fashionistas seeking a unique piece for their wardrobes.

LUCY'S LOUNGE

Map 1; 11 Lower Fownes Street, Temple Bar; ///paths.sudden.reveal; www.lucysloungevintage.com

A quirky gem, Lucy's Lounge has held a place in the hearts of locals since opening in the 1980s. This is where your mammy found her favourite gown for the local dance and where your best friend picked up that battered denim jacket she seems to wear whatever the weather. It's packed to the rafters with pieces (and whimsical decor), so go when you have the time to really root through the rails.

» Don't leave without heading downstairs to the basement to hunt for hidden gems. (Tip: owner Dee Macken knows where the best pieces are.)

TOLA VINTAGE

Map 1; 10 Fownes Street Upper, Temple Bar; ///assure.garage.skips; www.tolavintage.com

This store is a celebrity among Dubliners (and celebs themselves). Cool kids head here to rifle through the athleisure gear and shell jackets that promise them the throwback 1990s look that is oh-so-trendy right now. A browse is always a pleasure, but those in the know stalk their website to find out about the next kilo sale, which is where you'll see the stylish laden down with piles of clothes at €20 a kilo.

SIOPAELLA

Map 2; 30 Wicklow Street, Creative Quarter;
///empty.labs.tags; www.siopaella.com

Walking into this treasure trove feels like entering a seriously high-end boutique. The big differences are the rock-bottom prices and the unbelievable quality of second-hand stock. This consignment store is where trendy Dubliners trade in their finest pieces, like Birkin bags and Chanel coats, so that local style mavens can pick them up at just a fraction of the cost. It's not only the top designer gear you'll find here, either – you can also pick up pieces from the pricier end of the high street, from brands like Maje and Acne.

A STORE IS BORN

Map 2; 34 Clarendon Street, Creative Quarter;
///called.engine.tiger; 087 967 8033

You'd be forgiven for walking straight past this unassuming shop. It's only open on Saturdays, and the lack of an online presence makes it a bit of a well-guarded secret – which its staunch fans aren't complaining about. There's a gorgeous sense of old world glamour to the whole set-up: wafty kaftans and silk scarves line the walls, baskets brim with beaded clutch bags, and serious fashionistas welcome the calming ambience to joyfully sift through it all. This is the place to go if you're looking for ultra-glamorous vintage, like 1950s prom dresses and lace gowns to wear to an all-important meet-the-in-laws dinner party or fancy work ball.

» Don't leave without engaging in a lengthy chat with the owner to get the scoop about the fabulous customers they've had over the years.

Liked by the locals

"**Dublin style is very eclectic and diverse: the fashion scene is a really cool blend of high street and vintage. The clothes and bags we sell at Siopaella really reflect Dublin fashion.**"

ELLA DE GUZMAN, FOUNDER OF SIOPAELLA

Indie Boutiques

Whether they stock pieces made in Ireland or from talented creators around the globe, Dublin's indie boutiques are run by style mavens who know where to find the finest threads for fashion-conscious locals.

FRESH CUTS

Map 2; 13 Castle Market, Creative Quarter;
///humid.wins.looked; www.freshcutsclothing.com

The move away from fast fashion brands in favour of smaller, ethical shops is something Dubliners feel passionately about – so much so that the success of this gem's pop-up shop secured it a permanent store. Casual, minimal lifestyle attire keeps locals returning to stock up as the seasons change, while the brand's own graphic tees, hats

Try it!
UPCYCLE YOUR GARMS

Sustainable fashion advocates @theuselessproject run upcycling workshops, where you can learn how to make minor fixes or give old pieces a new lease of life.

and hoodies attract those seeking more abstract items. Everything is supplied by eco brands from around Europe, so you're allowed to feel smug as you stroll down the high street in your sustainable shirt.

BOW & PEARL

Map 5; Unit 33, Swan Centre, Rathmines; ///tone.admire.edge;
www.bowandpearl.com

Where does a Rathmines lady outfit her wardrobe? This lovely little store, where classy threads of premium quality come at an affordable price (find us a boutique in Rathmines that can say that). The dresses, blouses and knits that line the rails are cutesy but flattering, with pretty prints and fun colours that brighten up any dreary Dublin day. There's also a hard-to-resist jewellery section.

INDIGO & CLOTH

Map 1; 9 Essex Street E, Temple Bar; ///blocks.luck.accent;
www.indigoandcloth.com

Everything about this triple-threat boutique/café/studio screams cool. It stocks an excellent curation of swoon-worthy pieces from around the world, with brands you won't see anywhere else in town, all displayed in a manner so perfect you'll want to bribe the staff to reorganize your own wardrobe. You'll find the trendiest guys in the city here, picking up minimalist pieces before discussing the best pour-over methodology with the barista at the coffee stand.

» Don't leave without having a flat white from the ground floor coffee shop alongside a bar of the sea salt Bean & Goose chocolate.

OM DIVA

Map 2; 27 Drury Street, Creative Quarter; ///verge.inform.limbs;
www.omdivaboutique.com

It would be hard to find a Dubliner who doesn't adore this store.
An integral part of the city's style scene for 20 years, Om Diva is a
higgledy-piggledy shop filled with treasures. There's the added
bonus of the vintage stock, so you can pick up an abstract necklace
from a newly graduated art student before heading to the boudoir
basement for a pre-loved dress to match.

COSTUME

Map 2; 10 Castle Market, Creative Quarter; ///ally.elite.aside;
www.costumedublin.ie

Expect a well-dressed clientele hunting for something special at this
fashion landmark. The staff are fittingly artsy and genuinely talented
at picking out pieces for customers – half the joy of being here is
watching others wafting in and out of the changing rooms, modelling
the clothing pulled for them from the shop floor. The stunning clothes
themselves are designed by the best Irish and international talent.

FOLKSTER

Map 6; Dundrum Shopping Centre, Dundrum; ///limp.finishing.races;
www.folkster.com

There seem to be two worlds in this boutique – the land of casually
pretty dresses and cosy knits, and the one of fancy formalwear.
While those with three weddings to attend shuffle around the racks

of gowns, those on the lookout for more casual fare stick to the rails of laidback but covetable pieces, from buttery soft suede skirts to fuzzy, oversized jumpers.

» Don't leave without buying a few beautifully handmade gift cards (you know, for all those upcoming wedding ceremonies).

SPACE OUT SISTER

Map 4; 88 Francis Street, Liberties; ///humans.seats.start;
www.spaceoutsister.com

Tucked away among Francis Street's antique stores is this adorable lingerie shop with a loyal fanbase. Shopping in this calm space, decorated with sheepskin rugs and antique furniture, is an absolute dream (helped by the fact that you're often handed a glass of complimentary Babycham to enjoy as you browse). Whatever glam set you're looking for, be it a silk slip or a 1950s babydoll, owner Kiki always seems to be able to dig it out of a well-stocked drawer.

Nestled at the bottom of a lane in the coastal suburb of Fairview (in a renovated garage, of all places) lies hidden gem quack + dirk *(www.qplusd.com)*. As well as stocking vintage items, like voluminous 1980s dresses and chunky retro belts, this little store has a penchant for handmade clothing. In fact, owner Deirdre often sews the threads in-store while you browse the dresses, satchels, scarves – need we go on?

Gourmet Treats

Every neighbourhood in Dublin seems to have a little shop where foodies pick up their weekly staples. This is all thanks to artisans who've spent years finessing their craft, and locals who lap it up.

LISTONS FOOD STORE

Map 4; 25–6 Camden Street Lower, Portobello;
///agrees.agree.palms; www.listonsfoodstore.ie

Portobello locals only have one shop in mind when they need to stock their fridges, and that's Listons. The general vibe here is a love of good, healthy food, but there are some seriously decadent treats to hand, too, like gourmet sandwiches perfect for a luxe picnic in the park with friends and an excellent cheese counter that's full of delicacies guaranteed to impress guests at a dinner party.

LILLIPUT STORES

Map 3; 5 Arbour Hill, Stoneybatter; ///rinse.kite.loses;
www.lilliputstores.com

The kind of place where everyone who walks through the door is called "love", this charming little community shop is treasured by Stoneybatter residents. Shelves overflow with as much artisanal

Nip around the corner to independent publisher Lilliput Press to pick up a novel to enjoy with your treats.

treats as they can carry, from small-batch olive oil to the spicy peanut rayu from White Mausu that seems to fill the cupboards of every local in the area.

PEOPLE'S PARK MARKET

Map 6; Park Road, Glasthule, Dún Laoghaire; ///fires.reduce.custom;
www.dlrcoco.ie

Dublin has a bit of bad luck when it comes to markets (no thanks to redevelopment projects and a surge in online shopping), but this one has thankfully stood the test of time. A favourite haunt of Sunday strollers and weekday leisure-seekers, it supplies those lucky enough to live by the sea with local honey, fresh doughnuts and killer curries. Regulars head straight to the Arctic Stone cart for a hand-rolled ice cream to enjoy while perusing the good mix of produce.

MORTON'S

Map 5; 15-17 Dunville Ave, Ranelagh; ///clap.degree.dare; www.mortons.ie

While the well-to-do residents of Ranelagh pop into Morton's for their essentials (everyone needs organic steaks and fresh scallops, right?), other Dubliners only come here when they need to pick up fancy picnic supplies. Morton's freshly baked sourdough, truffle pecorino and homemade salted caramel tarts are always the most popular things on the blanket at outdoor gatherings.

» Don't leave without taking your spoils to nearby Dartmouth Square, a pretty park perfect for picnics.

ASIA MARKET

Map 2; 18 Drury Street, Creative Quarter;
///ducks.trucks.soil; www.asiamarket.ie

You wouldn't know it from the discreet doorway, but this supermarket is a Tardis, sprawling out to reveal an ever-bustling shop filled with in-the-know regulars stocking up on gyoza, nori and unusual vegetables. Both staff and shoppers move quickly, bustling between the aisles and calling out requests. Once you're done, it's a rite of passage to stop at the homemade mochi stand at the exit for some treats and a bubble tea – just the ticket for post-shopping fatigue.

SHERIDANS CHEESEMONGERS

Map 2; 11 Anne Street S, City Centre; ///react.snake.gentle;
www.sheridanscheesemongers.com

Cheese lovers: enter a paradise stocked with varieties from all over Ireland and Europe. You'll want to try everything from the Wicklow gooey brie to the Northern Irish pungent blue. Luckily, the staff are generous with the samples and encourage a nibble before committing, which is why you'll always see people hanging around the counter.

FALLON & BYRNE

Map 1; 11–17 Exchequer Street, Creative Quarter;
///slang.ideas.dates; www.fallonandbyrne.com

Grocery shopping has never been so fashionable. This iconic food hall is hallowed ground to Dubliners, who call in when the occasion warrants to pick up high-quality ingredients like gleaming heirloom tomatoes and treats such as edible flowers that impress any dinner guest. There's no pretention here, though: carefree banter always flows between locals and the experts behind the counter.

» Don't leave without popping into the restaurant upstairs. It seems fancy but surprisingly serves one of the best cheeseburgers in the city.

DUBLIN FOOD CO-OP

Map 6; The Old Chocolate Factory, Kilmainham Square, Kilmainham; ///whips.storms.chop; www.dublinfood.coop

Ostensibly a zero-waste shop, this is where eco-conscious locals come to fill their own Kilner jars with organic wholefoods and cleaning supplies. It's so much more than your average grocery store, though. This fantastic community hub brings the Kilmainham neighbourhood together, so much so that it's hard to find a local who isn't a member here (and doesn't revel in the discounts as a result) or who hasn't volunteered behind the counter. Devout fans tend to visit on a Saturday, so they can pick up a freshly squeezed juice and a crepe from the food trucks before stocking up.

Try it!
SHOP SUSTAINABLY

If the Food Co-Op has you motivated to adapt to a minimum-waste lifestyle, check out one of the frequent workshops. They include topics like zero-waste cooking and supporting cooking classes for refugees.

Irish Design

There's a strong tradition of art and craftsmanship in Ireland, but that doesn't mean old-fashioned tweeds and knitwear – modern Irish designers are at the top of their field, and every Dubliner wants a piece.

ARTICLE

Map 2; 59 William Street S, First Floor, Powerscourt Centre, Creative Quarter; ///tamed.combining.jungle; www.article.ie

The go-to spot to pick up a birthday present for artsy friends, this homeware-meets-funky-Irish-design store always has you leaving with a gift for yourself, too. Lining the shelves are amazing little items you never knew you wanted, much less needed: bamboo salad servers, ostrich feather dusters and high-end notebooks galore.

CHUPI

Map 2; 59 William Street S, Top Floor, Powerscourt Centre, Creative Quarter; ///tamed.combining.jungle; www.chupi.com

With a legion of chic fans, Chupi is the jewellery brand that feels at once classic and modern, as well as endlessly covetable. It's all inspired by Ireland's heritage and nature, from necklaces featuring old coins to ring bands modelled on hawthorn twigs. They're the

You'll find SO Fine Art Editions in the same shopping centre, so visit this gallery after to see original Irish art.

kind of pieces that you spot on your most stylish friend before getting addicted yourself, requesting an heirloom piece whenever big birthdays come around.

APRIL AND THE BEAR

Map 5; 213 Rathmines Road Lower; ///amused.force.door; www.aprilandthebear.com

When Dubliners are hunting for that next striking piece for their flat, they turn to this funky store. Owner and interior designer Siobhan Lam is a big believer in filling your home with items that you love, and she does the same with her store. Everything that April and the Bear stocks – quirky wall hangings, retro cocktail glasses, moss green lockers – is unique, cool and, above all, affordable.

SCOUT

Map 1; 5 Smock Alley Court, Temple Bar; ///songs.dating.bleat; www.scoutdublin.com

This unisex boutique leaves you wanting to unpack your bags and move in. Modern twists on timeless Irish pieces like Aran sweaters (they'll turn anyone into a sexy fisherman) and cosy hoodies share a space with locally designed linen slippers, handmade charcoal soap and hand-poured Irish candles that smell heavenly. Scout is practically a home away from home.

» Don't leave without buying the Bare Glow candle from Clean Slate. The scent will instantly transport you to the ocean.

IRISH DESIGN SHOP

Map 2; 41 Drury Street, Creative Quarter; ///cares.risky.wiping;
www.irishdesignshop.com

The space may be small and the name may be simple, but this shop is anything but. Handmade is at the core of everything here. The two women behind the store make their own range of bold, geometric jewellery in the workshop upstairs before displaying it among the vast range of items from other top-notch Irish designers downstairs – think cashmere beanies and tweed bow ties aimed at a cool crowd.

ARRAN STREET EAST

Map 3; 1 Little Green Street, Capel Street, North City;
///start.shop.descended; www.arranstreeteast.ie

Minimalists flock to this cool, Scandi-style modern pottery shop for its distinctive range of simplistic, sleek and contemporary ceramics. Before Arran Street East opened its doors, there was nothing quite like it in the city, so its range of muted tones and bold shapes quickly gained a strong following with first-time buyers and old-time renters

Try it!
THROW SOME CLAY

If Arran Street East ignites the inner ceramicist in you, book one of its weekend pottery workshops. You'll learn how to throw your own pot (and a lot of fun along the way is guaranteed).

seeking beautiful home touches. A lot of the items are designed with coffee in mind, including a ceramic filter pour-over that fits over the mugs they stock, and jumbo cups for the days when you need it most.

AVOCA

Map 2; 11–13 Suffolk Street, City Centre;
///daring.cities.crab; www.avoca.com

Mostly known for throws and scarves – all woven in a mill in the Wicklow countryside – the Avoca shop feels so cosy you almost want to wrap yourself in a blanket and make yourself at home. They make the kind of heritage pieces that last a lifetime, with cashmere and lambswool blended throws that brighten up even the dullest sofa. You'll visit to buy your co-worker a nice candle as a house-warming present and leave with a piece for the living room.

» Don't leave without buying a seaweed bath box from Voya, a Sligo-based brand. The hand-harvested seaweed makes for a heavenly soak.

INDUSTRY & CO

Map 2; 41 Drury Street, Creative Quarter; ///than.dishes.rested;
www.industryandco.com

You know you've struck gold when you can do all the shopping for your newly decorated bedroom under one roof and take a well-deserved break for a gooey brownie or two in the on-site café. Expect a blend of painstakingly hand-picked homewares, from pickle jar lamps to cool ceramics, and a lighting section that will make you rethink your whole house. You've been warned.

Book Nooks

Dublin has a literary heritage like no other. It's fitting, then, that bookshops dot every neighbourhood, and perusing the shelves of old and new is one of the best ways to spend an afternoon.

MARROWBONE BOOKS

Map 4; 78 The Coombe, Liberties; ///wants.blows.plant; www.marrowbone.ie

You can't miss this tiny second-hand book shop in the Liberties. For one, it's the only building on this residential street that's painted a vivid, Pokémon yellow. And it's always buzzing with Trinity students (it's owned by two alumni), who come here to check out the store's intimate gigs, readings and community events, and rifle through the piles upon piles of pre-loved books.

GUTTER BOOKSHOP

Map 1; Cow's Lane, Temple Bar; ///sticky.shape.detail; www.gutterbookshop.com

Named after the famous Oscar Wilde quote ("We are all in the gutter, but some of us are looking at the stars"), this charming store certainly leaves you feeling starry-eyed after a browse. Everything

Keep checking socials to find out when the next book launch is. (You might even get a free glass of wine.) from the name to the stock is about supporting fantastic Irish authors, so it's no wonder home-grown talents choose to hold their book launches here.

LAST BOOKSHOP

Map 4; 61 Camden Street Lower, Portobello; ///hats.muddy.fake; 086 851 7419

There are always a few people hanging around underneath the red awnings here, flipping through the novels displayed on the table outside. It's difficult to resist its charm when you walk past the door: the smell of second-hand books, the stacks of titles shoved haphazardly on shelves and in stacks on the floor, and, of course, the shop's adorable resident dog, Bertie. The genres available are wide-ranging, but the selection of Irish fiction at the front is always a winner.

TEMPLE BAR BOOK MARKET

Map 1; Temple Bar Square, Temple Bar; ///ranch.loving.blog; 016 772 255

Every weekend, rows of second-hand books appear on makeshift tables in the middle of Temple Bar, the shadows of the previous night's raucous festivities still clinging to the cobblestones. Before the rowdy tourists make their way back to the bars in the afternoon, a mix of students and bookworms can be found rifling through the boxes, rediscovering old classics and falling in love with new treasures.

» Don't leave without popping around the corner to the Temple Bar Food Market on a Saturday, for a crepe slathered in Nutella.

HODGES FIGGIS

Map 2; 56-8 Dawson Street, St Stephen's Green;
///fell.crate.expert; 016 774 754

Now owned by the Waterstones chain, this store has played a key role in Dublin's literary heritage. Founded in 1768, it was the bookshop of choice for many of the city's famed writers, and walking through its doors today feels like being a part of that history. While away a few hours browsing the huge collection alongside the next generation of writers in the form of Trinity students (the college is just up the road).

ULYSSES RARE BOOKS

Map 2; 10 Duke Street, City Centre; ///speaks.ties.slurs; www.rarebooks.ie

Your wallet might be intimidated by the first editions at the entrance, but worry not — while this museum-like shop has some of the rarest (and priciest) books in the country, it's not just about shelling out the big bucks. It feels special simply to be in the presence of these

Shh!

Books Upstairs *(www.books upstairs.ie)* is firmly on the radar of Dublin's most veracious readers, but hardly any of them know about the bookshop's regular events. Keep an eye on its calendar for readings, discussions and literary happenings. While you're here, swing by the beautiful restored Victorian café — laptops are banned, so people sit reading their new books under the stained-glass windows.

tomes, skimming your fingers over dusty hardbacks and ogling signed first editions from the likes of George R R Martin (which would set you back a massive €1,800).

THE WINDING STAIR

Map 3; 40 Ormond Quay Lower, North City;
///range.people.earth; www.winding-stair.com

This delightful little shop makes the most of its mishmash of new and second-hand titles with some lovely reading nooks in which to pore over them. You'll find the best new releases from Irish authors as well as an impressive poetry collection (to be expected from a shop named after a Yeats poem). Once you've purchased your title of choice, grab a cup of tea and a space in the sunny window seat and get reading.

>> Don't leave without heading up the actual winding stairs to the restaurant for potted crab and killer views over the Ha'penny Bridge.

THE COMPANY OF BOOKS

Map 5; 96 Ranelagh Road, Ranelagh; ///taxi.seated.truly;
www.thecompanyofbooks.ie

Brunchers making their lazy way around Ranelagh never fail to pop into this light and airy shop. The sleek design draws them in, but it's the excellent collection that makes them stay. Somehow, the passionate booksellers know exactly what you want to read before you do, and it'll be right there in the window display waiting for you. It's usually quiet enough to allow for a natter with the staff about the best books – chances are you'll leave with the perfect one.

An afternoon of
crate digging

There's no questioning Dublin's musical legacy (think U2 and Sinead O'Connor). Even today, you can hardly walk down the street without a busker strumming a guitar, nor enter a boozer without a sing-along. And in a city this dedicated to music, there's only one way to listen to it: on vinyl. The city centre is crammed with stores where music lovers sift through records old and new and chat about their favourites. There's no better way to spend an afternoon — just don't be surprised if you end up in a debate about obscure B-tracks.

1. Hen's Teeth
Blackpitts, Merchants Quay;
www.hensteethstore.com
///guard.orders.help

2. Tower Records
7 Dawson Street,
St Stephens Green;
www.towerrecords.ie
///funds.tried.free

3. All City Records
4 Crow Street, Temple Bar;
www.allcityrecords.com
///spirit.code.play

4. The R.A.G.E
8 Crow Street, Temple Bar;
www.therage.ie
///loops.mint.gravel

5. The Grand Social
35 Liffey Street
Lower, North City;
www.thegrandsocial.ie
///range.pram.curiosity

Bruxelles
///copy.lied.freed

Liffey

PATRICK STREET

THE LIBERTIES

KEVIN ST

NEW ROW SOUTH

1 Lunch at HEN'S TEETH
Grab a bite at this cool art collective that's part diner, part store, then browse the local art and excellent vinyl.

NORTH
CITY

Liffey

**Enjoy a gig at
THE GRAND SOCIAL**

Book tickets to this iconic
venue to end the day listening
to local artists. They also run
a vinyl fair once a month.

(5) *Ha'penny Bridge*

**Geek out at
THE R.A.G.E**

Enter this time machine for
second-hand vinyl and
retro computer games
(think Sega Megadrive).

**TEMPLE
BAR**

PEARSE
STREET

(4)
(3)

DAME STREET

COLLEGE
GREEN

SUFFOLK ST

*Trinity
College*

**Pop into
ALL CITY RECORDS**

Join the city's street artists
picking up their arty supplies
and underground records.

NASSAU ST

WICKLOW ST

GRAFTON ST

**CREATIVE
QUARTER**

DAWSON STREET

**(2) Rifle through
TOWER RECORDS**

Classical music fan? Into
obscure techno? You'll find it
all here: the king of Dublin's
vinyl scene. Browse the
cases, then check out the
turntables in the hi-fi room.

*A statue of Dubliner Phil
Lynott (frontman of Thin
Lizzy) stands outside one
of his favourite boozers,
Bruxelles – Dublin's
definitive rock pub.*

ST STEPHEN'S GREEN

ST STEPHEN'S GREEN

AUNGIER STREET

*St Stephen's
Green*

EVIN ST LOWER   CUFFE STREET

0 metres   200

0 yards   200

ARTS & CULTURE

Oozing with artistic heritage, Dublin is shaped by its fun-loving creative scene. Days are spent celebrating the talents of the past, while nights pass by applauding the new.

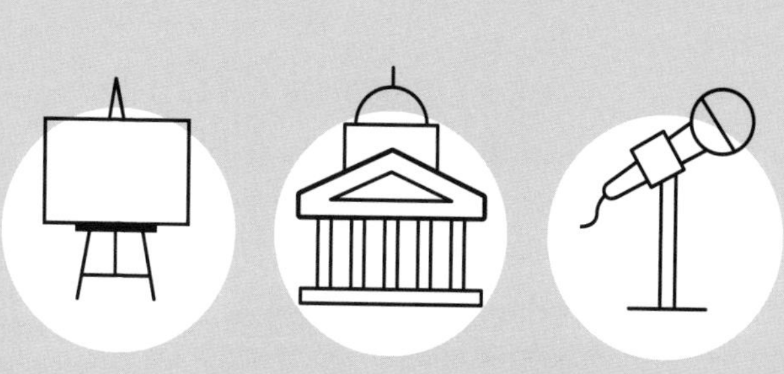

City History

Not a day goes by without grandparents sharing stories of the past and students hotly debating the issues of today. Giving these conversations ammunition are shrines to Irish ancestry in every crevice of the city.

EPIC THE IRISH EMIGRATION MUSEUM

Map 5; The chq Building, Custom House Quay, North City; ///lowest.crowds.decks; www.epicchq.com

People the world over can't resist pointing out that their grandmother twice removed was Irish, and this place shows how that came to be. Refusing to be a museum with just another list of long names, this interactive space invites you to listen to stories from over 300 emigrants to explore the impact of how, and why, 10 million people left Ireland. (You'll learn the steps of *Riverdance* along the way, too.)

SECRET STREET TOURS

Map 3; Meet outside Collins Barracks, Smithfield; ///loss.less.glory; www.secretstreettours.org

Smithfield may have a reputation as a hipster spot nowadays, but there's a complex history to the area and its residents. It makes sense, then, to tour it with someone who knows the secrets held within its

Head over the Liffey to Nicholas Street after to see plaques that quote stories from local residents.

colourful streets. Uniquely, these friendly guides are either homeless or formerly homeless, giving you a moving insight into a prevalent issue in the area and wider city.

IRISH NATIONAL WAR MEMORIAL GARDENS

**Map 6; Islandbridge, Kilmainham; ///soaks.wisley.waters;
www.heritageireland.ie**

While tourists flock to gardens in the centre, those seeking a moment of reflection head west to this charming, overlooked patch of green. Tucked away in Islandbridge, the gardens were erected in honour of 49,400 Irish soldiers who lost their lives in World War I. It's a tranquil spot, covered in rose bushes and centred around a large pond.

» Don't leave without arranging a visit to the granite book rooms to read the names of the fallen soldiers in the Harry Clarke manuscripts.

CHRIST CHURCH CATHEDRAL

**Map 1; Christchurch Place, Liberties; ///cheeks.card.shack;
www.christchurchcathedral.ie**

Daily services draw religious folk into this 1,000-year-old space, but it means more to the city than just a place of worship. Unbeknown to tourists, a 12th-century crypt lies beneath, harbouring key artifacts that have belonged to the cathedral for centuries. One of these most locals know all too well: the fondly named Tom and Jerry, a mummified cat and rat, thought to have become stuck in an organ during a chase.

Liked by the locals

"I love the warm, comforting smell of the library: centuries-old leather and paper mixed with a pinch of polish and a dash of ancient woodsmoke from the fireplace."

JASON MCELLIGOTT, DIRECTOR OF MARSH'S LIBRARY

MARSH'S LIBRARY

Map 4; St Patrick's Close, Liberties; ///spare.dine.tube; www.marshlibrary.ie

In all appearances just an old library, this oft-forgotten-about haven has more to it than sloping shelves and leather-bound tomes. If you know where to look, you'll find ancient manuscripts with bullet holes from the 1916 Rising: a bit of history in the history books.

» **Don't leave without** glimpsing the ancient pages on display that month – there's a rolling exhibition of open tomes according to theme.

GLASNEVIN CEMETERY

Map 6; Finglas Road, Glasnevin; ///hood.scars.sunset;
www.glasnevinmuseum.ie

The thought of ambling through a cemetery may give some people the creeps, but this place is intrinsic to Dublin's story. Take a tour to learn about the residents here or, if it's all feeling a bit morbid, follow those disappearing through a tiny door in the cemetery's walls to the National Botanic Gardens *(p161)* for a bit of zen.

KILMAINHAM GAOL

Map 6; Inchicore Road, Kilmainham; ///sticky.clots.twig;
www.kilmainhamgaolmuseum.ie

One of the most evocative places of Dublin's often turbulent past is a prison. The sense of history here is palpable: it's where the leaders of the 1916 Rising were executed, making it symbolic to the Irish rebellion. It's been empty since 1924, so you'll have no run-ins with inmates – just locals who live nearby walking the beautiful grounds.

Favourite Museums

The Irish are a talented (and proud) bunch, so the museums in the capital rightfully show off their greatest achievements. Most are delightfully free, too, so returning with visiting friends in tow is a given.

THE LITTLE MUSEUM OF DUBLIN

Map 2; 15 St Stephen's Green; ///scars.camp.sums; www.littlemuseum.ie

Shaking off any notion that a museum should be stuffy, this cosy townhouse is home to some of the quirkiest exhibits in Dublin. You'll learn everything you could possibly need to know about the city, from the 1916 Rising to Ireland's favourite puppets, Podge and Rodge. Tours are led by guides who are friendly, knowledgeable and deliciously eccentric – keep an eye out for themed options, particularly those about women's history, for more incredible stories.

WINDMILL LANE RECORDING STUDIOS

Map 5; 20 Ringsend Road, Ringsend; ///accent.good.future; www.windmilllanerecording.com

This white, stately building with its mint-green door may look more like a holiday home plucked out of the French Riviera but, inside, the walls echo with the blood, sweat and tears of artists like Kate Bush and U2. A tour of this working studio – the first of its kind in Ireland – attracts music lovers wanting to learn about the processes behind the most influential songs made over the last 40 years. You'll leave wanting to record the album you never knew you had in you here.

» Don't leave without mixing your own session with a virtual band – the first step in your own musical journey.

IRISH JEWISH MUSEUM

Map 4; 3 Walworth Road, Portobello; ///spoke.claims.retail; www.jewishmuseum.ie

Before Portobello became a hipster hub, it was Dublin's Jewish district. Locals are proud of the area's "Little Jerusalem" status and swing by this teensy museum, housed in an old synagogue, regularly to check out its talks, events and quirky collection. Look out for the former Lord Mayor of Dublin's yarmulke, which is hand painted with shamrocks.

NATIONAL MUSEUM OF IRELAND – ARCHAEOLOGY

Map 5; Kildare Street, St Stephens Green; ///staple.humid.sprint; www.museum.ie

There's always an excuse to pop into this city stalwart. Family visiting from out of town? Seeking refuge from the rain? This beloved museum is a hit thanks to its collection of some of Ireland's most famous (and fascinating) crafted artifacts. The exhibit they always come back to? Kinship and Sacrifice, where preserved Iron Age bodies are complete with fingernails, teeth and hair: creepy, but incredible, every time.

MUSEUM OF LITERATURE IRELAND

**Map 5; UCD Naughton Joyce Centre, 86 St Stephen's Green;
///tune.vibrate.artist; www.moli.ie**

Though housed in the original grounds of University College Dublin, where James Joyce and Mary Lavin once scribbled in their notebooks, this new museum refuses to be an old-fashioned time machine. MoLI is all about immersing visitors in the breadth of Ireland's old and new literary heritage. One minute you're ogling the first edition of *Ulysses*, the next you're uncovering the country's underrepresented female writers (there's so much more to Ireland's writing scene than Joyce, no matter how great he is). Retirees fittingly spend the day reading with a cup of tea in the stunning courtyard, so settle in on a bench alongside them and plug in to RadioMoLI, where interviews with contemporary writers continue the literary journey.

» **Don't leave without** browsing the fantastic MoLI shop, where books are stocked beside bespoke Irish crafts, art and jewellery.

CHESTER BEATTY LIBRARY

Map 1; Dublin Castle, City Centre; ///grid.today.spot; www.chesterbeatty.ie

Dublin Castle's worst-kept secret, this literary gem houses a renowned collection of centuries-old manuscripts from across the globe. Groups of schoolchildren clamouring to get inside, tourists embarking on the free tours and historians poring over the collection of Chinese jade books are regular sights in this Aladdin's cave. In the summer holidays, families flock in their droves for the art-making workshops, while the more sophisticated PhD students await the compelling seminars on topics like multiculturalism and identity. The best-kept secret,

Join a free Qigong and meditation session held on the rooftop of the library once a month.

though, is the unfussy Middle Eastern café, tucked away at the back of the museum, its delicious dishes satisfying many a hungry patron.

NATIONAL MUSEUM OF IRELAND – NATURAL HISTORY

Map 5; Merrion Street Upper, Merrion Square; ///sting.ashes.long; www.museum.ie

Providing fond memories of school trips, Dublin's "Dead Zoo", as it's affectionately known, is a beloved part of the city's fabric. A highly impressive artifact in its own right, this museum is a cabinet of curiosities, where mammals are housed in Victorian cases, a huge shark hangs from the ceiling and giant skeletons of Irish deer incite expressions of wonder. A calmness pervades the halls, where those escaping rainy days retreat and find themselves still lost in the maze of zoological exhibits long after the sun reappears from the clouds.

14 HENRIETTA STREET

Map 3; North City; ///oiled.tape.jolly; www.14henriettastreet.ie

Close to the hearts of Dubliners who have lived in the city centre for generations, this 18th-century house shows who they are and where they've come from. If the walls could talk, they'd tell stories of extreme hardship and camaraderie from the days when over 100 people once dwelled here. Luckily, previous residents tell those hidden histories of tenement living on the unmissable intimate tours.

Art Galleries

Dublin's art scene is about more than just, well, the art itself. Indie galleries and big hitters are all for asking challenging questions, honouring the artists of the past and inspiring the creatives of tomorrow.

DOUGLAS HYDE

Map 2; Trinity College Dublin, City Centre; ///sculpture.goat.boss; www. thedouglashyde.ie

At this too-often-forgotten tiny gallery on the Trinity College campus, a fitting approach to showcasing the works of unknown talent reigns. Displaying contemporary works that push boundaries, the space has become a magnet for free thinkers. As you explore this hidden gem, spare a thought for those queuing for the Book of Kells nearby.

IRISH MUSEUM OF MODERN ART

Map 6; Royal Hospital Kilmainham, Military Road, Kilmainham; ///usage.cared.forest; www.imma.ie

Small groups chill on the meadows that surround IMMA on sunny days, stepping inside after their catch-ups to get their fill of modern art. It's a social hub for budding creatives, who return for making workshops, artist-led seminars and a lot of Pablo Picasso.

ATELIER NOW

Map 5; Block 3, Charlemont Street, Portobello;
///clown.sobs.active; www.ateliernow.ie

Anything that acclaimed artist Maser touches draws out hipsters like moths to a flame, and his studio is no exception. Used as an exhibition space for his work and that of Dublin's up-and-coming artists, the atelier also hosts pop-up events like yoga and Pilates classes, attracting those in the need of a bit of culture and self-care.

» Don't leave without visiting the swanky, black-and-white-chequered bathroom. It's delightfully funky and a work of art in itself.

NATIONAL GALLERY OF IRELAND

Map 5; Merrion Square W; ///cave.rice.people; www.nationalgallery.ie

A national gallery may evoke images of highbrow critics and tourists filling quiet halls, but here a vibrant young crowd outnumbers the usual suspects. It has a lot to do with the cool events: design workshops, documentary screenings, networking opportunities and late-night openings on a Thursday, which all aim to foster budding creatives.

Try it!
GET CRAFTY

To create your own masterpiece, check out the workshop schedules at Hen's Teeth (*www.hensteethstore.com*), a cool art café in the Liberties. Depending on when you visit, you could be learning to crochet or collage.

HANG TOUGH CONTEMPORARY

Map 2; 4 Exchequer Street, Creative Quarter; ///senior.loss.rocket; www.hangtoughcontemporary.com

The artsy Creative Quarter was the obvious location for this fantastic new art gallery. Opened in 2021 by Hang Tough, the favourite framers of Dublin's artists and photographers, the relatively small space is dedicated to highlighting the best new talent in the city. The launch nights are one of the hottest (free) tickets in town, with guests spilling onto the street with their cocktails as live DJs play.

TEMPLE BAR GALLERY + STUDIOS

Map 1; 5–9 Temple Bar; ///tries.animal.chin; www.templebargallery.com

In the heart of Dublin's artistic quarter is this meeting place for creatives, who come to catch up over installations and performance art and make those all-important artist connections. The studios are

Shh!

You wouldn't expect it from a neighbourhood pub, but Lucky's *(www.luckys.ie)* in the Liberties doubles as a small art gallery, and is consequently perceived by in-the-know regulars as one of the coolest spots in town. As well as rotating art exhibitions that reflect local history, the pub also hosts regular art sales and launches from Epoch, the feminist collective *(www.epoch dublin.com)*. Epoch produces art filled with messages about homelessness, and profits go to charity, too.

occupied by over 30 creatives, from recent graduates to recognized names, but it's the gallery that draw the big crowds. There are five exhibitions a year with a strong emphasis on solo shows, which supportive friends, family and art lovers pack out without fail.

THE HUGH LANE
Map 3; Charlemont House, Parnell Square N, Rotunda;
///debate.falls.rich; www.hughlane.ie

It does this spot a disservice to call it a gallery in singular terms. Every room feels like its own mini museum: Francis Bacon's chaotic studio (yep, once his actual workspace), the banquet-esque sculpture hall, the sacred room full of kaleidoscopic stained-glass works. Pop in during the weekend for a treat, when a live pianist plays and the music filters beautifully into each of these rooms.

PHOTO MUSEUM IRELAND
Map 1; Meeting House Square, Temple Bar; ///fall.ozone.status;
www. photomuseumireland.ie

This tiny, inspiring gallery has had a huge impact on snap-happy locals. The rotating exhibitions feature the work of big names in the industry, but it's the talks and workshops that have built a small community of passionate photographers. Dark room, DSLR and smartphone photography training courses are regularly held here and promise to turn budding creatives into experts.

» Don't leave without checking out the adjoining shop, where over 3,000 inspiring photography books are waiting to be pored over.

Top Theatres

Some of the world's most impressive playwrights are from Dublin, so it fits that the theatre scene is at the centre of the city's culture today. Fresh talents are well on their way to surpassing their predecessors.

OLYMPIA THEATRE

Map 1; 72 Dame Street, Temple Bar; ///twig.dates.runner; www.olympia.ie

Despite its plush appearance, this isn't the kind of place you visit for a traditonal, classy theatre show – and that's exactly why it's a local favourite. Performances are always a belter, whether it's a musical dedicated to Ireland's favourite nightclub, the annual Christmas pantomime or a top comedy act on tour. Expect just as much craic as any bar-hopping night out: entertaining shows always end with crowds dancing and cheering before migrating to the bar inside.

THE NEW THEATRE

Map 1; 43 Essex Street E, Temple Bar; ///jobs.basic.frame; www.thenewtheatre.com

Productions always play to a packed house in this snug 66-seat space nestled at the back of a bookshop. That's probably to do with its strong ties to the Dublin Fringe Festival and that it does what it says on the tin

– promotes new theatre. There's a strong community feel to it all: the artistic director chooses productions written by rising playwrights, an on-site creative team helps to produce the work and direct new performers, and the seats fill out with friends supporting friends.

ABBEY THEATRE

**Map 5; 26–27 Abbey Street Lower, North City;
///cape.petty.video; www.abbeytheatre.ie**

Ireland's national theatre more than lives up to its well-regarded reputation. Founded by infamous theatre enthusiasts (W B Yeats, anyone?), the Abbey has long been a staple for an eclectic crowd of Dubliners – some of whom considered theatre too pretentious before visiting. Helping matters are the cheap tickets and a fitting emphasis on inclusiveness, diversity and ambitious new theatre work.

» Don't leave without taking a backstage tour to get into the fabric of Irish theatre, with a close look at productions and set design.

Shh!

The Abbey offers "Free First" tickets for the preview of all shows. They're distributed at 6:30pm outside the venue, so start queuing from about 6pm to guarantee a free ticket (it's first come, first served) and the smug feeling of being the first to see a new show. Check the website for the shows involved. Don't stress if you miss out: front row seats (row A) for every performance at the Abbey are a steal at just €13.

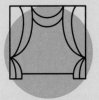

Liked by the locals

"Dublin's theatrical DNA comes from traditional storytellers, literary giants and political agitators. I love that audiences can choose from an immersive experience to a stirring revival and so much more."

AOIFE SPILLANE-HINKS, THEATRE/OPERA DIRECTOR

SMOCK ALLEY THEATRE

Map 1; 7 Exchange Street Lower, Temple Bar;
///pigs.sweet.quit; www.smockalley.com

It's easy to walk right past this unassuming building without realizing that a hub of dance and creativity lies inside. Once you cross the threshold, though, the quirky church-like set with Gothic windows and dazzling sculpted ceilings produces the wow-factor time and again.

THE LIR

Map 5; Trinity Technology and Enterprise Campus,
Pearse Street, Docklands; ///sands.hooked.spicy; www.thelir.ie

Providing a juxtaposition to the herds of suits in the Docklands are the trendy students of Ireland's National Academy of Dramatic Art. When classes at the Lir are over, however, the college opens its studio spaces to the public, who filter in for student shows, talks and workshops.

» Don't leave without visiting the wine bar on campus, which is a great way to rub shoulders with up-and-coming Irish talent.

THE GATE

Map 3; Cavendish Row, Parnell Square E, Rotunda;
///vets.mile.softly; www.gatetheatre.ie

You're close to the action wherever you sit in this intimate space. In spite of its small size, it's had a big impact on the careers of prodigious actors (Orson Welles, for one), so you may witness the next big thing performing in a classic play or musical. Wear your finest outfit for the occasion — it's an elegant venue with chandeliered ceilings.

Classic Cinemas

Rainy evenings call for a trip to the nearest cinema, where hot buttery popcorn and the latest release or oldest classic awaits. The next day, it's customary to discuss the flick with your work pals over a cuppa.

IRISH FILM INSTITUTE

Map 1; 6 Eustace Street, Temple Bar; ///sheet.digs.spots; www.ifi.ie

Without even a hint of superhero blockbusters on its calendar, the IFI is where you'll find movies that aren't showing anywhere else in the city. The theatres are rarely packed out (you won't find chatterbox teenagers here), so it's a calming hub for arty film buffs and budding film-makers who come for the mix of Irish and world cinema and stick around at the on-site bar after a showing to digest it all.

STELLA CINEMA

Map 5; 207, 209 Rathmines Road Lower, Rathmines;
///mobile.dared.pound; www.stellacinemas.ie

Everything about this converted old theatre is classic: the luxurious sofa seats, the cosy blankets, the traditional table service and the upstairs cocktail bar. With a 1920s flair, Stella is the fanciest cinema in town, made for date nights and special occasions. The latest

This place is no secret, so tickets are hard to come by. Book a week in advance to make sure of your spot.

blockbuster releases and cult classics are screened to a chic crowd every day, but come the weekend, night owls indulge in late-night viewings from midnight.

LIGHT HOUSE CINEMA

Map 3; Market Street S, Smithfield; ///shapes.extend.gone;
www.lighthousecinema.ie

This effortlessly cool and colourful modern venue is the place to be seen. Creatives and arthouse film enthusiasts congregate for a drink at the bar before settling in to an old classic or a new release on cosy couches. Sure, you can't see the vibrantly coloured seats once the lights go down, but you'll know you're sitting in style (and maybe alongside a wagging tail or two during the dog-friendly screenings).

» **Don't leave without** ordering some Nobó ice cream, dairy-free and made in Dublin, from the café to enjoy while watching the film.

CINEWORLD

Map 3; The Parnell Centre, Parnell Street, Rotunda;
///cove.pillow.pigs; www.cineworld.ie

A cinema chain may offer up haunting flashbacks of screaming kids and oh-so-outdated mainstream vibes, but this branch deserves your attention. It's the biggest cinema in Ireland, with four floors and 17 huge screens – including IMAX and 4DX – so all manner of crowds flock here to see guilty-pleasure new releases and superhero flicks with a big bucket of popcorn for a trusted good viewing.

SAVOY CINEMA

Map 3; 17 O'Connell Street Upper, North City;
///boots.middle.reply; www.imccinemas.ie

Ireland's oldest operational cinema may be a bit battered around the edges, but it's managed to hold onto its charm over the years. Though it focuses on new releases and often hosts movie premieres (and the stars of those flicks), old-time film lovers flock here for its irresistible old-school vibe, where nothing is over-complicated.

SASS MOUTH DAMES FILM CLUB

Map 2; 59 Drury Street, Creative Quarter; ///gains.aims.bliss;
www.sassmouthdames.com

Who doesn't love a sassy broad? Academic Megan McGurk, who runs this long-running film club and hosts its spin-off podcast, certainly does. Each season, she chooses a selection of movies made between 1929 and 1959 that all have one thing in common – a feisty woman

Shh!

It's always a surprise venue when Happenings (www.happenings. ie) are in charge, but the spontaneity is all part of the fun. This events team put on eco-friendly pop-up screenings in public outdoor spaces, but you don't know where – or what – it will be until 48 hours before. Think Goonies in Merrion Square or A Bug's Life in a Phibsborough park. Register on the website to join the community and be in the know.

(or women) at its heart, like Norma Shearer or Clara Bow. Screenings pop up all over town, but you'll usually find the club at Brooks Private Cinema; bag tickets for your girlfriends and celebrate girl power.

BROOKS PRIVATE CINEMA
Map 2; Brooks Hotel, 59 Drury Street, Creative Quarter;
///gains.aims.bliss; www.brookshotel.ie

Nestled in the basement of a tiny inner-city hotel is Dublin's best-kept secret, where entering feels like stumbling into an exclusive members' club. It's become a chic venue for groups of friends celebrating big birthdays or chilled hen parties, with just 26 seats that are only available for private hire. DVDs may be a thing of the past, but they're thriving here, where you can bring your own film to be screened.

» Don't leave without heading up to the Jasmine Bar upstairs after your film for a 16-year-old Bushmills whiskey to finish the night in style.

OMNIPLEX
Map 5; 210 Rathmines Road Lower, Rathmines;
///fight.skirt.ruled; www.omniplex.ie

Despite being a firm favourite among Rathmines locals, this little cinema remains under the radar of those living outside the area, so never gets too rammed. Parents pop by with their kids after browsing the neighbouring shopping centre, while friends arrive in the evening after having dinner nearby. It's most atmospheric at night, when the on-site bar opens and it's customary to grab a glass of wine to enjoy before (or with) the latest release or throwback film being screened.

Culture Live

Dublin's live cultural scene is centred on the community, where poetry slams, creative seminars and trad sessions provide a space for a range of voices to be heard, and a refuge for those who listen.

DOLCÁIN'S CELLAR

Map 6; The Laurel's Bar, 2 Main St, Clondalkin, S Dublin; ///dine.trains.smug

On the last Thursday of every month at 7pm, poets, troubadours and singer-songwriters pack into the cellar of The Laurel's Bar to show off their talent at the open mic night. What started as performances for the pub's regular punters has turned into a word-of-mouth victory: patrons tell their mates, who bring their dates, who gather their co-workers to soak up Irish talent while cracking jokes with each other.

IRISH WRITERS' CENTRE

Map 3; 19 Parnell Square N, Rotunda; ///barn.single.basket; www.irishwriterscentre.ie

Honouring Dublin's strong literary heritage while nurturing new writers is this beloved centre, at its best when hosting bimonthly Takin' the Mic. Stories of homelessness, poems about comical sexual escapades and songs dedicated to climate change are

If you want to show off your own talents, arrive at 7pm to sign up for a first come, first served spot.

performed by young writers of all backgrounds, so simply turn up (with your own booze in hand) and let the laughter (or tears) commence.

THE COBBLESTONE
Map 3; 77 King Street N, Smithfield; ///secret.silent.final; www.cobblestonepub.ie

It's all about the *seisiún* (session) here, self-styled as "a drinking pub with a music problem". Sure, many pubs host live trad – the pinnacle of Irish culture – but music has been part of The Cobblestone's fabric for more than five generations. Entering this old-fashioned, cosy space is like stumbling upon a private rehearsal: the band don't intend to entertain, but rather play for the love for it. A toe-tapping audience munching on a bag of crisps to upbeat jigs is simply a bonus.

» Don't leave without attending the Wednesday Balaclavas session to refine your own instrument playing and learn a trad tune or two.

PROJECT ARTS CENTRE
Map 1; 39 Essex Street E, Temple Bar; ///statue.tables.ramp; www.projectartscentre.ie

You never know what you'll get from the hundreds of annual events at this multidisciplinary arts centre, from rap performances covering mental health to thought-provoking live radio. Known affectionately as the "Big Blue Building", this non-profit is a hub for a super-local crowd of artists and thinkers who keep returning for the warm, supportive vibe.

THE TARA BUILDING

Map 5; Tara Street, City Centre; ///exists.submit.riches;
www.thetarabuilding.com

A vibrant mural on the outside, Dublin's most talented creatives on the inside and an exciting events calendar to boot make this co-working space one of the coolest places in town. Enticing journalists, stylists and designers to rise early are the free, monthly Creative Mornings: lectures led by cutting-edge innovators who share their bold ideas.

SWENY'S PHARMACY

Map 5; 1 Lincoln Place, City Centre; ///friday.market.newest; www. sweny.ie

It may be unusual for a pharmacy to have a cult following, but this is no usual chemist. Featured in James Joyce's *Ulysses*, it's a meeting place for fans who come for daily live readings. Expect a niche crowd of regulars and volunteers cradling cups of tea while discussing the masterpiece.

» Don't leave without buying the famous lemon-scented soap that Leopold Bloom smells – and goes on to purchase – in the book.

POETRY IRELAND

Map 6; DCU St Patrick's Campus, Drumcondra;
///analogy.curiosity.sock; www.poetryireland.ie

Banishing exam sweat flashbacks at the mere mention of poetry is this inviting non-profit. Currently between homes, and based in a temporary office space in DCU for the next few years, it hosts a range of open mics across the city from passionate soapbox poetry on the streets to cosy and contemplative indoor affairs.

Liked by the locals

"Dublin is a city of colour, character and creativity, and somewhere that showcases this really well is The Tara Building. We feel so lucky to be able to host our events in this bright open space."

GERALDINE CARTON, THE USELESS PROJECT

Head up to
STIRRUP LANE

Don't stare at collective Subset's eye-wobbling mural of a boy on a horse for too long – it's seriously trippy (and cool).

SMITHFIELD

5

6

Drinks and dinner at
THE HENDRICK

Finish the day in this street art-themed hotel, checking out the collection of urban art and enjoying some food.

PHIBSBOROUGH ROAD

NORTH KING ST

DORSET ST UPPER

CHURCH ST

CAPEL STREET

SMITHFIELD

NORTH CITY

GARDINER ST LOWER

Look out for
THE TARA BUILDING

Stroll down Tara Street to this co-working space, its exterior emblazoned with a vibrant mural by iconic Irish street artist Maser.

Butt B

2

Liffey

Grattan Bridge

TEMPLE BAR

COLLEGE ST

Trinity College

4

Amble down
LOVE LANE

Head north to this little alleyway filled with art, an initiative set up by the council to turn Dublin's lanes into open-air galleries.

SOUTH GREAT GEORGES ST

NASSAU ST

CREATIVE QUARTER

GRAFTON STREET

CITY CENTRE

ST STEPHEN'S GREEN

AUNGIER ST

THE LIBERTIES

PORTOBELLO

WEXFORD ST

Continue to the
U ARE ALIVE MURAL

Camden Street is a canvas for art, but pause at this favourite by Aches and Maser and let the message – U Are Alive – sink in.

3

CAMDEN ST LOWER

HARCOURT ST

*Known for his Repeal the 8th mural in 2016, Maser is Dublin's most famous street artist – he even has his own studio, **Atelier Now** (p117).*

0 metres 500

0 yards 500

A morning exploring
Dublin's street art

It's hard to turn a corner without stumbling across some killer street art, from multimedia works that incorporate sculpted metal to large-scale murals that defy belief. Dublin is a canvas for creative pieces, all of which tell stories about community and life at large. As is the nature of the game, street art doesn't always stick around here (to the dismay of Dubliners who count on it to liven up their commutes). But, as more Dublin artists get their names known on the global scene, that's starting to change. Always keep your eyes peeled.

Embrace your inner artist at ALL OUT DESIGN
Start by learning the ropes on a street art workshop. Your canvas? The warehouse walls of this agency, so go wild with the spray paint.

N-STRAND RD

STREET

Liffey

PEARSE STREET

Grand Canal

1. All Out Design
1A Hyacinth Street, North Strand; www.allout.ie
///burst.frozen.feel

2. The Tara Building
Tara Street, City Centre;
www.thetarabuilding.com
///exists.submit.riches

3. U Are Alive Mural
77 Camden Street Lower, Portobello
///bills.member.admiral

4. Love Lane
Crampton Court, Temple Bar
///rush.trucks.ritual

5. Stirrup Lane
Stirrup Lane, Smithfield
///alien.coffee.oath

6. The Hendrick
6 Hendrick Street, Smithfield;
www.hendrickdublin.ie
///finely.region.fast

Atelier Now
///image.cones.moth

NIGHTLIFE

With their love of banter, music and the odd tipple, Dubliners need little excuse for a "session". No matter what day it is, there's always a Friday night buzz to the city.

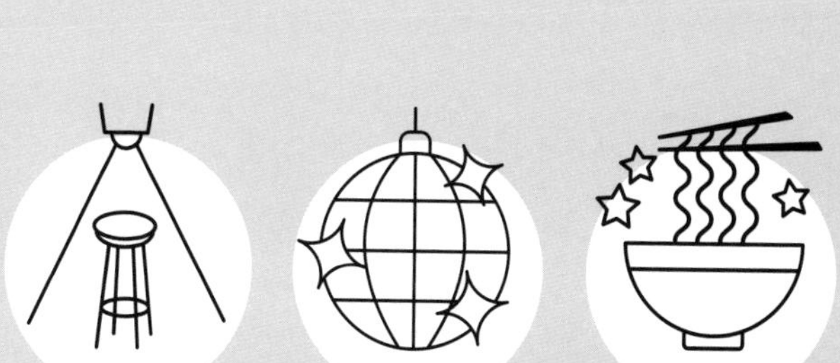

Cool Clubs

Clubbing in Dublin is an experience to be reckoned with. Socializing, getting the "shift" (sparking up a romance) and becoming best buds with DJs are all part and parcel of a night spent dancing.

XICO

Map 5; 143 Baggot Street Lower, St Stephen's Green;
///club.odds.pints; www.xico.ie

Hosting one of the wildest nights out in Dublin, Xico is the only place where you'll find yourself dancing beside the table you just ate from, wearing an obnoxiously large sombrero and sipping frozen margaritas. This cavernous venue starts out as a popular place for Mexican food, yet as the hour gets late and the diners get tipsy, the floor is transformed into a lively nightclub. It's a hotspot for fun-filled fiestas and live music, the highlight being the bongo and saxophone duo.

DICEY'S GARDEN

Map 4; 21–5 Harcourt Street, City Centre; ///guilty.lifted.games; 01 478 4066

Students on an all-important budget own the night at this notorious, no-frills joint. The DJ set is always eclectic, with the likes of pop, rap and hip-hop playing out to two major dance floors and a huge beer

For a swankier club night, head upstairs to celebrity haunt Krystle. It requires a separate entry fee, mind.

garden. Between dances, groups of friends tuck into unbelievably cheap food at the BBQ area while sipping on pints for a glorious €3.

PANTIBAR

Map 3; 7–8 Capel Street, North City; ///decent.backed.bubble; 01 874 0710

The "Queen of Ireland", drag queen legend Panti Bliss rules the roost at this Capel Street haunt. Drawing in swathes of weekly regulars are Panti's karaoke nights and pub quizzes, but weekends are reserved – and renowned – for partying. Amid the neon lights and luscious red decor, a community of welcoming staff and fun-loving patrons dance to gay anthems, cheesy tunes and a whole lot of pop.

» Don't leave without trying Panti's Pale Ale, a homemade and refreshing pint that's made at the nearby Trouble Brewing.

IZAKAYA BASEMENT

Map 1; 12 S Great George's Street, Creative Quarter; ///names.hired.closet; www.yamamori.ie/izakaya-basement

A Japanese speakeasy in Dublin may come as a surprise, but catch the rowdy crowds of late-night revellers queuing at 1am and you'll see it's certainly caught on. At first glance, this is a top-class sushi joint, but descend into the basement and you'll be swept into a sea of sweaty youngsters dancing to EDM until 3am (it's one of the latest clubs in the city, after all). The interior matches the crowd: edgy and grungy, with black bamboo shoots lining the bar and worn-down wooden walls.

Liked by the locals

"There's a genuine electricity in the air on a good night in Dublin. People will pack eight or nine hours of partying into a quarter of that time. I've been lucky enough to play all over the world, and there is nowhere like Dublin."

MARCUS O'LAOIRE, DUBLIN DJ

MOTHER

**Map 2; Lost Lane, Adams Court, Grafton Street, City Centre;
///locate.escape.chefs; www.motherclub.ie**

This funky disco club is the reason you've been stocking up on
groovy glad rags from Dublin's vintage stores. City slickers and an
older, more alternative crowd party to their hearts' content at this
legendary LGBTQ+ venue, where synth-pop tunes blast from the
DJ's speakers and themed nights are a regular occurrence.

PYGMALION

**Map 2; 59 William Street S, Powerscourt Centre, Creative Quarter;
///flown.robe.cult; www.pyg.ie**

An eclectic atmosphere defines this ever-bustling spot, where the buzz
from the outdoor terrace radiates down the street. Friends catch up
around alfresco tables cluttered with glasses, heading inside when it
gets dark to dance to thumping house music spun by a DJ every night.
» Don't leave without trying the two-for-one pygtails, Pyg's signature
cocktails that are ideal for quenching the thirst.

OPIUM

Map 4; 26 Wexford Street, Portobello; ///noisy.curvy.detect; www.opium.ie

The place to see and be seen, Opium is where the stylish masses
head when they're in the mood to go "out out". It's expensive and
performative, but you get what you pay for: a vibrant manga-
inspired dance club with live music and themed nights that spans
three floors, topped off with a botanical beer garden.

Live Music

As far as Dubliners are concerned, their city is the home of the singer-songwriter. It follows that music is the lifeblood here and nights are spent worshipping bold vocals, guitar strums or heavy beats.

THE SUGAR CLUB

Map 5; 8 Leeson Street Lower, St Stephen's Green; ///pink.album.bronze; www.thesugarclub.com

As dusk sweeps across Dublin, athleisure fashions are swapped out for more sophisticated outfits for a night at this luxurious hotspot. In the plush red auditorium, couples settle in to banquette seating around small tables, feeling somewhat smug about nabbing a ticket to see international or home-grown artists perform. The music ranges from jazz to hip-hop, but whatever the genre, this arena never lets you down.

THE GRAND SOCIAL

Map 3; 35 Liffey Street Lower, North City; ///range.pram.curiosity; www.thegrandsocial.ie

Judging by the name, you might walk in here expecting a huge venue, but take "grand" in the Irish sense of the word and you'll understand the title – it's the perfect social hub. At this cosy, fairy light-lit bar, you'll rub shoulders with after-work crowds and old friends racing to the rooftop beer garden for pre-gig drinks. Once refreshed, everyone heads to the atmospheric loft space to listen to popular indie bands and lesser-known alternative acts that they've been waiting weeks to hear (you'll need to buy tickets online beforehand to join them).

>> **Don't leave without** heading downstairs after a gig to dance to a bit of techno. It's a great way to end the night.

WHELAN'S

Map 4; 25 Wexford Street, Portobello; ///covers.runner.slides;
www.whelanslive.com

As any and every local will tell you, a night in this gritty but beloved institution is never a bad idea. In the labyrinth of tiny rooms, hipsters drink the place dry, dates cuddle up in cubby holes and photographs of some of the pub's most famous performers, from Jeff Buckley to the Arctic Monkeys, grace the walls. Book tickets for any of the upcoming gigs and make a bee-line for the main stage – you might just witness the next big artist to become musical royalty here.

Try it!
BRAVE THE STAGE

If you'd rather be the new talent that the punters rave about, sign up for Whelan's "Song Cycle" every Monday at 9pm. The atmosphere is electric and the crowd supportive, so get writing that next hit.

VICAR STREET

Map 4; 58–9 Thomas Street, Liberties; ///soda.keen.washed;
www.vicarstreet.com

For big-name acts, you can't beat this venue. Smack bang in the middle of the cool Liberties neighbourhood, there's a rock 'n' roll vibe to this place, where, oddly, you'll find Bono's old motorbike. Surprisingly, it's not all alternative gigs: an assortment of genres cater to an assortment of patrons, who heave into the bar before shows start every night of the week. Just book ahead like the rest of them.

ANSEO

Map 4; 18 Camden Street, Portobello; ///sailor.pushy.noble

A classic pub by day, Anseo is conquered by music lovers on weekend nights in what feels like an extension of their own living room. With no website, often no queue and a quieter vibe than its neighbouring bars, only those in the know frequent this cosy oasis. Rock up before 8pm to nab a seat for the live gigs, then follow the musicians down to the bar after a show when DJs spin funk and reggae records.

THE ACADEMY

Map 3; 57 Middle Abbey Street, North City;
///forced.sake.transit; www.theacademydublin.com

Combine live music with a dance floor to enjoy it on and Dubliners will keep coming back. The snug main room at this multi-floor club means no matter where you are, you'll be up close to the acts on stage (and your fellow spectators, so prepare to dodge the odd

Come on Saturday for Circus, a club night with free candyfloss and tunes ranging from grime to R&B.

splash of beer and tipsy twirling neighbour). You can just rock up impulsively, but save the disappointment of a gig being at full capacity and book in advance.

RUBY SESSIONS

Map 5; Doyle's Pub, College Street, City Centre;
///sushi.landed.crown; www.rubysessions.com

If Dublin is the home of the singer-songwriter, this Tuesday music night is the bricks and mortar of the scene. Since 1999, Ruby's has championed pared-back acoustic sets, enforcing absolute silence and respect for talented artists in an intimate space. All proceeds for the night go to charity, so whether it's Damien Rice making a surprise appearance or a lesser-known singer starting out, they're all playing for the love of music, rather than to line their pockets.

THE WORKMAN'S CLUB

Map 1; 10 Wellington Quay, Temple Bar; ///hedge.token.data;
www.theworkmansclub.com

Behind the walls of this granny-chic building is something akin to Dublin's biggest house party, where indie students and beatniks congregate by the stage with pints or head to the outdoor smoking area to chat. It's the live performers, such as First Aid Kit and Royal Blood, that keep those with pre-bought tickets vibing till the early hours.
» Don't leave without tucking into a cheeseburger and the iconic garlic butter fries from Wowburger, located in the beer garden.

Comedy Nights

An indefinable and irreverent humour defines the DNA of both Dublin and its locals. With everything from stand-up to improv gracing the comedy circuit, there's an excuse to have a bit of craic every night.

THE COMEDY CRUNCH

Map 1; The Stag's Head, 1 Dame Lane, City Centre;
///dating.monday.bigger; www.thecomedycrunch.com

Visit The Stag's Head pub on a Sunday or Monday night and the queues forming outside at 8pm hint at something unmissable. While punters chatter at the bar, the knowledgeable head downstairs, grabbing whatever spare seat they can find and awaiting the presence of returning comedians such as Bill Burr and David O'Doherty. It's a chilled out night (helped by the free ice cream during the break).

LAUGHTER LOUNGE

Map 5; 8 Eden Quay, North City; ///motor.export.labels;
www.laughterlounge.com

A professional, sophisticated feel befits a venue where some of the biggest names in the Irish comedy scene perform Friday to Saturday. This is one for the planners, who book ahead to see their favourite comedians and make an entertaining night of it, filling their dimly lit tables with drink pitchers and munching on pizza as four acts grace the quirky redbrick stage. The seats are first come, first served, so if you dread getting picked out (and picked on) during a set, get here early and stake out a place at the back.

» Don't leave without getting your picture taken in the free photo booth to capture the evening you saw your comedy hero.

MOB THEATRE

Map 3; Wigwam, 54 Middle Abbey Street, North City;
///rush.games.energy; www.mobtheatre.ie

Every Thursday night is different in the downstairs area at Wigwam restaurant. One week, you're watching comedy improv shows based on a single audience suggestion; the next, a fantasy role-playing event known as Dungeons and Naggins. Started by a group of friends needing an outlet for their passions, Mob has grown into a sociable community group, where intimate events draw new attendees each week and encourage theatre and comedy lovers to connect.

Try it!
IMPROVE YOUR IMPROV

Mob Theatre runs a range of friendly workshops and classes on everything from sketch comedy to improv, taught by professionals. Keep an eye on its website for upcoming dates.

CHERRY COMEDY

Map 4; Whelan's, 25 Wexford Street, Portobello;
///wicked.basis.drip; www.cherrycomedy.ie

What started as a comedy night in college by a group of friends has now graduated along with them, becoming one of the most talked-about nights in Dublin. A young crowd pack out the intimate upstairs space in Whelan's *(p141)* every Monday, when up-and-coming comedians draw out constant giggles with comical anecdotes.

DUBLIN COMEDY IMPROV

Map 2; The International Bar, 23 Wicklow Street, Creative Quarter;
///wires.help.wells; 01 677 9250

Of the three brilliant comedy nights that The International Bar hosts, this Sunday event is the jewel in the crown. The show runs completely based off of random suggestions from the audience, so it feels like having a bit of banter with your flatmates (albeit with some pretty prolific comedians instead).

» Don't leave without asking about the other nights hosted at The International Bar, like live blues sessions and Latin music evenings.

ANSEO COMEDY CLUB

Map 4; 18 Camden Street, Portobello; ///sailor.pushy.noble

Anseo's open mic nights are the talk of the town come Wednesday. Set up for budding comedians to evolve their material, they draw energetic, dry-witted regulars and good-humoured friends hoping to witness the comedy stars of tomorrow before they hit the big time.

Liked by the locals

"By far my favourite show to attend and perform at is Cherry Comedy in Whelan's. The quality is always stellar, the atmosphere is electric and you never know what big name might pop by to do a set."

LOLSY BYRNE, IRISH COMEDIAN

Karaoke Joints

It's not a Dublin night out without a sing-along. When friends find a way of gathering after too long apart, they opt for clambering into private booths, flicking eagerly through song books and fighting for the mic.

WOOLSHED BAA AND GRILL

Map 3; The Parnell Centre, Parnell Street, Rotunda; ///hotels.pose.remedy; www.woolshedbaa.com

Anything for a free shot, right? Brave the stage here on a Thursday night and the bartenders will reward you with just that. A rowdy, lively atmosphere is to be expected at this sports bar, where raucous applause from the regular punters egg shy performers on (though you won't find many here) before they take the mic themselves and belt out a classic rock anthem between swigs of beer.

MANEKI

Map 2; 43 Dawson Street, St Stephens Green; ///cure.sorry.jazzy; www.manekiktv.com

Given that karaoke originates in Japan, it's no surprise this Japanese restaurant knows how to do it well. Pop-hungry revellers tuck into dinner before heading into one of the private booths to celebrate

Opt for the dinner and karaoke package for sushi platters, a bottle of prosecco and two hours of singing time.

hen dos and birthdays. The 1990s club vibe decor is a bit tacky, but that simply adds to the carefree vibes of a night filled with pitching issues and incorrect lyrics.

MARRAKESH
Map 3; 121–2 Capel Street, North City;
///radar.yappy.fired; www.marrakesh.ie

The perfect mash-up of Moroccan heritage and pop culture, this spot attracts large parties seeking a lively evening out without the venue-hopping most Dublin nights entail. Hang-outs here begin with sharing plates of couscous and tagine against a backdrop of live jazz and belly dancing (depending on the day), and end with mates shuffling into a private room styled with slick microphones, leather sofas and glass tables to belt out their best Britney number.

UKIYO
Map 1; 7–9 Exchequer Street, Creative Quarter;
///pram.brand.cherry; www.ukiyobar.com

Somewhat surprisingly, not every Dubliner has a voice to match the city's singer-songwriter credentials. That's where Ukiyo's private booths come in, where groups clamber on the sofas and sing tunes (there's over a whopping 14,000 to choose from) in the most imperfect way without the embarrassment of an entire bar hearing.

» Don't leave without heading out to the dance floor when your hour slot is up, where a live DJ sees you through the rest of the night.

Solo, Pair, Crowd

Karaoke is pretty much made for all manner of crowds, whether you can hold a tune or not.

FLYING SOLO
Work for it
The Workman's Club *(p143)* is known for its live music scene, so those after a supportive audience will find it among the music lovers at the Sunday karaoke sessions. Just pick your guilty-pleasure favourite and sing.

IN A PAIR
It takes two
Enjoy a banh mi and a papaya bubble tea before you hit the mic at Boba Bar on Parnell Street. Channel your inner Simon and Garfunkel and choose a song made for a duo.

FOR A CROWD
Hit the jackpot
If there's one thing that will tempt your friends to belt out classic tunes in front of a pub full of punters, it's a cash prize. Head to The Lower Deck in Portobello on Saturday and hopefully those drinks will buy themselves.

THE GEORGE

Map 1; 89 S Great George's Street, Creative Quarter;
///novel.wooden.event; www.thegeorge.ie

A sing-along isn't just a crowd-pleasing pastime at this popular LGBTQ+ institution: it's a full-on event every Saturday night. This isn't one for mic-shy singers, with private booths swapped out for a spotlit stage and an accompanying audience who cheer you on even when you stumble over a word (or seven). Drawing a raucous, eccentric and welcoming crowd are the pop-centric drag hosts, Veda and Davina Devine, so you can expect lots of brutal (but harmless) teasing and sass if you take to the stage with even an ounce of nerves. It's all a lot of fun, though, where the only sounds that stand a chance of ousting your vocals is all the laughter.

WIGWAM

Map 3; 54 Middle Abbey Street, North City;
///rush.games.energy; www.wigwamdublin.com

Saturday afternoons at bar/restaurant Wigwam always seem to go the same way: groups of girlfriends filter in for bottomless brunch, prosecco flows freely, and before you know it, the halloumi fries are all gone and you're making your way downstairs to the colourful karaoke den. Competition heats up between the solo singer doing a sassy Lizzo cover and the chosen five who've *finally* decided which Spice Girl they are, but it's all in the name of fun. Not keen on showcasing your dulcet tones to everyone? Book a private box.

» Don't leave without ordering a fruity cocktail and exploring the rest of Wigwam – think ping pong tables, DJ club nights, tempting food.

Late-Night Bites

*It's a rite of passage to stop for some easy-going bites
on your way home, whether to soak up a night of
drinking or stave off hunger after a long show, all
the while gossiping about the evening's antics.*

NAMASTE INDIA

Map 3; 88 King Street N, Smithfield;
///bucked.cloth.shout; www.namasteindia.ie

This Tandoori and Balti house serves the best creamy butter
tandoori chicken in Dublin – or so say its dedicated fans who pop
by for a late-night snack after bar-hopping in Smithfield. It's takeway
only, so follow the locals down to the Liffey to eat your saucy trays of
chips and naan while soaking up the 3am revelry.

DIFONTAINE'S PIZZERIA

Map 1; 22 Parliament Street, Temple Bar;
///pints.angel.smoke; www.difontainespizzeria.ie

This New York-style pizza joint is so beloved that Dubliners will walk
across the city to get their hands on a slice. It's a grab 'n' go setting
and the queue moves quickly, so be prepared to seize your slice
(they're bigger than your head) and exit swiftly. They also run a "pay

If there's a particular homeless shelter that you'd like to donate your pre-paid slice to, let the staff know. it forward" scheme which allows you to buy another slice for someone in need, so you're doing good for the community, even when you're slightly inebriated.

ZAYTOON

Map 1; 15 Parliament Street, Temple Bar;
///once.punt.tested; www.zaytoon.ie

No ordinary kebab shop, this modern Persian-style kitchen cooks up the healthiest meal you'll find after a night out. The long queues at the weekend are testament to the incredibly fresh grub, which draws pub goers around 11pm and a more rowdy post-clubbing pack around the 1am mark. Most places operate as takeaway only in the early hours, but you can have a proper sit-down meal here, extending your night out with chance for a good gossip.

» Don't leave without trying the chicken shish marinated with Iranian saffron – it's truly bursting with flavour.

DOLLARD MARKET

Map 1; 2–5 Wellington Quay, Temple Bar;
///nest.slowly.organ; www.dollardpizza.ie

By day, Dollard Market is a swish food hall and deli, but by night, it opens up its quirky pizza hatch, passing bespoke slices through to hungry locals until the wee hours. The gourmet wood-fired pizza is top quality, so you're getting a good feed after skipping dinner to make that theatre show or music gig.

Liked by the locals

"You spend the night dancing your socks off in The George, spill out onto the street and then it's time for the main event. Everyone flocks down to Gay Spar for a chicken fillet roll, bottle of water and tipsy laughs with mates."

BRIAN DILLON, JOURNALIST AND
GAY SPAR ENTHUSIAST

SPAR

Map 1; 19–20 Dame Street, City Centre; ///vast.pops.calculating;
01 633 9070

This might be the most random spot on the list, but it wouldn't be a true reflection of Dublin nightlife if it didn't make the cut. It's unusual for a supermarket to hold such a special place in the hearts of locals, but the Spar on Dame Street isn't your average branch. Lovingly nicknamed Gay Spar by fans because of its proximity to The George *(p151)*, the famous LGBTQ+ bar, this is an institution for post-clubbers. They all come for one thing: the chicken fillet roll, which has achieved its popularity through word of mouth. If you don't go to Gay Spar after a night out, you're not getting the real Dublin clubbing experience.

MCGUINNESS TRADITIONAL TAKE AWAY

Map 4; 84 Camden Street Lower, Portobello;
///famous.doing.button; www.mcguinnesstakeaway.ie

This family-owned spot ticks all the boxes for a late-night snack. First off, it's great value: €7.50 for a pizza slice, a bag of chips and a can of coke. Secondly, they have a vegan menu – something that is nearly impossible to come by at 4am. (They even put their vegan food in white bags and the non-vegan in brown bags, ideal for those who may need a helping hand after a night of drinking.) Despite brimming with a raucous mass of hungry revellers every night, the staff remain super friendly and are always up for a chat in the late hours.

» Don't leave without ordering the vegan pizza – it's a game-changer, with cheese as stringy and delicious as the real thing.

NORTH
CITY

*The iconic **Workman's Club** has been the setting for legendary album recordings and gigs, including a Cillian Murphy DJ set.*

TEMPLE
BAR

Liffey

WELLINGTON QUAY

④

A bite to eat at
DOLLARD MARKET

This hatch is open until 4am, so don't go to bed hungry. Get a monster slice of pizza with tiny meatballs, and you'll be all set.

EUSTACE STREET

*A nightlife institution, the Dame Street **Spar** is known as "Gay Spar". It adopted this nickname at Pride in 2019, using the title in its posters.*

DAME STREET

DAME STREET

Dance in
THE GEORGE

③

It's not a night out until you throw some shapes in the city's most beloved gay bar.

CREATIVE
QUARTER

GEORGE'S ST

② EXCHEQUER ST

WIC

SOUTH GREAT

Grab the mic at
UKIYO

Get the night off to a belting start – literally. Book a private room at this karaoke joint and sing some tunes with your pals.

0 metres   100
0 yards   100

Liffey

COLLEGE STREET

'FOLK STREET

REET

STREET

① Swing by
GRAFTON STREET
Many musicians made their
mark busking here, and
aspiring artists still draw
crowds day and night. Stop
by and you may witness
the next Glen Hansard.

**CITY
CENTRE**

An evening of
Irish craic

Dublin sure has a reputation as a great city for a
knees-up. Okay, locals may shudder at the thought
of partying around stag-and-hen-do-central
Temple Bar, but just a few streets away from the
tourist traps there lie beloved institutions. The
convivial atmosphere in the centre is infectious,
with anyone and everyone filling the streets with
laughter as they hop between pubs, clubs and
music venues in search of the best craic. Oh, and
don't expect to sneak off with an "Irish Goodbye"
– you'll be having too much fun to duck out.

1. Grafton Street
Grafton Street, City Centre
///paper.metro.random

2. Ukiyo
7–9 Exchequer Street,
Creative Quarter;
www.ukiyobar.com
///pram.brand.cherry

3. The George
89 S Great George's
Street, City Centre;
www.thegeorge.ie
///novel.wooden.event

4. Dollard Market
2–5 Wellington
Quay, Temple Bar;
www.dollardandco.ie
///nest.slowly.organ

Workman's Club
///hedge.token.data

Spar
///vast.pops.calculating

OUTDOORS

A passion for the great outdoors is in the blood of the Irish. After days spent working in the centre, locals rely on coastal walks and picnics in the park for weekend escapism.

Green Spaces

Ireland's national colour is taken seriously here. Pretty gardens in the suburbs and lush rolling parks in the centre are a taste of the country in the city, where days are spent leisurely on green grounds.

ST STEPHEN'S GREEN

Map 2; enter at Fusilier's Arch, St Stephen's Green; ///leads.flips.party; www.ststephensgreenpark.ie

The most famous park in Dublin is slap bang in the middle of town. On a sunny day, you'll see gaggles of Dubliners lounging on the grass with picnic lunches and coffees, between perfect flower gardens and bronzed statues. Keep an eye on the duck pond – Dublin's infamously angry seagulls have decided to take up shop and pose as ducks, in order to get fed by hapless visitors. They're surprisingly convincing.

IVEAGH GARDENS

Map 5; enter at Clonmel Street, St Stephen's Green; ///feast.idea.loft; www.iveaghgardens.ie

Known as Dublin's "secret garden", this tucked-away nook feels worlds away from the always-booming St Stephen's Green around the corner. Workers from the surrounding offices come for a spot of

Pick up a sandwich and a coffee to go from nearby Green Bench Café to enjoy in the gardens.

lunch while friends gossip over classy picnics and a bottle of wine post-work. Gushing waterfalls and singing birds provide a blissful soundtrack.

DARTMOUTH SQUARE PARK

Map 5; enter at Dartmouth Square N, Ranelagh; ///luck.fled.hotels; 01 222 5278

This pretty, leafy park is so beloved by Ranelagh residents that they stepped in to save it when it was under threat a few years ago. The elegant heart of the chichi neighbourhood, this park is frequented by well-heeled locals who come to spy on the glam houses that surround it. On summer weekends, attention shifts inwards, when yogis come for free yoga sessions before heading to brunch nearby.

NATIONAL BOTANIC GARDENS

Map 6; enter at the car park, Glasnevin; ///deputy.held.sheet; www.botanicgardens.ie

Located next to Glasnevin Cemetery (p111), these tranquil gardens have long been a staple for those who live in the neighbourhood. The fresh scent of blossoming plants wafting through the air and the sound of squirrels scuttling through the trees is enough to draw retirees and parents with pushchairs here, to set up stations on the benches and watch the world go by. It's a botanic haven.

» **Don't leave without** heading inside the Orchid House to get your fill of these tropical, brightly coloured beauties.

THE PEOPLE'S PARK

Map 6; enter at Park Road, Glasthule, Dún Laoghaire;
///vase.case.resort; 01 205 4817

Visit this beachside park on a Sunday and you'll be lucky to find a patch of green to settle on, with mismatched blankets and pushchairs taking up every inch of space. After a morning stroll along the nearby pier, residents pick up locally sourced produce from the market *(p93)* for picnics in the adjoining park. There's always a buzz here.

PHOENIX PARK

Map 6; enter at Parkgate Street (Main Gate), North City;
///taken.hired.amuse; www.phoenixpark.ie

There's something special about Europe's largest enclosed park in the autumn. As soon as the trees burst into vivid crimson colours, a calm descends: sun worshippers swap the vast lawns for cosy pub couches while leaf-peepers embark on crisp strolls, where the only

Hidden behind Wexford Street, St Kevin's Park *(Camden Row)* is relatively unknown to many Dubliners. It's always pretty empty, adding to the eerie feel you get when walking through (it's the former graveyard for St Kevin's Church, after all). Surrounded by high walls covered in ivy, and home to the skeletal ruins of the 18th-century church, it's a pretty spot for an impromptu picnic if you're not too creeped out.

sounds are of leaves crunching beneath their feet. Autumn also brings with it the start of rutting season, when the park's fallow deer roam the fields in the glow of the setting sun. If the autumn air is too chilly, retreat inside one of the stately homes that dot the park.

ST ANNE'S PARK

Map 6; enter at the car park, All Saints Road, Clontarf East, Raheny; ///soft.frozen.herb; 01 222 8933

There are two sides to this whopping expanse of green: the buzzing sports scene and the relaxed residential character. While teenagers fill out the playing pitches and families enjoy a set on the tennis courts, those hoping to escape the buzz get lost among the ancient trees and idyllic gardens. The Rose Garden is a place of pilgrimage in the summer months, when the beautiful flowers are at their peak.

» Don't leave without visiting the City Farm and Ecology Centre, where you might catch a class on plant life or caring for animals.

MERRION SQUARE PARK

Map 5; enter at Merrion Square E, Merrion Square; ///afford.wiring.target; 01 661 2369

You know you've made it to Merrion Square Park when you see the statue of Oscar Wilde reclining on a rock. It won't be long before you recline yourself, settling in on the grassy surrounds to admire the Georgian architecture that frames the garden. Everything from the hundred-year-old streetlights to the paintings hung on the railings at the Sunday market gives the feeling of stepping back in time.

Beautiful Beaches

It doesn't matter if the sun is shining or the rain is pouring: the beach is a magnet for locals. The charm of Dublin is its coastal location, with the promise of fresh sea air in easy reach of the hustle and bustle.

SANDYMOUNT STRAND

Map 6; enter at car park 1, Strand Road, S Dublin; ///pens.steer.reduce

A spectacular sunrise behind the iconic Poolbeg Towers is all it takes to persuade urbanites to rise before dawn, don their athleisure and hit this beach. Given its close proximity to the centre (it's a short ride on the Dart), Sandymount Strand has become a firm favourite with city slickers, who jog the long promenade when the tide is out in the morning and make it back into town for those 9am starts.

PORTMARNOCK

Map 6; enter at Velvet Strand, Portmarnock, N Dublin; ///pepper.cluster.debugging

This large beach more than lives up to its nickname of "Velvet Strand", its smooth and spotless sands stretching for 5 miles (8 km). With hardly a rock in sight, Portmarnock is the favoured beach for families with kids in tow. Parents sprawl across the smooth sands

The beach is a bit of a trek from the village, so stock up on picnic supplies before you hit the sands.

to sunbathe and watch the little ones play when it's sunny, and grandparents join windy walks along the strand in their cosiest beanies during the winter.

SANDYCOVE

Map 6; Forty Foot, Sandycove, S Dublin; ///caviar.breeds.futuristic

It's testament to the popularity of this beach that it overshadows the ultra-swish nearby neighbourhood of Dalkey – the Beverly Hills of Dublin, where many Irish celebrities (Bono, Enya and Van Morrison, to name a few) have set up home. That's all thanks to the iconic swimming promontory, Forty Foot, at the very back of Sandycove Beach. While post-exam revellers jump in from the rocks during the warmer months, thick-skinned swimmers arrive at 5am every morning for a sunrise swim, no matter the time of year.

LOUGHSHINNY

Map 6; enter at the car park, Loughshinny, Rockabill View, N Dublin;
///benchmark.folds.glimmers

Think of Ireland and it's the character of Loughshinny you'll have in mind: a quaint, charming fishing village, home to fishmongers and a small but mighty community feel. Pop into the tiny village to grab some supplies from the shops and perch yourself by the beach's picnic area alongside other leisurely locals with the same idea.

» Don't leave without taking a post-picnic coastal walk around the famous folding cliffs, formed by layers of limestone and shale.

BULL ISLAND

Map 6; enter at North Bull Island Interpretative Centre, Dublin Bay, N Dublin; ///intervals.soap.phones

You know you've arrived when you spot the colourful kites dancing through the sky on the weekends. One of the windiest places in Dublin, Bull Island attracts those who can brave the elements: thrill-seekers kitesurfing in the cold sea to bird-watchers on the lookout for rare species. All this activity creates a fine backdrop for a run along the vast strand or a catch-up stroll with a coffee from beloved Happy Out *(p74)*.

SEAPOINT

Map 6; enter at Martello Tower off Brighton Vale, Dún Laoghaire, S Dublin; ///adding.darker.retain

Drawing hardy regulars who hang up their towels on the Martello Tower before easing their way into the freezing sea is this ultimate swimming spot. It becomes one of the busiest places in the summer, when families, friends and couples lay out their towels and spend the day dipping in and out of the water. After a swim, it's mandatory to get a 99 ice cream from the van at the side of the beach – it may not cost 99c anymore, but that nostalgia lives on.

KILLINEY

Map 6; enter at Killiney Beach car park, S Dublin; ///recollect.lizards.graphs

Despite its picturesque curved bay, this beach doesn't draw as many crowds as nearby Forty Foot *(p165)*. It's a welcoming quiet alternative, where the only people you'll likely bump into are dog walkers, tracking up and down the pebbly seafront while their dogs skip in and out of the water. This strand also offers one of the most scenic vistas of Bray Head to the south and Howth Head to the north – spare a thought for those packing into the nearby beaches as you take in the impeccable views in peace.

» **Don't leave without** walking up Killiney Hill before hitting the beach for even more stunning views of Dublin Bay.

SKERRIES SOUTH BEACH
Map 6; enter off Manning's Opening, Skerries S Beach, N Dublin; ///strung.exists.unpainted

A day trip to this quintessential seaside resort feels just like stepping into a postcard scene: couples stroll hand in hand along the vast promenade, students lounge by the harbour with a book and friends sip a coffee while looking out at the nearby islands and the iconic Rockabill Lighthouse. On sunny weekends, it seems like the whole of Dublin flocks to this idyllic beach for a city escape, only heading back to the centre once the sun has set.

Try it!
CLEAN AND CONSERVE

To help keep Dublin's beaches beautiful, volunteer for Clean Coasts (www.clean coasts.org) and take part in a beach clean-up. You'll meet other locals and explore the beaches at the same time: it's a win-win.

Scenic City Strolls

Every quarter in Dublin has its own character, from the rustic canal stretches to the cosmopolitan skyline along the Liffey. Sauntering the patchwork of streets is the best way to get to know the city and its locals.

THE GREAT SOUTH WALL

Map 6; start at The Great South Wall parking; ///sleepy.image.senses

Sure, everyone raves about the views at the end of the promenade here, but the walk along one of Europe's longest sea walls to get there is what it's all about. Every Dubliner has at some point braved the strong winds that make you feel like you're on the brink of being swept away and followed the walkway all the way out to the iconic red Poolbeg Lighthouse. It'll take you about 40 minutes to reach, so draw breath when you do and look back at the cityscape in all its glory.

DÚN LAOGHAIRE PIERS

Map 6; E Pier, Dún Laoghaire; ///funds.burns.washed

Ask any Dubliner where to go for a cracking first date and they'll direct you to Dún Laoghaire's East Pier, where romance blossoms along a dreamy walk past boats on the glistening Irish Sea. There's always a great buzz on this side of the pier, especially on Sunday

Get an ice cream from Teddy's, known by locals as one of the city's best ice cream parlours, for your walk.

afternoons when everyone makes the most of the last few hours of the weekend. Those seeking a quiet stroll tend to head to the forgotten-about West Pier instead.

GRAND CANAL, PORTOBELLO

Map 4; start at Atlas Language School, Portobello; ///asserts.input.lately

The beauty of Dublin's Grand Canal is how the vibe changes as it traverses each neighbourhood. Portobello is where every Dubliner wishes they lived, and it has a lot to do with the picture-perfect part of the canal here. During the summer months, it's flooded with students drinking cans, stoic businessmen with pints from The Barge *(p68)* and groups of girlfriends dining alfresco on a picnic blanket. Autumn sees the canal covered in orange leaves as swans and herrings glide between the reeds, mirroring a scene from a Monet painting.

BLESSINGTON STREET BASIN

Map 3; 28 Primrose Avenue, Phibsborough; ///title.energy.pizza

This idyllic walled park is the kind that you pop into when you have time to kill between coffee dates before realizing you've circled it three times already. It's a short walk around what locals call the "duck pond", but there's always something magical to catch your eye – a "fairy zone" with little painted mushrooms and tiny houses, ducklings following their mother and quirky old doors in the walls.

>> Don't leave without continuing your stroll down Geraldine Street to peek at the classic Georgian architecture of the houses here.

GRAND CANAL, DOCKLANDS

Map 5; start at The Lir Academy, Grand Canal Dock, Docklands;
///spice.mock.cherry

This tech hub may be known as Dublin's "Silicon Docks", but it's not
your average office district. Cool architecture and edgy street art draw
crowds after work, when the area buzzes with young professionals.
Take the scenic route to join them: start at the houseboats beside
The Lir Academy and walk along the water, spying the iconic Bolands
Mill before reaching Hanover Quay and its bustling restaurants.

RIVER LIFFEY

Map 3; start at O'Connell Bridge, City Centre; ///major.insect.hung

Any Dubliner will tell you that there's a rivalry between the north
and south, from the different accents to which side has the better
attractions. Splitting the two is the River Liffey, and acting as the
perfect weaver between them are its various bridges. Walking
along the banks aimlessly may feel like the ultimate tourist activity,
but start before the sun begins to set and you'll be joined by workers

Try it!
BOARD A BOAT

Give your feet a rest and glide along the
water instead with Liffey River Cruises
(www.dublindiscovered.ie), passing all the
landmarks and learning about Dublin's past
in relation to the Liffey and Docklands.

making their way home across the O'Connell and Ha'penny bridges, channelling their own inner tourist as they take in the gorgeous skyline of high buildings. Start by walking over O'Connell Bridge from the north side and continue west, zigzagging between the sides to decide for yourself – are you a Northsider or a Southsider?

DOLLYMOUNT STRAND

Map 6; Bull Island, Clontarf E, Dollymount; ///blank.enhancement.risks

Dublin may be full of walkable coastal suburbs, but "Dollyer", as it's affectionately known to the locals, was made for strolls – Sunday strolls, to be specific. With stunning views across Dublin Bay, cute coffee shops peppered along the way for a pick-me-up and a straight route that doesn't require much thought or planning to follow, it's a no-brainer for a weekend wind-down.

» **Don't leave without** grabbing some good old fish and chips from Beshoff Bros to eat while looking out to Dublin Bay.

DODDER RIVER

Map 6; start at Lansdowne Road; ///watch.quiet.slams

When Churchtown and Rathgar residents are seeking a lunchtime stroll or a post-work head-clearing session, they follow the route along their local river, passing small waterfalls and thick trees. Expect to see the same faces here daily, politely nodding at one another as they pass by. In the summer, the sights get more interesting, with groups of friends gathering on the green with their bikes, teenagers kicking a football around and fishermen knee-deep in the river.

Rural Walks

For everyone from hardy hikers to Sunday strollers,
weekends in Dublin are all about donning walking
boots, reaching new heights and seeing the city from
a different angle – a much higher one.

HOWTH CLIFF PATH

Map 6; start at Howth Dart station, Howth Road, Howth;
///notepad.headquarters.raising

One for the thrill-seekers, this 6-km (4-mile) walk hugs the coastline
of the Howth Head peninsula, weaving along the edge of the cliffs
and providing killer views of the waves below. It's steep, rocky and
gets pretty windy, so only the brave (and the fit) give it a go. Hike out
until you see the Baily Lighthouse and then descend into Howth
Village to find some well-deserved grub.

TICKNOCK FAIRY CASTLE LOOP

Map 6; start at Ticknock Forest, Ticknock Road, Ticknock; ///fails.rare.type

Chillingly fresh mountain air and throbbing calves aren't a deterrent
for those who repeatedly hike this 6-km (4-mile) trail. The most
popular summit in the Dublin Mountains, Ticknock rewards those
who push through the muscle cramp with impressive views at the

Visit Ireland's highest pub, Johnnie Fox's, in Glencullen for post-walk grub (and take the bus back home).

top (making up for the less-than-magical Fairy Castle itself along the way). Do as the locals do and bring a flask of hot whiskey to reward yourself with.

DONABATE TO PORTRANE LOOP

**Map 6; start at Donabate Beach car park, Balcarrick, Portrane;
///runway.coaching.perfume**

Keeping health-obsessed Dubliners fit is this 12-km (7.5-mile) route connecting the two beautiful beaches of Donabate and Portrane. Spectacular views of Lambay Island are slightly overshadowed by the colony of wallabies that you're likely to spot along the way, but if they're hiding, black-bellied plovers and greenfinches are guaranteed to keep you company from the skies and trees above.

» Don't leave without stopping in Donabate Town to grab a bite to eat (and prevent any stomach grumbles on the two-hour journey home).

SHANKILL TO SCALP LOOP

Map 6; start at Brady's pub, Shankill; ///sipped.loiter.barons

Skirting through the lush forests of Rathmichael and Carrickgollgan before reaching the Lead Mines, this 11-km (7-mile) route attracts serious nature lovers. What this moderate two-hour route lacks in height, it more than makes up for in the unique sights and tranquil vibe along the way: rabbits and badgers run through the birch and larch trees while birds flit above. Those with a head for heights can detour to the Carrickgollgan summit, a small hill with big views.

BRAY TO GREYSTONES CLIFF WALK

**Map 6; start at the bandstand on Bray Promenade,
Ballynamuddagh, Wicklow; ///desktop.crab.unzips**

As you hike along the cliffside, sporty families and friends will pass you by, catching up as they do without pausing for breath. Their stamina is a sign that they constantly return to repeat this trek. The 7-km (4.5-mile) route feels pretty long, so get the train back to the city centre when you're done — like the path, it hugs the cliffside so you can continue taking in the impeccable views as you rest your legs.

KILLINEY HILL

**Map 6; start at Killiney Hill car park, Killiney Hill Road, Killiney;
///mistreat.simpler.yearns**

The route of choice for those who hate breaking a sweat, lacing up hefty boots or have limited mobility but nonetheless want to brag about their hiking escapades, Killiney Hill is the ticket. You'll reach

Shh!

Down from Killiney's White Rock beach lies the secluded Vico Bathing Place *(Vico Road)*. This lesser-known swimming cove is the perfect antidote for tired legs (okay, Killiney Hill isn't strenuous, but if you need an excuse for a dip). Old stone steps lead straight into the sea and there's always a gaggle of local swimmers knocking around, many of whom take to the water "in the nip" – this is one of Dublin's few nudist spots.

the summit in just 20 minutes, giving you ample time to relax and spy on the millionaires' mansions that dot the landscape when the skies are bright and the day still young.

» Don't leave without seeing if you can spot what is known as Manderley Castle, the elegant home of famous singer Enya. As a heads-up, it's in the southern portion of Killiney.

THE MONTPELIER LOOP TRAIL
Map 6; start at Montpelier Hill car park, S Dublin; ///skills.voice.oppose

The walk up Montpelier Hill is one to make your thighs scream – fitting given that you'll reach an abandoned church-like building called the Hell Fire Club at the top. This lodge was home to a society of the same name, and legend has it that the devil himself once made an appearance here. With high trees and dark drumlins, it's the most haunting walk you can do – tackle the steep 4-km (2-mile) climb as the sun begins to set for an even eerier experience.

THE SUGARLOAF TRAIL
Map 6; start at Red Lane car park; ///cookers.seaside.redirected

Given its name, it's easy to imagine what the Great Sugar Loaf Mountain looks like. The conical formation tempts families and couples to drive down from Dublin at the weekend, but don't be fooled by the short 2.5-km (1.5-mile) length of the route – it's intense, with a steep upper section. If it hasn't already taken your breath away, the stunning views of Wicklow from the top certainly will.

Dreamy Viewpoints

There's no need to climb a mountain or head to the coast for picturesque views and panoramas. Nothing is more idyllic than witnessing the sun set and rise over the urban skyline.

SKYLINE CROKE PARK

Map 6; Cusack Stand, Croke Park, St Joseph's Avenue, Drumcondra; ///quite.less.tins; www.crokepark.ie/skyline

This thrilling rooftop walkway is no place for those with a fear of heights. While sports fans head to this huge stadium for the Gaelic games, work parties and friends bypass the rowdy chants in favour of the 17-storey-high Skyline and its tour. Sure, it has a touristy reputation, but it still draws a local crowd at sunset who revel in the panoramic views of Dublin's landmarks and mountains as day turns into night.

ST PATRICK'S CATHEDRAL

Map 4; St Patrick's Close, Liberties; ///train.guilty.lined; www.stpatrickscathedral.ie

Proving that gorgeous views don't always equal city-wide panoramas is Dublin's main cathedral – well, its gardens. Settle on a grassy patch and let a picture-perfect scene play out, as friends chatter animatedly,

Head inside the cathedral for a view just as dreamy. Think vibrant stained glass and patterned tiles.

budding photographers crouch for the perfect shot of the high steeple and workers sip on a coffee beside the dainty water fountain. It's a true snapshot of local life.

SAMUEL BECKETT BRIDGE

Map 5; start at Sir John Rogerson's Quay, S of the Liffey;
///people.empire.showed; www.bridgesofdublin.ie

This harp-shaped bridge, linking the south of the Liffey to the north, seems always to be alive with the hurried steps of office workers commuting to and from work. Despite this daily routine, the view never gets old, tempting them to look up from their phones for even a split second. When the bustle slows down in the evening, find the perfect bench to perch and watch the city lights reflect in the water.

» Don't leave without popping into the rooftop bar at The Mayson, for even better river views (and great cocktails to boot).

O'CONNELL TOWER

Map 6; Glasnevin Cemetery, Finglas Road, Glasnevin;
///vote.hotel.spell; www.glasnevinmuseum.ie/tower

Rewarding those who make the 222-step pilgrimage to the top of Ireland's tallest round tower is a unique 360-degree view of the city proper, its neighbouring counties and the glistening Irish Sea. The beautifully restored tower has a commanding presence over Glasnevin Cemetery (p111), so when visitors are seeking a moment of reflection after trawling the grounds, this is just the ticket.

ALOFT DUBLIN CITY OPEN TERRACE

Map 4; 7th Floor, 1 Mill Street, Liberties; ///jukebox.dine.follow;
www.aloftdublincity.com

A favoured haunt with Liberties residents, this rooftop bar sits on top of an unassuming hotel and is rarely frequented by those living outside the area. The contemporary, stylish terrace fits perfectly in the trendy neighbourhood, attracting glamorous groups of friends, sophisticated daters and a post-work crowd seeking killer cocktails and even better sunset views. As one of the highest buildings in the Liberties, you'll see a side of the city that you won't find anywhere else, with the added bonus of a distinct lack of tourists. A sweeping view of the centre's landmarks (think the Guinness Storehouse and St Patrick's Cathedral) and out towards the Wicklow Mountains is the perfect backdrop for animated catch-ups.

» **Don't leave without** heading inside to the WXYZ bar once the sun sets and the temperature drops for a dinner to complement the fine view (you can still see it through the window).

Shh!

Ireland's golf courses tend to always offer sweeping views of rolling hills and the coastline, but Deer Park Golf Course *(www.deerparkgolf.ie)* takes its views to another level. Golfers are treated to all of this with the additional magnificent view of Howth Castle (which tends to distract even the most dedicated from their game). You don't have to be a member to visit – simply book onto a course and enjoy the views.

HA'PENNY BRIDGE
Map 1; start at the N side, Bachelors Walk, Temple Bar; ///skill.hood.safe; www.bridgesofdublin.ie

Ask any local to pick their favourite landmark and this is sure to top the list. Chances are if you're strolling through Dublin's city centre, you'll walk across this beautiful cast-iron bridge along with thousands of others to get from the north to the south, or vice versa. Even though you don't need to pay a ha'penny nowadays to cross the bridge (hence the name), once you lean up against the railings underneath the period lanterns and take in the views of the buildings along the Liffey to Dublin Bay, you'd happily pay a toll to stay there all day. (To avoid any grief from commuters and passersby, though, you should probably get a shuffle on and not linger for too long.)

WELLINGTON MONUMENT
Map 6; St James's, E Phoenix Park, North City; ///spoil.vent.roof; www.phoenixpark.ie

When friends agree to gather in Phoenix Park (p162), the Wellington Monument near the eastern edge of the grounds is the meeting spot of choice. It's the kind of place where you greet your buddy with a hug but end up staying, caught up in watching the world go by. The towering obelisk is the local and less crowded version of The Spire, Dublin's best-known landmark, so you can perch on the steps around the base without elbowing others out of the way for the clearest views. One minute you might see friends dancing to music blasting from portable speakers, the next dogs chasing the city's joggers on the fields. It's an ideal spot to indulge in a leisurely afternoon of people-watching.

Sporty Adventures

When GAA, hurling and rugby matches aren't on at the arenas, sports withdrawals are staved off by the countless waterways, large parks and dedicated venues that turn the city into a playground.

ROCK CLIMBING IN DALKEY QUARRY

Map 6; Dalkey Quarry, Dalkey; ///hamstring.notebook.sharing; www.adventure.ie

A disused quarry may not sound like a great location for a day out, but this Dalkey spot is far more picturesque than the name implies, with giant sheets of rock covered in thickets of greenery. Stags, hens and groups of mates come here to learn how to rock climb and abseil, before heading for a pint to toast their new heights.

KAYAKING TO DALKEY ISLAND

Map 6; Bullock Harbour, Glenageary, Dalkey; ///pounds.immaculate.array; www.kayaking.ie

Nature lovers rejoice at the chance to share space with some of Dublin's favourite locals: the seals that call Dalkey Island home. After a 20-minute kayak from Dalkey Harbour, you'll enter prime seal territory, where these beautiful creatures bask in the sun. Pull

This popular activity tends to book up quickly, so reserve your spot in advance to avoid disappointment.

your kayak into the beach to embrace the wilderness, feel the strong breeze in your hair and gallivant up through the grassy hills before hopping back in your kayak.

TANDEM BIKING IN PHOENIX PARK

Map 6; Phoenix Park Bikes, Gate House, Chesterfield Avenue, Phoenix Park, North City; ///taken.hired.amuse; www.phoenixparkbikes.com

When locals are looking to spruce up a conventional date or occupy the kids in the school holidays, they head for the bike rental shop in Phoenix Park (p162) and get strap in on a tandem bike. There are numerous routes to choose from (it is the biggest park in Europe, after all), so riders can show off their skills to passersby or hide from the few sniggering at their attempts to cycle in unison. Once they do get the hang of it, you can expect to see them gliding through the trees together, stopping off to peek at the resident wild deer.

SKI CLUB OF IRELAND

Map 6; Killegar, Kilternan; ///surface.giggled.immovable; www.skiclub.ie

Skiing holidays are highly popular among Dubliners, so most head to the artificial revolving ski slopes in Kilternan to brush up on their skills before their trips to the Alps and beyond. Classes are available but things really hot up on a Friday, when like-minded regulars come for a freestyle night of music, breathtaking tricks and a whole lot of fun.

» Don't leave without sitting on the bonnet of your car and waiting for the sun to set over Dublin. Absolute scenes, as the locals would say.

Solo, Pair, Crowd

Whether you're hoping to gain a new skill or let loose, Dublin offers up activities to suit all manner of crowds.

FLYING SOLO
Grow wings
If you're a real thrill-seeker, give wingsurfing in the Grand Canal Dock a go. The sheltered docklands are the perfect place to learn the basics before heading to the waves.

IN A PAIR
On the ball
Ireland is a dream golfing destination, with a huge range of courses to choose from. Plan a catch-up with your BFF while you play a leisurely game at Stepaside Golf Centre, a perfect course for beginners.

FOR A CROWD
Get messy
Stags, hen parties, work events or simple weekend fun: paintballing is the perfect competitive activity. Head to Courtlough Outdoor Adventure Centre for a course that puts you through your paces.

KAYAKING ON THE RIVER LIFFEY

Map 5; City Kayaking, Dublin City Moorings, Custom House Quay;
///along.softly.woes; www.citykayaking.com

It's not uncommon to see a kayak making its way down the Liffey in the summer when water levels are low. Friends hop in a kayak to see the city from a new perspective, all while trying not to fall in the water after a wobble. There are many outfitters to go with, but for something different, book a Music Under the Bridges tour with City Kayaking and enjoy a gig from the comfort of your vessel.

CYCLE THE DOCKLANDS

Map 5; start at DublinBikes, Guild Street; ///back.flank.fuels

For those who don't own a bike, Dublin's rental schemes *(p12)* are a saviour. Leisurely weekend cyclists avoid the centre in favour of a ride through the Docklands to Ringsend, where hip cafés provide a stop-off excuse from which to watch locals racing row boats on the Liffey.
» Don't leave without cycling through Ringsend Park. It's an oft-overlooked oasis of green with a real neighbourhood, family vibe.

STAND-UP PADDLEBOARDING

Map 6; Dún Laoghaire Harbour; ///acute.slug.crunch; www.bigstyle.ie

Combining exercise with socializing, SUPing has Dubliners falling hard and fast – literally. You can try it at most waterways – the Liffey, Dalkey, the Grand Canal – but water sports mecca Dún Laoghaire is the most popular choice for a reason. BigStyle SUP School makes it easy to pick up, leaving more time to admire the views as you navigate the sea.

NORTH CITY

Hit up the DOCKLANDS

Glide through Dublin's hip tech hub, taking in the cutting-edge modern architecture and buzzing restaurants.

Liffey

DOCKLANDS

Liffey

TEMPLE BAR

3 RINGSEND RD

IRISH ROAD

River Dodder

CITY CENTRE

Stop off at the PATRICK KAVANAGH STATUE

Pause at the memorial for this Irish poet, sitting on a bench. There's space for you to sit next to him and gaze at the water.

Pick up a DUBLINBIKE

Rent a bike *(p12)* from Grantham Street (it's a cinch to get one), then make your way down to the canal.

Grand Canal

In the early days, Guinness – Ireland's most famous drink – was actually made with water from the Grand Canal.

PORTOBELLO

1

ADELAIDE RD

2

Grand Canal

5

RANELAGH RD

DARTMOUTH RD

LEESON ST UPPER

CLYDE ROAD

MERRION RD

SERPE

BALLSBRIDGE

Cheers with a pint at THE BARGE

Pop your bike back at the Charlemont Street station, then enjoy an alfresco Guinness above the water at this local favourite.

RANELAGH

RATHMINES

DONNYBROOK

River Dodder

0 metres   500
0 yards   500

An afternoon cycle along
the Grand Canal

The Liffey may hog the headlines, but the Grand Canal is the city's true heart – just look to the Irish poets and songwriters who've used it as their muse. It actually stretches the whole width of Ireland, and while there are plans to create a cycle path that spans the entire length, the idyllic portion that flows through Dublin is all you need. At the weekend, Dubliners love nothing more than gathering for "canal cans", hopping in a kayak or walking their dogs along the pretty banks. There's no better way to see the real Dublin than cycling along the canal, the city's vast social playground.

1. Dublinbikes
Grantham Street;
www.dublinbikes.ie
///model.took.assure

2. Patrick Kavanagh Statue
Wilton Terrace,
Grand Canal Dock
///woven.bells.index

3. Docklands
Grand Canal Dock
///spice.mock.cherry

4. Sandymount
Sandymount Strand
///pens.steer.reduce

5. The Barge
42 Charlemont Street,
Ranelagh;
www.thebarge.ie
///result.grit.pans

BEACH ROAD

Dublin Bay

SANDYMOUNT

CLAREMONT RD

GILFORD ROAD

STRAND ROAD

4

**Take a moment at
SANDYMOUNT**
Enjoy the view of the
Poolbeg Towers – a tall
power plant known for its
distinctive chimneys –
from this pretty coastline.

MERRION

With a little research and preparation, this city will feel like a home away from home. Check out these websites to ensure a healthy, safe stay in Dublin.

Dublin
DIRECTORY

SAFE SPACES

Dublin is a friendly and inclusive city but, should you feel uneasy or want to find your community, there's a host of spaces catering to different ages, genders, sexualities, demographics and religions.

www.inar.ie
The Irish Network Against Racism, a nationwide civil society offering support.

www.islamicfoundation.ie
The definitive guide to mosques and prayer halls in Ireland.

www.jewishireland.org
A guide to times of services at the city's three synagogues.

www.outhouse.ie
A welcoming centre for the LGBTQ+ community to come together.

HEALTH

Healthcare in Ireland isn't free so make sure you have comprehensive health insurance; emergency healthcare is covered by the European Health Insurance Card (EHIC) for EU residents and the UK Global Health Insurance Card (GHIC) for those from the UK. If you do need medical assistance, there are pharmacies and hospitals across town.

www.dentalhospital.ie
Dublin Dental University Hospital, serving emergency dental needs.

www.hickeyspharmacies.ie
A central city pharmacy that opens until 9pm every day.

www.hse.ie
Ireland's health service, with information on all local clinics and general advice.

www.stjames.ie
St James is the main hospital in the city centre, with a 24-hour A&E department.

www.wellwomancentre.ie
Clinics for women across the city that provide sexual healthcare, family planning and counselling services.

TRAVEL SAFETY ADVICE
Dublin is generally a safe city. Before you travel – and while you're here – always keep tabs on the latest regulations in Ireland.

www.dfa.ie
Latest safety advice and onward travel regulations from the Department of Foreign Affairs in Ireland.

www.drcc.ie
Information and support in regards to sexual violence from the Dublin Rape Crisis Centre, with a 24-hour helpline.

www.garda.ie
Useful information from An Garda Síochána, the Irish police.

www.gov.ie
The official Irish government website is the first port of call for all COVID-19 regulations.

www.itas.ie
The Irish Tourist Assistance Service, helping those who have been the victim of a crime while visiting Ireland.

ACCESSIBILITY
Dublin has come along leaps and bounds when it comes to accessibility, but some medieval streets can prove tricky for wheelchair users and some attractions may be lacking in facilities. It's always best to check ahead.

www.iwa.ie
The Irish Wheelchair Association runs various accessible organizations including gyms and community centres.

www.ireland.com
Find an up-to-date accessibility charter on the official Tourism for Ireland website.

www.irishdeafsociety.ie
Excellent resource for Deaf people, with information on booking interpreters.

www.ncbi.ie
A great source of support and advice on travel assistance for those with sight loss.

www.transportforireland.ie
Keep tracks on accessible stations and services for all transport across Dublin.

INDEX

ACKNOWLEDGMENTS

Meet the illustrator

Award-winning British illustrator David Doran is based in a studio by the sea in Falmouth, Cornwall. When not drawing and designing, David tries to make the most of the beautiful area in which he's based; sea-swimming all year round, running the coastal paths and generally spending as much time outside as possible.

With thanks

DK Eyewitness would like to thank the following people for their contribution to the first edition of this book: Nicola Brady, Éadaoin Fitzmaurice, Lucy Richards, Tania Gomes, Zoë Rutland and Casper Morris.

THIS EDITION UPDATED BY

Contributor Nicola Brady
Senior Editor Lucy Richards
Senior Designer Stuti Tiwari
Project Editor Rebecca Flynn
Project Art Editor Ankita Sharma
Designer Jordan Lambley
Indexer Helen Peters
Senior Cartographic Editor Casper Morris
Cartography Manager Suresh Kumar
Jacket Designer Sarah Snelling
Jacket Illustrator David Doran
Senior Production Editor Jason Little
Senior Production Controller Samantha Cross
Managing Editor Hollie Teague
Managing Art Editors Sarah Snelling, Priyanka Thakur
Art Director Maxine Pedliham
Publishing Director Georgina Dee

This book was made with Forest Stewardship Council™ certified paper — one small step in DK's commitment to a sustainable future. **For more information go to** www.dk.com/our-green-pledge

MIX
Paper | Supporting responsible forestry
FSC™ C018179
www.fsc.org

First edition 2021
Published in Great Britain by Dorling Kindersley Limited,
DK, One Embassy Gardens, 8 Viaduct Gardens,
London SW11 7BW.
The authorised representative in the EEA is
Dorling Kindersley Verlag GmbH. Arnulfstr. 124,
80636 Munich, Germany.
Published in the United States by DK Publishing,
1745 Broadway, 20th Floor, New York, NY 10019.
Copyright © 2021, 2023 Dorling Kindersley Limited
A Penguin Random House Company
23 24 25 26 10 9 8 7 6 5 4 3 2 1
All rights reserved.

A CIP catalog record for this book is available from the British Library.
A catalog record for this book is available from the Library of Congress.
ISSN: 1542 1554
ISBN: 978 0 2415 6900 9
Printed and bound in China.
www.dk.com

A NOTE FROM DK EYEWITNESS

The world is fast-changing and it's keeping us folk at DK Eyewitness on our toes. We've worked hard to ensure that this edition of Dublin Like a Local is up-to-date and reflects today's favourite places but we know that standards shift, venues close and new ones pop up in their place. So, if you notice something has closed, we've got something wrong or left something out, we want to hear about it. Please drop us a line at travelguides@dk.com

THE
OFFICE OF COMPLINE

In Latin and English

From the

SAINT LOUIS ANTIPHONARY
FOR THE HOURS

Chant settings by
Fr. Samuel F. Weber, O.S.B.
Institute of Sacred Music
Archdiocese of Saint Louis

IGNATIUS PRESS   SAN FRANCISCO

NIHIL OBSTAT

San Francisco, July 9, 2010

Rev. Msgr. J. Warren Holleran
S.T.D.

IMPRIMATUR

San Francisco, July 16, 2010

† Most Reverend George Niederauer
Archbishop of San Francisco

Contents

Acknowledgments

The editor gratefully acknowledges those who have assisted in bringing this book to completion.

Fr. Joseph Fessio, S. J., first suggested the need for a book that would contain the Office of Compline in Latin and English, arranged for chanting, and has been an invaluable help in moving the project along and bringing it to completion. Archbishop Raymond L. Burke encouraged this book in its various stages, especially as an aid to prayer in parishes and families.

Finally, the editor wishes to thank the Rev. Dylan Schrader, the Rev. Mr. Henry Purcell, James Clark, Daniel C. Gill and David Voss, of the Kenrick School of Theology, Archdiocese of Saint Louis, who, in various ways, have rendered invaluable assistance in preparing this book for publication.

Fr. Samuel F. Weber, O.S.B.
Editor

Foreword

The Church, through the Liturgy of the Hours, an important part of her public prayer, sanctifies each hour of every day of our lives. She indeed makes all time holy. Among the Hours, the Office of Compline has a distinct importance. It is the Church's last prayer of the day, her prayer before retiring. It embraces the experience of the whole day which has passed and, at the same time, the experience of sleep, the abandonment of self to unconsciousness, which is, for us, a daily anticipation of death, of the passage from this life to the life which is to come.

Abbot Prosper Guéranger, O.S.B., commenting on the Office of Compline for the Season of Advent, in what is now known as the Extraordinary Form of the Roman Rite, observed:

> This Office, which concludes the day, commences by a warning of the dangers of the night: then immediately follows the public confession of our sins, as a powerful means of propitiating the divine justice, and obtaining God's help, now that we are going to spend so many hours in the unconscious, and therefore dangerous, state of sleep, which is also such an image of death.[1]

The Christian pilgrimage of each day, through the Office of Compline, is consistently placed within the context of the pilgrimage of a lifetime, which reaches its destiny in death, in the passage, with Christ, from our earthly home to the lasting home which He has prepared for us in Heaven.[2]

Given the importance of the Office of Compline as the Hour which ends the day before sleep, the Church, in her liturgical discipline, has insisted that Compline should always be her final public prayer of the day. In the General Rubrics of the *Breviarium Romanum*, as it was restored by decree of the Ecumenical Council of Trent, we read:

> *Compline* is most fittingly said by all who are obliged to the recitation of the Divine Office, but, above all, in religious families,

[1] Prosper Guéranger, O.S.B., *The Liturgical Year*, Volume 1 – Advent, tr. Laurence Shepherd, O.S.B., Fitzwilliam, New Hampshire: Loreto Publications, 2000, p. 110.
[2] Cf. *Heb* 13:14.

as the final prayer at the end of the day, even if, for a just reason, Matins of the following day will have already been anticipated. [3]

The Fathers at the Second Vatican Ecumenical Council, likewise, gave the following norm regarding Compline in the reform of the Divine Office: "Compline is to be so composed that it will be a suitable prayer for the end of the day." [4] Accordingly, the *General Instruction of the Liturgy of the Hours*, published after the Council, stipulates: "Night prayer is the last prayer of the day, said before retiring, even if that is after midnight." [5]

At the end of each day, the Office of Compline uncovers for us, once again, the nature of our Christian pilgrimage on this earth, that is, the daily conversion of life to Christ, which is, at one and the same time, the daily turning away from sin and death. The Examination of Conscience with which Compline begins permits the Christian to see most clearly the profound truth of the gift of life and time, the truth revealed in Jesus Christ, through the outpouring of the Holy Spirit into the Christian soul. Having confronted his sins, his failure to turn to Christ throughout the day, the Christian, by the Act of Contrition, turns to Christ, turns away from sin and death once more, one final time in the day, before falling to sleep.

Compline, in a particular way, underlines for the Christian the reality of Satan and his cohorts at work in the world and in his own life. Dom Cipriano Vagaggini, O.S.B., commenting on the struggle against Satan, as it is reflected in the Liturgy of the Hours, in general, and in the Hour of Compline, in particular, declared: "The Roman Liturgy of

---

[3] *"Completorium*, ab omnibus qui ad recitationem divini Officii obligantur, praesertim autem in familiis religiosis, valde opportune dicitur tamquam ultima precatio in fine diei, etiam si, ob iustam causam, Matutinum diei sequentis iam anticipatum fuerit." *Breviarium Romanum* ex Decreto SS. Concilii Tridentini restitutum Summorum Pontificum cura recognitum, Editio typica 1961, ed. Manlio Sodi and Alessandro Toniolo, Città del Vaticano: Libreria Editrice Vaticana, 2009, p. 32, no. 147.

[4] "Completorium ita instruatur, ut fini diei apte conveniat; …" Concilium Oecumenicum Vaticanum II, "Constitutio de Sacra Liturgia, *Sacrosanctum Concilium*," 4 December 1963, *Acta Apostolicae Sedis*, vol. 56 (1964), p. 122, no. 89b. English translation from: *Documents on the Liturgy 1963-1979: Conciliar, Papal, and Curial Texts*, ed. International Commission on English in the Liturgy, Collegeville: The Liturgical Press, 1982, p. 19, no. 89.

[5] "Completorium est ultima diei oratio, ante nocturnam quietem facienda, etiam post mediam noctem si casus ferat." *Instructio Generalis de Liturgia Horarum*, 1 November 1970, no. 84. English translation from: *Documents on the Liturgy 1963-1979: Conciliar, Papal, and Curial Texts*, ed. International Commission on English in the Liturgy, Collegeville: The Liturgical Press, 1982, p. 1108, no. 3514.

the ferial breviary reminds us of the struggle against Satan in a special way in the last canonical hour of the day, which is Compline."[6]

The *Lectio brevis* for Compline on every day before the reform after the Second Vatican Ecumenical Council and, since the reform, for Compline on Tuesday, taken from the *First Letter of Peter*, gives clear expression to the battle against Satan, which is at heart of the Christian life:

> Be sober, be watchful. Your adversary the devil prowls around like a roaring lion, seeking some one to devour. Resist him, firm in your faith.[7]

The prayer at the conclusion of Compline on solemnities other than Sundays, likewise, gives expression to the Christian's consciousness of the real danger which Satan constitutes in his life and, therefore, of his need to turn to Christ Who, especially through the ministration of His angels, will not fail to safeguard and save the soul who places his trust in Him:

> Lord, we beg you to visit this house and banish from it all the deadly power of the enemy. May your holy angels dwell here to keep us in peace; and may your blessing be upon us always. We ask this through Christ our Lord. Amen.[8]

The Christian is deeply conscious that, in the struggle to live in Christ who conquers sin and death in our human nature, he faces a formidable enemy in Satan and his cohorts. At the same time, he knows that God has dispatched His angels to watch over and assist him. In the daily Prayer to One's Guardian Angel, we acknowledge the supreme love of God Who commits us to the care of the angels, "to light and guard, to rule and guide."[9]

[6]Cyprian Vagaggini, O.S.B., *Theological Dimensions of the Liturgy: A General Treatise on the Theology of the Liturgy*, tr. Leonard J. Doyle and W. A. Jurgens, Collegeville: The Liturgical Press, 1976, p. 448.

[7]"Sobrii estote, vigilate. Adversarius vester Diabolus tamquam leo rugiens circuit quaerens quem devoret. Cui resistite fortes in fide." (*1 Pt* 5:8-9). English translation: Revised Standard Version Catholic Edition.

[8]"Visita, quaesumus, Domine, habitationem istam, et omnes insidias inimici ab ea longe repelle; angeli tui sancti habitent in ea, qui nos in pace custodiant; et benedictio tua sit super nos semper. Per Christum Dominum nostrum. Amen." *Liturgia Horarum* iuxta Ritum Romanum, "Ad Completorium: Post I Vesperas Dominicae et Sollemnitatum."

[9]"illumina, custodi, rege et guberna." "Prayer to One's Guardian Angel" (*Angele Dei*/Angel of God).

Dom Vagaggini observes well that neither the Christian life itself nor its highest expression, the Sacred Liturgy, make ultimate sense, if the reality of the struggle against Satan is ignored or forgotten. [10] Psalm 90, one of the three "proper and specific psalms of Compline, in the monastic tradition, the tradition in which this hour was born," [11] addresses powerfully the struggle against Satan, expressing confidence in the particular assistance and protection which God provides for us in the struggle through the ministration of His angels:

[N]o evil shall befall you,
　no scourge come near your tent,
For he will give his angels charge of you,
　to guard you in all your ways. [12]

While the Office of Compline makes the Christian deeply conscious of his daily combat against Satan, with the concomitant danger to the eternal salvation of his soul, even as Our Lord was tempted by Satan in the desert at the beginning of His public ministry, it also leads him to trust in the protection and guidance of God, provided through His angels. [13]

Praying the Canticle of Compline, which is the prayer of Simeon at the Presentation of the Lord, the Christian goes to rest at peace, because he has placed all his trust in the Lord Who never fails in His love of man and Who covers the Christian with the protection of the angels. Abbot Guéranger comments:

The canticle of the venerable Simeon – who, while holding the divine Infant in his arms, proclaimed him to be *light of the Gentiles*, and then slept the sleep of the just – admirably expresses the rest which a good Christian, whose heart is united to God, enjoys in Jesus; for, as the apostle says, whether we wake or sleep, we live together with Him who died for us. [14]

The Christian, through the indwelling of the Holy Spirit, lives in Christ, and, even as Simeon who held the Christ Child in his arms, finds his

[10] Cf. Vagaggini, p. 450.

[11] Vagaggini, p. 449.

[12] "Non accedet ad te malum, et flagellum non appropinquabit tabernaculo tuo, quoniam angelis suis mandabit de te, ut custodiant te in omnibus viis tuis." (*Ps* 90:10-11). English translation: Revised Standard Version Catholic Edition.

[13] Cf. Vagaggini, p. 450.

[14] Guéranger, p. 115.

lasting, that is, eternal, joy and peace in the living presence of Christ. Having prayed the Canticle of Simeon, he can with confidence conclude his night prayer, knowing that Christ dwells within him through the Holy Spirit, by asking God to give him "a restful night and a peaceful death."[15]

Finally, Compline concludes with an antiphon calling upon the intercession of the Mother of God. Contemplating the reality of another day of his Christian pilgrimage, the Christian experiences the company of the Mother of God, whom the Lord has given to us, when He was dying on the Cross, as the Mother of the Church, the Mother of all of the members of His Mystical Body. Before retiring for the night, he rightly turns to his Heavenly Mother to thank her for her unfailing care and to beg, once again, her protection and intercession, during the night.

Compline can well be called the Church's family prayer before retiring. Even as children gather around their father and mother to pray before going to bed, so, too, the whole Church places herself before her Heavenly Father, in the company of the Blessed Virgin Mary, and the angels and all the Saints, to pray before retiring for the night. Like children in the company of their parents, as they, with fear, face the darkness of the night, the Church, before God the Father, knows the faithful and enduring protection of God Who loves us unconditionally and safeguards us against the assaults of the Evil One. It is most important, therefore, that a worthy book containing the Office of Compline be accessible to all in the Church, to religious communities, seminaries, parishes, families, and, in sort, to all who wish to be one with the Church in her final public prayer of the day.

Father Samuel Weber, O.S.B., director of the Institute of Sacred Music of the Archdiocese of Saint Louis, responding to the need of a readily accessible Book of Compline for English-speaking Catholics, has carefully prepared the volume which you now have in your hands. The *Office of Compline* is an important and integral part of his bigger work, the Saint Louis Antiphonary for the Hours, which provides beautiful and yet accessible chant settings for the fuller praying of the Liturgy of the Hours in the Church, both at home and in the wider community of parishes, religious communities, seminaries and other groups of the faithful. The Institute of Sacred Music has for its purpose the promotion of fitting Sacred Music for the Church's public prayer, especially Gregorian Chant and Sacred Polyphony, in accord with the

[15] "Noctem quietam et finem perfectum…." *Liturgia Horarum* iuxta Ritum Romanum, «Ordinarium : Ad Completorium.»

xii

deeper appreciation of the organic unity of Sacred Liturgy, as it has been celebrated throughout the Christian centuries.

Father Weber's *Office of Compline* offers to all the faithful the richness of the Church's night prayer. It is complete, that is, it contains all the texts of the Church's public night prayer, both in Latin and in English. It fully respects the integrity of those texts in the original Latin and in the approved English translation from the Latin.

The *Office of Compline* also provides all of the chants for those who are able to pray the Hour more fully by singing. The musical texts, which Father Weber has arranged for ease of chanting, are beautiful and can be learned also by the family who wants to pray with the universal Church before retiring for the night. The chants are set, as just noted, to the original Latin text or its approved English translation.

In summary, the *Office of Compline* satisfies the requirements for the fitting and indeed beautiful celebration of the last Hour of the day, in every community of the Church, from the little Church of the home and family to the bigger Church of the parish, the religious community or the seminary. It provides a most worthy instrument for the praying of Compline with renewed faith, hope and love.

In the name of all who will use the *Office of Compline*, I express the deepest esteem and gratitude to Father Samuel Weber, O.S.B., for his great care in preparing a volume which certainly will serve well the public prayer of the Church, her Sacred Liturgy. In our gratitude, let us pray for God's continued blessing upon the important work of Father Weber for the restoration of the Sacred Liturgy, especially sacred music, as it was mandated by the Second Vatican Council, in continuity with the perennial Tradition of the Church.

It is my hope, as a shepherd of the flock, that the *Office of Compline* will inspire a new appreciation of the importance of the last Hour of the day and a new participation in the public prayer of the Church, at the end of each day. It is my hope that the *Office of Compline* of the Saint Louis Antiphonary for the Hours will contribute a significant part to the greater sanctification of the time which concludes every day for us, the time before we give ourselves over to sleep. So may we all be safeguarded from the wiles of Satan and protected by the saving grace of Christ through the ministration of the holy angels. So may we all, through the intercession of the Blessed Virgin Mary, attain "a restful night and a peaceful end."

† Raymond Leo Burke
Archbishop Emeritus of Saint Louis
Prefect of the Supreme Tribunal of the Apostolic Signatura

Directions for Compline

1. *Introductory rite.* STAND.

   Make the sign of the cross when the presider begins the opening verse, *O God, come to my assistance.* Bow while the Persons of the Blessed Trinity are mentioned during the *Glory be.*

   A brief examination of conscience may be made. In the communal celebration of the office, a penitential rite using the formulas of the Mass may be inserted here.

2. *Hymn.* STAND.

   Bow during the Trinitarian doxology in the last verse of the hymn.

3. *Psalmody.* SIT.

   Sit when the first verse of the first psalm begins. Bow during the *Glory be* at the end of each psalm.

4. *Reading.* SIT.

5. *Responsory.* SIT.

   Bow during the *Glory be* in the responsory.

6. *Gospel canticle.* STAND.

   All stand before the antiphon for the Gospel canticle.
   Make the sign of the cross when the first verse of the canticle begins. Bow during the *Glory be* at the end of the canticle.

7. *Prayer.* STAND.

   The presider says this prayer alone.

8. *Concluding rite.* STAND.

   The presider gives the blessing alone.

9. *Antiphon in honor of the Blessed Virgin.* STAND.

   According to custom this antiphon may be sung kneeling Monday through Friday. After I and II Vespers of Sunday, however, it is always sung standing.

I

Ordinarium / Ordinary

ORDINARIUM AD COMPLETORIUM

IN PRINCIPIO HORÆ

℣. D E- us in adiutó-ri- um me- um inténde. ℟. Dómine   ad adiu-

vándum me   festína.   Gló-ri- a Pa-tri, et Fí- li- o, et Spi-rí-tu- i

Sancto.   Sicut e-rat in princí-pi- o, et nunc et semper,   et. in sǽ-

cu-la sæcu-ló-rum. Amen.   Alle-lú- ia.

TEMPORE QUADRAGESIMÆ

℣. D E- us in adiutó-ri- um me- um inténde. ℟. Dómine   ad adiu-

vándum me   festína. Gló-ri- a Pa-tri, et Fí- li- o, et Spi-rí-tu- i

Sancto.   Sicut e-rat in princí-pi- o, et nunc et semper,   et in sǽ-

cu-la sæcu-ló-rum. Amen.

ORDINARY AT COMPLINE

AT THE BEGINNING OF THE HOUR

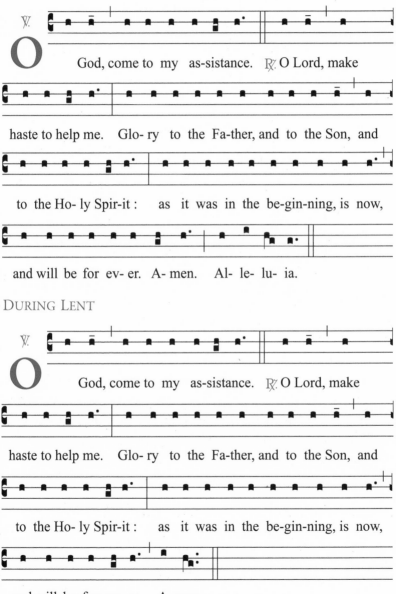

℣. O God, come to my as-sistance. ℟. O Lord, make haste to help me. Glo-ry to the Fa-ther, and to the Son, and to the Ho-ly Spir-it: as it was in the be-gin-ning, is now, and will be for ev-er. A-men. Al-le-lu-ia.

DURING LENT

℣. O God, come to my as-sistance. ℟. O Lord, make haste to help me. Glo-ry to the Fa-ther, and to the Son, and to the Ho-ly Spir-it: as it was in the be-gin-ning, is now, and will be for ev-er. A-men.

Postea laudabiliter fit conscientiæ discussio, quae in celebratione communi inseri potest in actum paenitentialem, iuxta formulas in Missa adhibitas.

HYMNUS

Tonus Hymni Te lucis ante terminum, vel Christe, qui, splendor et dies, variatur secundum Tempora aut Festa, 90-132.

> Te lucis ante términum,
> Rerum creátor, póscimus,
> Ut sólita cleméntia
> Sis præsul ad custódiam.
>
> Te corda nostra sómnient,
> Te per sopórem séntiant,
> Tuámque semper glóriam
> Vicína luce cóncinant.
>
> Vitam salúbrem tríbue,
> Nostrum calórem réfice,
> Tætram noctis calíginem
> Tua collústret cláritas.
>
> Præsta, Pater omnípotens,
> Per Iesum Christum Dóminum,
> Qui tecum in perpétuum
> Regnat cum Sancto Spíritu. Amen.

Vel, iuxta rubicas in Proprio de Tempore descriptas :

> Christe, qui, splendor et dies,
> Noctis tenébras détegis,
> Lucísque lumen créderis,
> Lumen beátis prædicans,
>
> Precámur, sancte Dómine,
> Hac nocte nos custódias ;
> Sit nobis in te réquies,
> Quiétas horas tríbue.
>
> Somno si dantur óculi,
> Cor semper ad te vígilet ;
> Tuáque dextra prótegas
> Fidéles, qui te díligunt.

A brief examination of conscience may be made. In the communal celebration of the office, a penitential rite using the formulas of the Mass may be inserted here.

Hymn

The Chant of the Hymn Before the Ending of the Day, or O Christ, Who Art the Light and Day, varies according to the Seasons and Feasts, 91-133.

Before the ending of the day,
Creator of the world, we pray,
That with thy constant favor thou
Wouldst be our Guard and Keeper now.

Allow our hearts to dream of thee,
Thee through the sleep of night to see,
Then, with the light of dawn may we
Thy glory praise unceasingly.

O grant us health of life once more ;
The warmth of day to us restore,
And pierce the gloomy dark of night
With splendid beams of thy pure light.

O Father, that we ask be done,
Through Jesus Christ, thine only Son ;
Who, with the Holy Ghost and thee,
Doth live and reign eternally. Amen.

Or, according to the rubrics given in the Proper of the Time :

O Christ, who art the Light and Day,
Thou drivest darksome night away !
We know thee as the Light of light,
Illuminating mortal sight.

All-holy Lord, we pray to thee,
Keep us tonight from danger free ;
Grant us, dear Lord, in thee to rest,
So be our sleep in quiet blest.

And while the eyes soft slumber take,
Still be the heart to thee awake ;
Be thy right hand upheld above
Thy servants resting in thy love.

Defénsor noster, áspice,
Insidiántes réprime,
Gubérna tuos fámulos,
Quos sánguine mercátus es.

Sit, Christe, rex piíssime,
Tibi Patríque glória,
Cum Spíritu Paráclito,
In sempitérna sǽcula. Amen.

Tempore vero paschali :

Jesu, redémptor sǽculi,
Verbum Patris altíssimi,
Lux lucis invisíbilis,
Custos tuórum pérvigil :

Tu fabricátor ómnium
Discrétor atque témporum,
Fessa labóre córpora
Noctis quiéte récrea.

Qui frangis ima tártara,
Tu nos ab hoste líbera,
Ne váleat sedúcere
Tuo redémptos sánguine,

Ut, dum graváti córpore
Brevi manémus témpore,
Sic caro nostra dórmiat
Ut mens sopórem nésciat.

Iesu, tibi sit glória,
Qui morte victa prǽnites,
Cum Patre et almo Spíritu,
In sempitérna sǽcula. Amen.

PSALMODIA

Post I Vesperas dominicarum et sollemnitatum dicuntur psalmi 4 et 133 (134), 20 ; post II Vesperas, psalmus 90 (91), 38.

Alterutrum Completorium de dominica dicitur etiam infra octavam Nativitatis et octavam Paschæ.

Ceteris diebus, psalmi cum suis antiphonis, inveniuntur in Psalterio. Licet tamen resumere alteruturm Completorium de dominica.

Yea, our Defender, be thou nigh
To bid the pow'rs of darkness fly ;
Keep us from sin, and guide for good
Thy servants purchased by thy Blood.

All praise, eternal Son, to thee
Whose advent sets thy people free ;
Whom with the Father we adore
And Holy Ghost, for evermore.   Amen.

Paschaltide :

Jesus, Redeemer of the earth,
The Father's Word of heav'nly birth,
Bright splendor of the unseen light,
Protect thine own throughout this night.

O Maker blest, thou Lord sublime,
Who judgest wisely space and time,
Though daily toil hath worn us through,
Our weary frame this night renew.

Thou breakest Hell's fierce pow'rs below ;
Make haste to free us from the foe
Lest by his crafty lures be caught
Those whom thy Precious Blood hath bought.

Though mortal bodies tire and strain,
How briefly do we thus remain !
And while these bodies lie asleep,
Grant that our minds their watch may keep.

O Jesus, be all glory thine,
Who over death in triumph shine,
Whom with the Father we adore
And Holy Ghost for evermore. Amen.

PSALMODY

After I Vespers of Sundays and solemnities, psalms 4 and 133 (134) are said, 21 ; after II Vespers, psalm 90 (91), 39, is said.

Both forms of Compline for Sunday may be used within the octave of Christmas and the octave of Easter.

On all other days, the psalms and antiphons are found in the Psalter. One may, however, use Compline from Sunday during the week.

LECTIO BREVIS

Post psalmodiam fit lectio brevis, quæ sumitur eodem loco quo psalmi in Psalterio. Deinde sequitur responsorium breve.

RESPONSORIUM BREVE

Per annum :

6.

IN ma-nus tu- as, Dó-mi-ne, * Comméndo spí- ri- tum

me- um.   In ma-nus. ℣. Re-de- mí-sti nos, Dó-mi- ne,   De- us

ve- ri- tá- tis.   * Comméndo. ℣. Gló-ri- a Pa-tri,   et Fí- li- o,

et Spi- rí- tu- i Sancto.   In ma-nus.

Tempore adventus :

4.

IN ma-nus tu- as, Dó-mi-ne, * Comméndo spí- ri- tum

me- um.   In ma-nus. ℣. Re-de-mí-sti nos, Dó-mi- ne,   De- us

ve- ri- tá- tis. * Comméndo. ℣. Gló-ri- a Pa- tri,   et Fí- li- o,

READING

A brief reading, found in the Psalter, and a responsory follow the psalmody.

RESPONSORY

Through the Year :

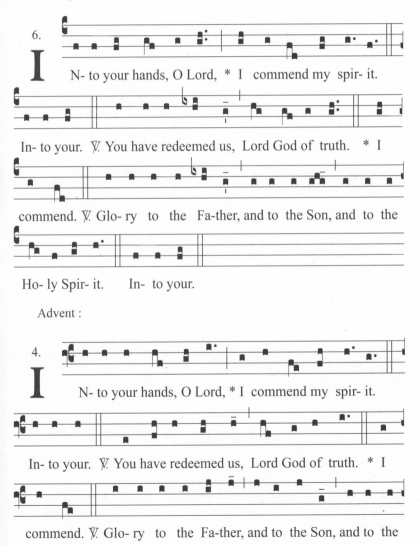

IN- to your hands, O Lord, * I commend my spir- it.

In- to your. ℣. You have redeemed us, Lord God of truth. * I

commend. ℣. Glo- ry to the Fa-ther, and to the Son, and to the

Ho- ly Spir- it. In- to your.

Advent :

IN- to your hands, O Lord, * I commend my spir- it.

In- to your. ℣. You have redeemed us, Lord God of truth. * I

commend. ℣. Glo- ry to the Fa-ther, and to the Son, and to the

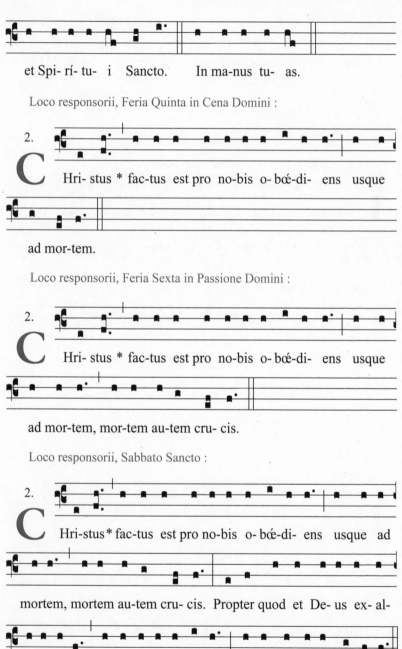

et Spi- rí- tu- i Sancto.   In ma-nus tu- as.

Loco responsorii, Feria Quinta in Cena Domini :

2. C Hri- stus * fac-tus est pro no-bis o- bœ-di- ens usque

ad mor-tem.

Loco responsorii, Feria Sexta in Passione Domini :

2. C Hri- stus * fac-tus est pro no-bis o- bœ-di- ens usque

ad mor-tem, mor-tem au-tem cru- cis.

Loco responsorii, Sabbato Sancto :

2. C Hri-stus * fac-tus est pro no-bis o- bœ-di- ens usque ad

mortem, mortem au-tem cru- cis. Propter quod et De- us ex- al-

tá-vit il-lum, et de-dit il-li nomen, quod est su-per omne nomen.

Ho- ly Spir- it.   In- to your hands.

In place of the responsory, Holy Thursday :

2.
F OR our sake * Christ was o- be- di- ent,   ac-cept-ing

e- ven death.

In place of the responsory, Good Friday :

2.
F OR our sake * Christ was o- be- di- ent,   ac-cept-ing

e- ven death, death on   a   cross.

In place of the responsory, Holy Saturday :

2.
F OR our sake * Christ was o- be- di- ent,   ac-cept-ing

e- ven death, death on   a cross. Therefore God raised him on

high and gave him the name   a-bove all   o- ther names.

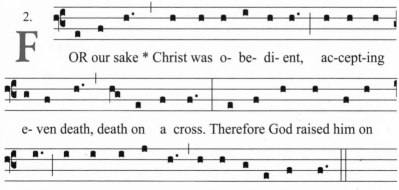
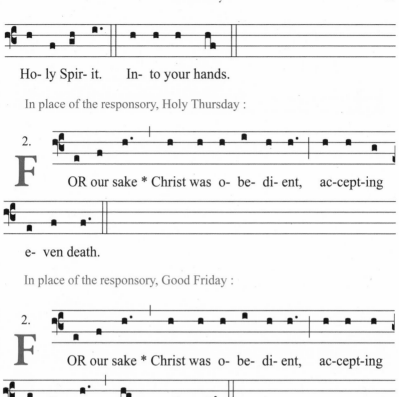

Loco responsorii, per octavam Paschae :

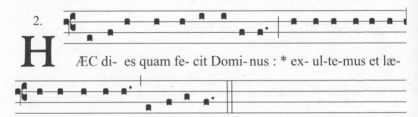

2.

HÆC di- es quam fe- cit Domi- nus : * ex- ul-te-mus et læ-

te-mur in e- a, al- le- lu- ia.

Tempore paschale :

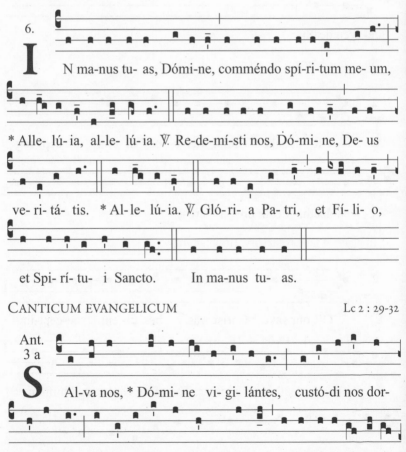

6.

IN ma-nus tu- as, Dómi-ne, comméndo spí-ri-tum me- um,

* Alle- lú- ia, al-le- lú-ia. ℣. Re-de-mí-sti nos, Dó-mi- ne, De- us

ve- ri- tá- tis. * Al-le- lú- ia. ℣. Gló-ri- a Pa- tri, et Fí- li- o,

et Spi- rí- tu- i Sancto.   In ma-nus tu- as.

CANTICUM EVANGELICUM   Lc 2 : 29-32

Ant.
3 a

SAl-va nos, * Dó-mi- ne vi- gi- lántes, custó-di nos dor-

mi- én-tes, ut vi- gi- lé-mus cum Chri-sto, et requi- escámus in

In place of the responsory, during the Easter Octave :

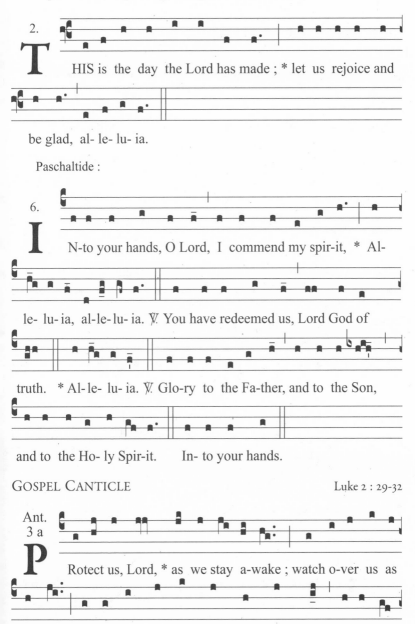

2.

THIS is the day the Lord has made ; * let us rejoice and

be glad, al- le- lu- ia.

Paschaltide :

6.

IN-to your hands, O Lord, I commend my spir-it, * Al-

le- lu- ia, al-le-lu- ia. ℣. You have redeemed us, Lord God of

truth.   * Al- le- lu- ia. ℣. Glo-ry to the Fa-ther, and to the Son,

and to the Ho- ly Spir-it.   In- to your hands.

GOSPEL CANTICLE   Luke 2 : 29-32

Ant.
3 a

PRotect us, Lord, * as we stay a-wake ; watch o-ver us as

we sleep, that a-wake, we may keep watch with Christ, and a-sleep,

pa- ce. T. P. Alle- lú- ia.

Christus lumen gentium et gloria Israel

1. Nunc dimít-tis servum tu- um Dó-mi- ne, * secúndum ver-bum

tu-um in pa-ce ; 2. Qui- a vi-dé-runt ó- cu- li me- i * sa- lu-

tá-re tu- um, 3. Quod pa-rá- sti * ante fá-ci- em ómni- um po-pu-

ló-rum : 4. lumen ad re-ve-la- ti- ó-nem gén-ti- um, * et gló-ri- am

ple-bis tu- æ Is-ra- el. 5. Gló-ri- a Pa-tri, et Fí- li- o, * et Spi- rí-

tu- i Sancto. 6. Si-cut e-rat in princí-pi- o, et nunc et semper, *

et in sǽcu-la sæcu-ló-rum. A-men.

Anti-
phona

Sal-va nos, Dó-mi- ne vi- gi- lántes, custó-di nos dor-

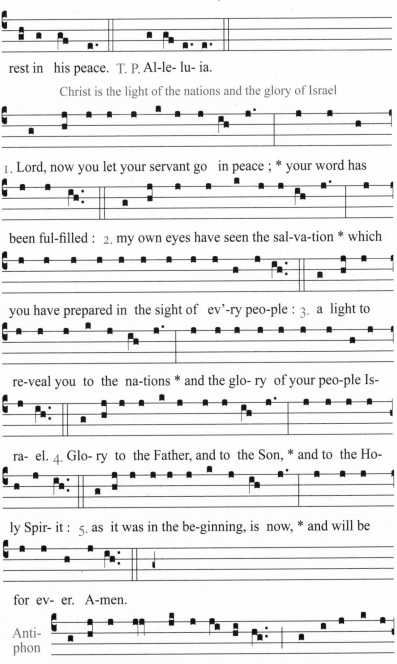

rest in his peace. T. P. Al-le- lu- ia.

Christ is the light of the nations and the glory of Israel

1. Lord, now you let your servant go in peace ; * your word has

been ful-filled : 2. my own eyes have seen the sal-va-tion * which

you have prepared in the sight of ev'-ry peo-ple : 3. a light to

re-veal you to the na-tions * and the glo- ry of your peo-ple Is-

ra- el. 4. Glo- ry to the Father, and to the Son, * and to the Ho-

ly Spir- it : 5. as it was in the be-ginning, is now, * and will be

for ev- er. A-men.

Anti-
phon

Protect us, Lord,   as we stay a-wake ; watch o-ver us as

mi- én-tes, ut vi- gi- lé-mus cum Chri-sto, et requi- escámus in

pa- ce. T. P. Alle- lú- ia.

ORATIO CONCLUSIVA

Postea dicitur oratio ut in Psalterio, cui præmittitur invitatio Orémus. Et respondetur Amen.

Deinde dicitur, etiam a solo, benedictio :

Octem qui- é- tam et fi-nem perféctum concédat no-bis

Dómi-nus omnípo- tens. ℟. A-men.

Deinde dicitur una ex antiphonis in honorem B. Mariæ Virginis.

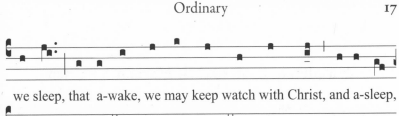

we sleep, that a-wake, we may keep watch with Christ, and a-sleep,

rest in his peace. P.T. Al-le- lu- ia.

CONCLUDING PRAYER

Afterward the prayer, with the invitation Let us pray, as given in the Psalter is said. The response at the conclusion of the prayer : Amen.

The blessing is said, even in individual recitation :

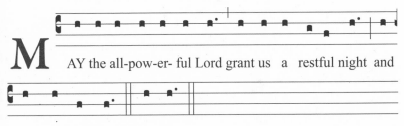

a peaceful death. ℟. A-men.

Then is said one of the antiphons in honor of the Blessed Virgin Mary.

Antiphonæ finales ad B. Mariam Virginem

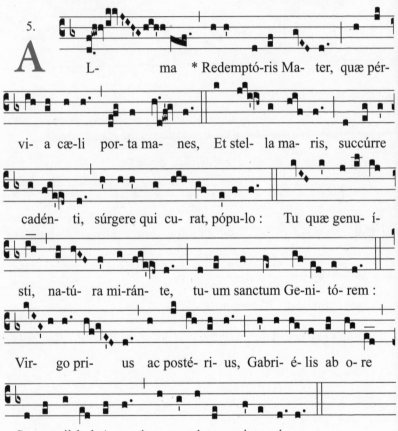

AL- ma * Redemptó-ris Ma- ter, quæ pér-

vi- a cæ-li por- ta ma- nes, Et stel- la ma- ris, succúrre

cadén- ti, súrgere qui cu- rat, pópu-lo : Tu quæ genu- í-

sti, na-tú- ra mi-rán- te, tu- um sanctum Ge-ni- tó- rem :

Vir- go pri- us ac posté- ri- us, Gabri- é- lis ab o- re

Sumens il-lud A-ve, * pecca- tó-rum mi-se- ré- re.

Antiphons in Honor of the Blessed Virgin Mary

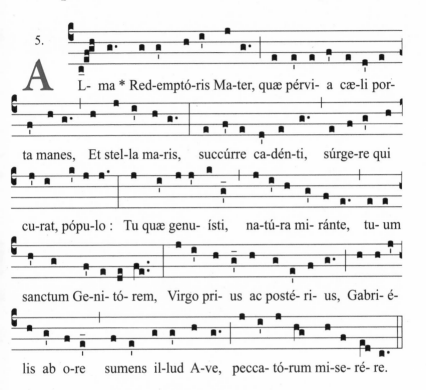

5.

AL- ma * Red-emptó-ris Ma-ter, quæ pérvi- a cæ-li por-ta manes, Et stel-la ma-ris, succúrre ca-dén-ti, súrge-re qui cu-rat, pópu-lo : Tu quæ genu- ísti, na-tú-ra mi- ránte, tu- um sanctum Ge-ni- tó- rem, Virgo pri- us ac posté- ri- us, Gabri- é-lis ab o-re sumens il-lud A-ve, pecca- tó-rum mi-se- ré- re.

Loving Mother of our Redeemer Lord,
Star of the sea and portal of the skies,
Unto thy fallen people help afford—
Fallen, but striving still anew to rise.

Thou who didst once, while wondering worlds adored,
Bear thy Creator, Virgin then as now,
O by thy holy joy at Gabriel's word,
Pity the sinners who before thee bow.

6.

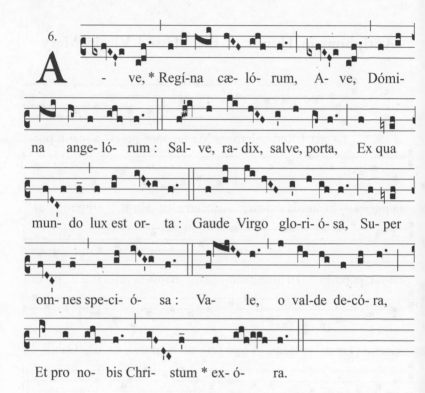

A - ve, * Regí-na cæ- ló- rum, A- ve, Dómi-

na ange- ló- rum : Sal- ve, ra- dix, salve, porta, Ex qua

mun- do lux est or- ta : Gaude Virgo glo-ri- ó- sa, Su- per

om- nes spe-ci- ó- sa : Va- le, o val-de de-có- ra,

Et pro no- bis Chri- stum * ex- ó- ra.

6.

A - ve, Re- gí-na cæ-ló- rum, * A-ve, Dó-mi-na ange-ló-

rum : Salve, ra-dix, sal-ve, por-ta, Ex qua mundo lux est or-ta :

Gaude Virgo glo- ri- ó- sa, Su- per omnes spe-ci- ó- sa : Val-e,

o valde de-có- ra, Et pro no- bis Christum ex- ó- ra.

Hail, O Queen of Heaven enthroned !
Hail, by angels Mistress owned !
Root of Jesse, Gate of morn,
Whence the world's true Light was born :

Glorious Virgin, joy to thee,
Loveliest whom in heaven they see :
Fairest thou where all are fair,
Plead with Christ our sins to spare.

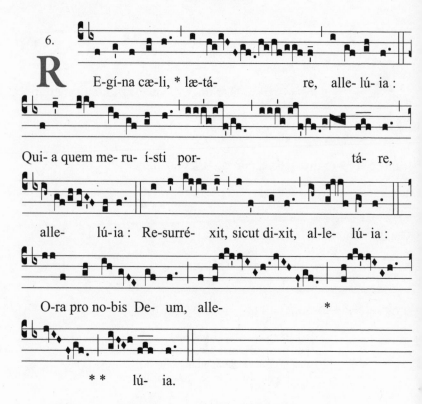

6.

R E-gí-na cæ-li, * læ-tá- re, alle- lú- ia :

Qui- a quem me- ru- í-sti por- tá- re,

alle- lú- ia : Re-surré- xit, sicut di-xit, al-le- lú- ia :

O-ra pro no-bis De- um, alle- *

** lú- ia.

6.

R E-gí-na cæ-li, * læ-tá-re, alle-lú- ia : Qui- a quem me-

ru- í-sti por-tá- re, alle-lú-ia : Re-surré-xit, si-cut di-xit, al-le-

lú- ia : O-ra pro no-bis De- um, alle- lú- ia.

Joy to thee, O Queen of heaven ! Alleluia.
He whom it was thine to bear ; Alleluia.
As He promised, hath arisen ; Alleluia.
Plead for us a pitying prayer ; Alleluia.

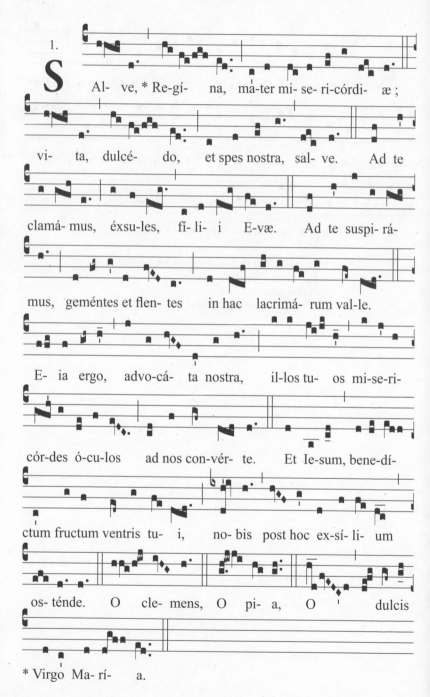

1.

SAl- ve, * Re-gí- na, ma-ter mi- se- ri-córdi- æ ;

vi- ta, dulcé- do, et spes nostra, sal- ve. Ad te

clamá- mus, éxsu-les, fí- li- i E-væ. Ad te suspi- rá-

mus, geméntes et flen- tes in hac lacrimá- rum val-le.

E- ia ergo, advo-cá- ta nostra, il-los tu- os mi-se-ri-

cór-des ó-cu-los ad nos con-vér- te. Et Ie-sum, bene-dí-

ctum fructum ventris tu- i, no- bis post hoc ex-sí- li- um

os- ténde. O cle- mens, O pi- a, O dulcis

* Virgo Ma- rí- a.

5.

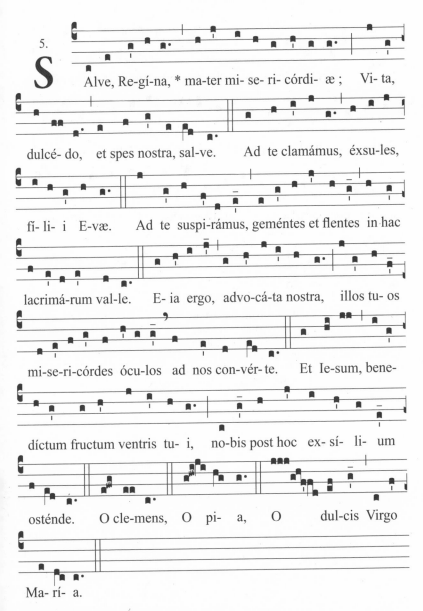

Alve, Re-gí-na, * ma-ter mi- se- ri- córdi- æ ; Vi- ta,

dulcé- do, et spes nostra, sal-ve. Ad te clamámus, éxsu-les,

fí- li- i E-væ. Ad te suspi-rámus, geméntes et flentes in hac

lacrimá-rum val-le. E- ia ergo, advo-cá-ta nostra, illos tu- os

mi-se-ri-córdes ócu-los ad nos con-vér-te. Et Ie-sum, bene-

díctum fructum ventris tu- i, no-bis post hoc ex- sí- li- um

osténde. O cle-mens, O pi- a, O dul-cis Virgo

Ma- rí- a.

Hail, holy Queen, Mother of mercy, our life, our sweetness, and our hope. To thee do we cry, poor banished children of Eve. To thee do we send up our sighs, mourning and weeping in this valley of tears. Turn then, most gracious Advocate, thine eyes of mercy towards us. And after this our exile, show unto us the blessed Fruit of thy womb, Jesus. O clement, O loving, O sweet Virgin Mary.

7.

SUB tu- um præ-sí- di- um confú-gimus, * sancta De- i Gé-ne-trix ; nostras depre-ca-ti- ó-nes ne despí-ci- as in neces-si- tá- ti-bus, sed a per- í- cu- lis cunctis lí- be- ra nos sem-per, Virgo glo- ri- ó-sa et be- ne- dí- cta.

We fly to thy protection,
O holy Mother of God ;
despise not our petitions
in our necessities,
but deliver us always from all dangers,
O glorious and blessed Virgin.

II

Psalterium / Psalter

POST I VESPERAS DOMINICÆ
ET SOLEMNITATUM

Omnia ut in Ordinario, 2, praeter sequentia :

Per annum :

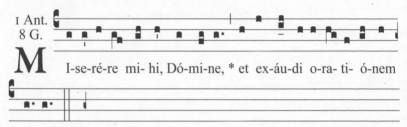

I Ant.
8 G.

M I-se-ré-re mi- hi, Dó-mi-ne, * et ex-áu-di o-ra- ti- ó-nem

me- am.

Tempore paschali :

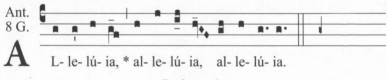

Ant.
8 G.

A L- le- lú- ia, * al- le- lú- ia,   al- le- lú- ia.

Psalmus 4

Gratiarum actio

Admirabilem fecit Dominus, quem suscitavit a mortuis (S. Augustinus).

1. Cum in-vo-cá- rem, ex-au-dí-vit me De-us iustí- ti- æ **me**- æ. *

In tri-bu-la-ti- ó- ne di-la-*tá-sti* **mi**- hi. *Flex:* peccá- re : †

2. miserére **mei** *
   et exáudi oratió*nem* **me**am.

3. Filii hominum, úsquequo gravi **cor**de ? *
   Ut quid dilígitis vanitátem et quæri*tis men***dá**cium ?

AFTER I VESPERS
ON SUNDAYS AND SOLEMNITIES

All as in the Ordinary, 3, except the following :

PSALMODY

During the Year :

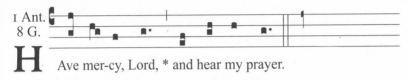

I Ant.
8 G.

HAve mer-cy, Lord, * and hear my prayer.

Paschaltide :

Ant.
8 G.

AL- le- lú- ia, * al- le- lú- ia,   al- le- lú- ia.

Psalm 4

Thanksgiving

The resurrection of Christ was God's supreme and wholly marvellous work (Saint Augustine).

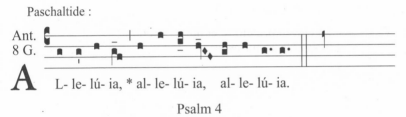

1. When I call, answer me, O *God of* **jus**tice ; * from anguish you re-

leased me ; have mer-*cy and* **hear** me ! *Pause :* do not sin : †

2. O men, how long will your *hearts be* **closed**, *
   will you love what is futile and seek *what is* **false** ?

3. It is the Lord who grants favors to those *whom he* **loves** ; *
   the Lord hears me whenev*er I* **call** him.

4. Et scitóte quóniam mirificávit Dóminus sanctum **su**um ; *
   Dóminus exáudiet, cum clamáve*ro ad* **e**um.

5. Irascímini et nolíte pec**cá**re ; †
   loquímini in córdibus **ve**stris, *
   in cubílibus vestris et *conqui***é**scite,

6. Sacrificáte sacrifícium iust**í**tiæ *
   et speráte *in* **Dó**mino.

7. Multi dicunt : « Quis osténdit nobis **bo**na ? ». *
   Leva in signum super nos lumen vultus *tui,* **Dó**mine !

8. Maiórem dedísti lætitiam in corde **me**o, *
   quam cum multiplicántur fruméntum et vi*num e***ó**rum.

9. In pace in idípsum dórmiam et requi**é**scam, *
   quóniam tu, Dómine, singuláriter in spe cons*titu***í**sti me.

10. Glória Patri, et **Fí**lio, *
    et Spirí*tui* **San**cto.

11. Sicut erat in princípio, et nunc et **sem**per, *
    et in sæcula sæcu*lórum.* **A**men.

Per annum :

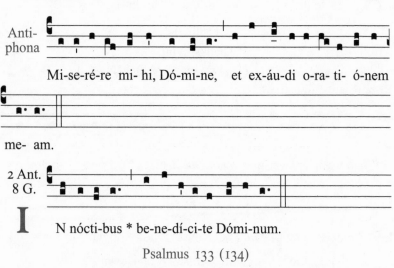

Anti-
phona
Mi-se-ré-re mi- hi, Dó-mi-ne,   et ex-áu-di o-ra- ti- ó-nem

me- am.

2 Ant.
8 G.

I N nócti-bus * be-ne-dí-ci-te Dómi-num.

Psalmus 133 (134)

Vespertina oratio in templo

Laudem dicite Deo nostro, omnes servi eius et qui timetis eum, pusilli et magni ! (Ap 19 : 5).

4. Fear him ; do not sin : †
   ponder on your bed *and be* **still**. *
   Make justice your sacrifice and trust *in the* **Lord**.

5. " What can bring us happiness ? " *many* **say**. *
   Let the light of your face shine on *us, O* **Lord**.

6. You have put into my heart a *greater* **joy** *
   than they have from abundance of corn *and new* **wine**.

7. I will lie down in peace and sleep *comes at* **once** *
   for you alone, Lord, make me *dwell in* **safety**.

8. Glory to the Father, and *to the* **Son**, *
   and to the *Holy* **Spir**it :

9. as it was in the begin*ning, is* **now**, *
   and will be for ev*er. A*men.

During the Year :

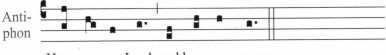

Anti-phon

Have mer-cy, Lord, and hear my prayer.

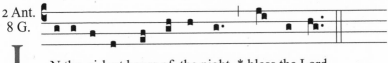

2 Ant.
8 G.

I N the si-lent hours of the night, * bless the Lord.

Psalm 133 (134)

Evening prayer in the temple

Praise our God, all you his servants, you who fear him, small and great (Revelation 19 : 5).

1. Ecce be-ne-dí-ci- te Dómi-num, omnes ser-vi **Dómi-ni,** * qui

sta-tis in do-mo Dómi-*ni per* **noc-** tes.

2. Extóllite manus vestras ad sanctuárium *
et bened*ícite* **Dó**minum.

3. Benedícat te Dóminus ex **Sion,** *
qui fecit cæ*lum et* **ter**ram.

4. Glória Patri, et **Fí**lio, *
et Spirí*tui* **San**cto.

5. Sicut erat in princípio, et nunc et **sem**per, *
et in sæcula sæcu*lórum.* **A**men.

Per annum :

Anti-
phona

In nócti-bus be-ne-dí-ci-te Dómi-num.

Tempore paschali :

Anti-
phona

Al-le- lú- ia, al- le- lú- ia, al- le- lú- ia.

LECTIO BREVIS   Deut 6 : 4–7

A
U-di Is-ra- el : Dómi-nus De- us noster Dómi-nus u-nus

est. Dí- liges Dóminum De- um tu- um ex to-to corde tu- o et ex

1. O come, bless the Lord, * all you who serve the Lord,

2. who stand in the house *of the* **Lord**, *
   in the courts of the house *of our* **God**.

3. Lift up your hands to the *holy* **place** *
   and bless the Lord *through the* **night**.

4. May the Lord bless *you from* **Zi**on, *
   he who made both heav*en and* **earth**.

5. Lift up your hands to the *holy* **place** *
   and bless the Lord *through the* **night**.

6. Glory to the Father, and *to the* **Son**, *
   and to the *Holy* **Spir**it :

7. as it was in the beginn*ing, is* **now**, *
   and will be for ev*er. A*men.

Through the Year :

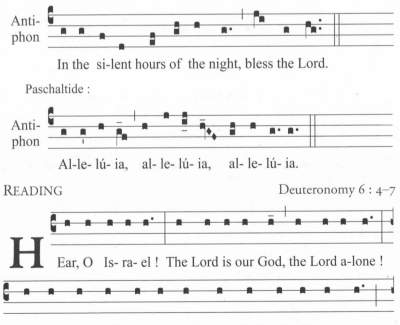

In the si-lent hours of the night, bless the Lord.

Paschaltide :

Al-le- lú- ia,   al- le- lú- ia,   al- le- lú- ia.

READING   Deuteronomy 6 : 4–7

HEar, O Is- ra- el ! The Lord is our God, the Lord a-lone !

Therefore, you shall love the Lord, your God, with all your heart,

to-ta ánima tu- a   et ex to-ta forti-tú-dine tu-a. † Erúntque verba

hæc, quæ e-go præ-cí-pi- o ti-bi hó-di- e, in corde tu- o,   *   et in-

culcábis e- a fí-li- is tu- is   et loqué- ris e- a sedens in domo

tu- a   et ámbu-lans in i-tí-ne-re,   decúmbens atque consúrgens.

Ordinarium, 8.

Oratio

Dominicis et per octavam Paschæ :

V I-si-ta nos, quæ-sumus, Dómi-ne, hac nocte præsénti, *

ut, di- lú-cu-lo tu- a virtú-te surgéntes, de re-surrecti- ó-ne Christi

tu- i gaudé-re va-le- á-mus. Qui vi-vit et regnat in sæcu-la

sæcu- ló-rum. ℟ A-men.

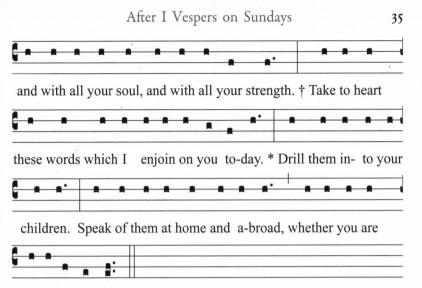

and with all your soul, and with all your strength. † Take to heart

these words which I   enjoin on you to-day. * Drill them in- to your

children. Speak of them at home and a-broad, whether you are

bus-y or   at rest.

Ordinary, 9.

Prayer

On Sundays and through the octave of Easter :

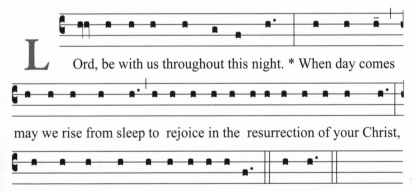

L Ord, be with us throughout this night. * When day comes

may we rise from sleep to rejoice in the resurrection of your Christ,

who lives and reigns for ev- er and ev-er.   ℟. A-men.

In solemnitatibus :

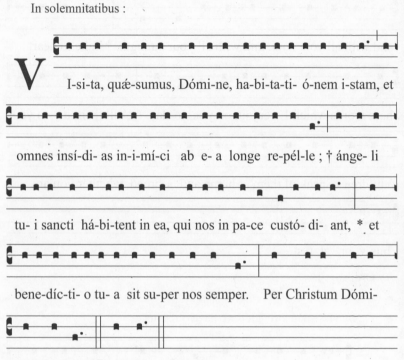

VI-si-ta, quǽ-sumus, Dómi-ne, ha-bi-ta-ti- ó-nem i-stam, et omnes insí-di- as in-i-mí-ci ab e- a longe re-pél-le ; † ánge- li tu- i sancti há-bi-tent in ea, qui nos in pa-ce custó- di- ant, * et bene-díc-ti- o tu- a sit su-per nos semper.   Per Christum Dómi-num nostrum. ℟. A-men.

Conclusio Horæ et antiphona ad B. M. V., ut in Ordinario, 16.

On solemnities :

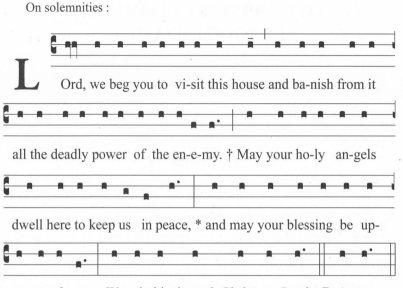

Lord, we beg you to vi-sit this house and ba-nish from it

all the deadly power of the en-e-my. † May your ho-ly   an-gels

dwell here to keep us   in peace, * and may your blessing be up-

on us always.   We ask this through Christ our Lord.   ℟. A-men.

Conclusion of the Hour and antiphon to the B. V. M., as in the Ordinary, 17.

POST II VESPERAS DOMINICÆ
ET SOLEMNITATUM

Omnia ut in Ordinario, 2, praeter sequentia :

PSALMODIA

Per annum :

Ant.
8 G.

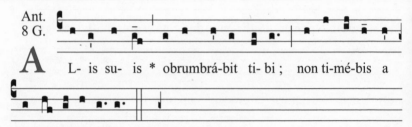

A L- is su- is * obrumbrá-bit ti- bi ; non ti-mé-bis a

ti-mó- re noctúrno.

Tempore paschali :

Ant.
8 G.

A L- le- lú- ia, * al- le- lú- ia,   al- le- lú- ia.

Psalmus 90 (91)

In protectione Altissimi

Ecce dedi vobis potestatem calcandi supra serpentes et scorpiones
(Lc 10 : 19)

1. Qui há-bi-tat in pro-tecti- ó-ne Al-**tís**-si-mi, * sub umbra Om-

ni-po-téntis *commo-***rá**- bi- tur. *Flexa :* Di-cet **Dó**-mi-no : †

2. Dicet **Dómino** : †
    « Refúgium meum et fortitúdo **me**a, *
    Deus meus, sper**á***bo in* **e**um ».

AFTER II VESPERS
ON SUNDAYS AND SOLEMNITIES

All as in the Ordinary, 3, except the following :

PSALMODY

During the Year :

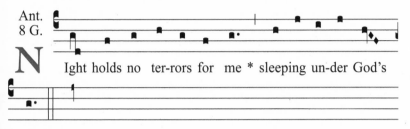

Ant.
8 G.

Night holds no ter-rors for me * sleeping un-der God's

wings.

Paschaltide :

Ant.
8 G.

AL- le- lú- ia, * al- le- lú- ia, al- le- lú- ia.

Psalm 90 (91)

Safe in God's sheltering care

I have given you the power to tread upon serpents and scorpions (Luke 10 : 19).

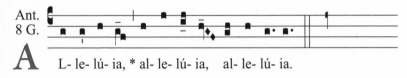

1. He who dwells in the shelter of *the Most* **High** * and a- bides

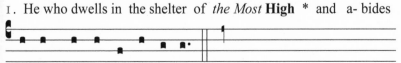

in the shade of *the Al***might**y

2. says to the *Lord :* " *My* **re**fuge, *
my stronghold, my God in *whom I* **trust** ! "

3. Quóniam ipse liberábit te de láqueo ve**nán**tium *
et a ver*bo ma*lígno.

4. Alis suis obumbrábit **ti**bi, *
et sub pennas e*ius con***fú**gies ;

5. scutum et loríca véritas **e**ius. *
non timébis a timó*re no***ctúr**no,

6. a sagítta volánte in **die**, †
a peste perambulánte in **té**nebris, *
ab extermínio vastánte *in me***rí**die.

7. Cadent a látere tuo **mil**le, †
et decem milia a dextris **tu**is ; *
ad te autem non ap*propin***quá**bit.

8. Verúmtamen óculis tuis conside**rá**bis, *
et retributiónem peccató*rum vi***dé**bis.

9. Quóniam tu es, Dómine, refúgium **me**um. *
Altíssimum posuísti habitá*culum* **tu**um.

10. Non accédet ad te **ma**lum, *
et flagéllum non appropinquábit taberná*culo* **tu**o.

11. Quóniam ángelis suis mandávit **de** te, *
ut custódiant te in ómnibus *viis* **tu**is.

12. In mánibus por**tá**bunt te, *
ne forte offéndas ad lápidem *pedem* **tu**um.

13. Super áspidem et basilíscum ambu**lá**bis, *
et conculcábis leónem *et dra***có**nem.

14. Quóniam mihi adhæsit, liberábo **e**um ; *
suscípiam eum, quóniam cognóvit *nomen* **me**um.

15. Clamábit ad me, et ego exáudiam **e**um ; †
cum ipso sum in tribulatió**ne**, *
erípiam eum et glorific*ábo* **e**um.

16. Longitúdine diérum replébo **e**um, *
et osténdam illi salu*táre* **me**um.

17. Glória Patri, et **Fí**lio, *
et Spirí*tui* **San**cto.

18. Sicut erat in princípio, et nunc et **sem**per, *
et in sæcula sæcu*lórum*. Amen.

3. It is he who will free you *from the* **snare** *
   of the fowler who seeks *to de***stroy** you ;

4. he will conceal you *with his* **pin**ions *
   and under his wings you *will find* **re**fuge.

5. You will not fear the terror *of the* **night** *
   nor the arrow that *flies by* **day**,

6. nor the plague that prowls *in the* **dark**ness *
   nor the scourge that lays *waste at* **noon**.

7. A thousand may fall *at your* **side**, *
   ten thousand fall *at your* **right**,

8. you, it will nev*er ap***proach** ; *
   his faithfulness is buck*ler and* **shield**.

9. Your eyes have on*ly to* **look** *
   to see how the wicked *are re***paid**,

10. you who have said : " *Lord, my* **refuge** ! " *
    and have made the Most *High your* **dwell**ing.

11. Upon you no e*vil shall* **fall**, *
    no plague approach *where you* **dwell**.

12. For you has he command*ed his* **an**gels, *
    to keep you in *all your* **ways**.

13. They shall bear you up*on their* **hands** *
    lest you strike your foot a*gainst a* **stone**.

14. On the lion and the viper *you will* **tread** *
    and trample the young lion *and the* **drag**on.

15. Since he clings to me in love, *I will* **free** him ; *
    protect him, for he *knows my* **name**.

16. When he calls, I shall answer : " *I am* **with** you. " *
    I will save him in distress and *give him* **glo**ry.

17. With length of life I *will con***tent** him ; *
    I shall let him see my *saving* **pow**er.

18. Glory to the Father, and *to the* **Son**, *
    and to the *Holy* **Spir**it :

19. as it was in the beginn*ing, is* **now**, *
    and will be for ev*er. A***men**.

Per annum :

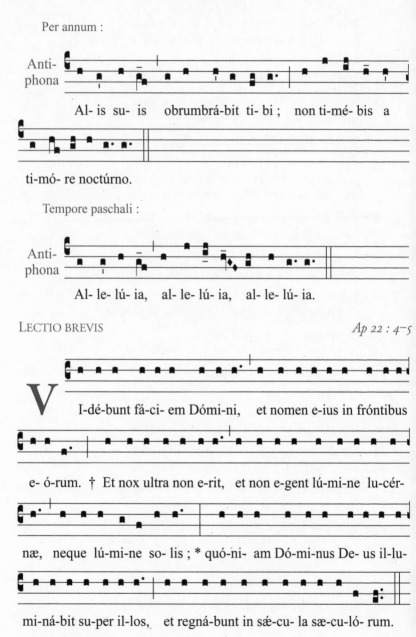

Anti-
phona

Al- is su- is   obrumbrá-bit ti- bi ;   non ti-mé- bis a

ti-mó- re noctúrno.

Tempore paschali :

Anti-
phona

Al- le- lú- ia,   al- le- lú- ia,   al- le- lú- ia.

LECTIO BREVIS   *Ap 22 : 4-5*

V I-dé-bunt fá-ci- em Dómi-ni,   et nomen e-ius in fróntibus

e- ó-rum. † Et nox ultra non e-rit,   et non e-gent lú-mi-ne lu-cér-

næ,   neque lú-mi-ne so- lis ; * quó-ni- am Dó-mi-nus De- us il-lu-

mi-ná-bit su-per il-los,   et regná-bunt in sǽ-cu- la sæ-cu-ló- rum.

Ordinarium, 8.

Through the Year :

Anti-
phon

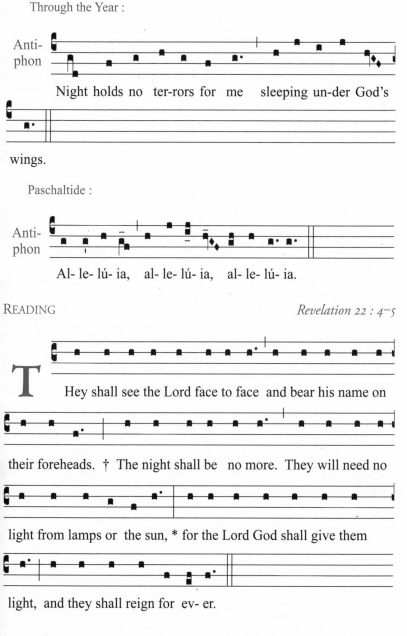

Night holds no ter-rors for me   sleeping un-der God's

wings.

Paschaltide :

Anti-
phon

Al- le- lú- ia,   al- le- lú- ia,   al- le- lú- ia.

READING   *Revelation 22 : 4–5*

T Hey shall see the Lord face to face and bear his name on

their foreheads. † The night shall be no more. They will need no

light from lamps or the sun, * for the Lord God shall give them

light, and they shall reign for ev- er.

Ordinary, 9.

Oratio

Dominicis et per octavam Paschæ :

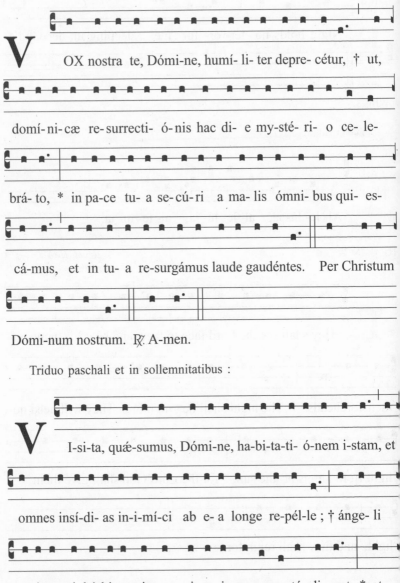

VOX nostra te, Dómine, humí- li- ter depre- cétur, † ut, domí-ni-cæ re-surrecti- ó-nis hac di- e my-sté- ri- o ce- le-brá- to, * in pa-ce tu- a se-cú-ri a ma- lis ómni- bus qui- es-cá-mus, et in tu- a re-surgámus laude gaudéntes. Per Christum Dómi-num nostrum. ℞. A-men.

Triduo paschali et in sollemnitatibus :

VI-si-ta, quǽ-sumus, Dómi-ne, ha-bi-ta-ti- ó-nem i-stam, et omnes insí-di- as in-i-mí-ci ab e- a longe re-pél-le ; † ánge- li tu- i sancti há-bi-tent in ea, qui nos in pa-ce custó- di- ant, * et

Prayer

On Sundays and through the octave of Easter :

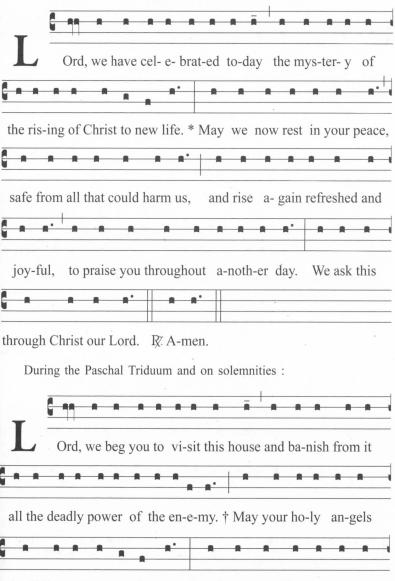

Lord, we have cel- e- brat-ed to-day the mys-ter- y of

the ris-ing of Christ to new life. * May we now rest in your peace,

safe from all that could harm us,   and rise a- gain refreshed and

joy-ful,   to praise you throughout a-noth-er day.   We ask this

through Christ our Lord.   ℟. A-men.

During the Paschal Triduum and on solemnities :

Lord, we beg you to vi-sit this house and ba-nish from it

all the deadly power of the en-e-my. † May your ho-ly   an-gels

dwell here to keep us   in peace, * and may your blessing be up-

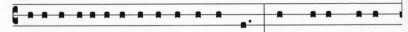

bene-díc-ti- o tu- a sit su-per nos semper.   Per Christum Dómi-

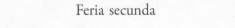

num nostrum. ℟. A-men.

Conclusio Horæ et antiphona ad B. M. V., ut in Ordinario, 16.

FERIA SECUNDA

Omnia ut in Ordinario, 2, praeter sequentia :

Psalmodia

Per annum :

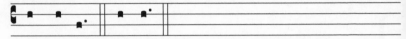

Ant.
8 G.

TU, Dómine De- us,*pá-ti- ens et multæ mi-se- ri-córdi-æ.

Tempore paschali :

Ant.
8 G.

AL- le- lú- ia, * al- le- lú- ia,   al- le- lú- ia.

Psalmus 85 (86)

Pauperis in rebus adversis oratio

Benedictus Deus, qui consolatur nos in omni tribulatione nostra (2 Cor 1 : 3, 4)

1. Inclí-na, Dómi-ne, au-rem tu- am et ex-**áu**-di me, * quó-ni- am

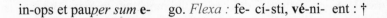

in-ops et pau*per sum* e-   go. *Flexa :* fe- cí-sti, **vé**-ni- ent : †

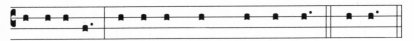

on us always.   We ask this through Christ our Lord.   ℟ A-men.

Conclusion of the Hour and antiphon to the B. V. M., as in the Ordinary, 17.

MONDAY

All as in the Ordinary, 3, except the following :

PSALMODY

Through the Year :

Ant.
8 G.

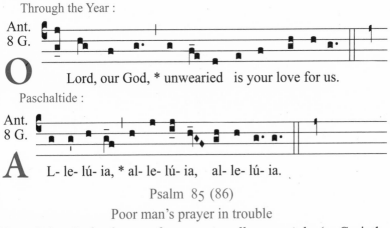

O Lord, our God, * unwearied   is your love for us.

Paschaltide :

Ant.
8 G.

A L- le- lú- ia, * al- le- lú- ia,   al- le- lú- ia.

Psalm 85 (86)

Poor man's prayer in trouble

Blessed be God who comforts us in all our trials (2 Corinthians 1 : 3, 4).

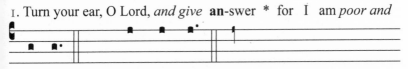

1. Turn your ear, O Lord, *and give* **an**-swer * for Ī am *poor and*

need- y. *Pause :* Lord, your way †

2. Custódi ánimam meam, quóniam **sanc**tus sum ; *
   salvum fac servum tuum, Deus meus, sper*ántem* **in** te.

3. Miserére mei, **Dó**mine, *
   quóniam ad te clamávi *tota* **di**e.

4. Lætífica ánimam servi **tu**i, *
   quóniam ad te, Dómine, áni*mam le*vá**v**i.

5. Quóniam tu, Dómine, suávis et **mi**tis *
   et multæ misericórdiæ ómnibus invo*cánti***bus** te.

6. Auribus pércipe, Dómine, oratiónem **me**am *
   et inténde voci deprecati*ónis* **me**æ.

7. In die tribulatiónis meæ clamávi **ad** te, *
   quia ex*áudi*es me.

8. Non est símilis tui in diis, **Dó**mine, *
   et nihil sicut ó*pera* **tu**a.

9. Omnes gentes, quascúmque fecísti, **vé**nient †
   et adorábunt coram te, **Dó**mine, *
   et glorificábunt *nomen* **tu**um,

10. quóniam magnus es tu et fáciens mira**bí**lia : *
    tu es *Deus* **so**lus.

11. Doce me, Dómine, viam **tu**am, *
    et ingrédiar in veri*táte* **tu**a ;

12. simplex fac cor **me**um, *
    ut tímeat *nomen* **tu**um.

13. Confitébor tibi, Dómine Deus meus, in toto corde **me**o *
    et glorificábo nomen tuum *in* æ**tér**num,

14. quia misericórdia tua magna est **su**per me, *
    et eruísti ánimam meam ex inférno in*feri***ó**ri.

15. Deus, supérbi insurrexérunt **su**per me, †
    et synagóga poténtium quæsiérunt ánimam **me**am, *
    et non proposuérunt te in con*spéctu* **su**o.

16. Et tu, Dómine, Deus miserátor et mi**sé**ricors, *
    pátiens et multæ misericórdiæ et *veri***tá**tis,

2. Preserve my life, for *I am* **faith**ful : *
   save the servant who *trusts in* **you**.

3. You are my God ; have mercy *on me*, **Lord**, *
   for I cry to you all *the day* **long**.

4. Give joy to your ser*vant, O* **Lord**, *
   for to you I lift *up my* **soul**.

5. O Lord, you are good *and for*gi**v**ing, *
   full of love to *all who* **call**.

6. Give heed, O Lord, *to my* **prayer** *
   and attend to the sound *of my* **voice**.

7. In the day of distress *I will* **call** *
   and surely you *will re*p**ly**.

8. Among the gods there is none like *you, O* **Lord** ; *
   nor work to com*pare with* **yours**.

9. All the nations shall come *to a*dore you *
   and glorify your *name, O* **Lord** :

10. for you are great and do mar*vellous* **deeds**, *
    you who a*lone are* **God**.

11. Show me, Lord, your way †
    so that I may walk *in your* **truth**. *
    Guide my heart to *fear your* **name**.

12. I will praise you, Lord my God, with *all my* **heart** *
    and glorify your *name for* **ever** ;

13. for your love to me *has been* **great** : *
    you have saved me from the depths *of the* **grave**.

14. The proud have risen against me ; †
    ruthless men *seek my* **life** : *
    to you they *pay no* **heed**.

15. But you, God of mercy *and com*pas**s**ion, *
    slow to an*ger, O* **Lord**,

16. abounding in *love and* **truth**, *
    turn and take pi*ty on* **me**.

17. réspice in me et miserére **me**i ; †
da fortitúdinem tuam púero **tu**o *
et salvum fac fílium an*cíllæ* **tuæ**.

18. Fac mecum signum in **bo**num, †
ut vídeant, qui odérunt me, et confun**dán**tur, *
quóniam tu, Dómine, adiuvísti me et conso*látus* **es** me.

19. Glória Patri, et **Fí**lio, *
et Spir*ítui* **San**cto.

20. Sicut erat in princípio, et nunc et **sem**per, *
et in sæcula sæcu*lórum*. **Amen**.

Per annum :

Tu, Dómine De- us, pá- ti- ens et multæ mise- ri-córdi-æ.

Tempore paschali :

Al- le- lú- ia, al- le- lú- ia, al- le- lú- ia.

LECTIO BREVIS   *1 Th 5 : 9–10*

Posu- it nos De- us in acqui-si-ti- ónem sa-lú-tis per Dómi-

num nostrum Ie-sum Christum, † qui mórtu- us est pro no-bis, * ut

sive vi-gi-lémus si-ve dormi- á-mus, si-mul cum il- lo vi-vá-mus.

Ordinarium, 8.

17. O give your strength *to your* **ser**vant *
    and save your *handmaid's* **son**.

18. Show me a sign of your favor †
    that my foes may see *to their* **shame** *
    that you console me and give *me your* **help**.

19. Glory to the Father, and *to the* **Son**, *
    and to the *Holy* **Spir**it :

20. as it was in the beginn*ing, is* **now**, *
    and will be for ev*er. A*men.

Through the Year :

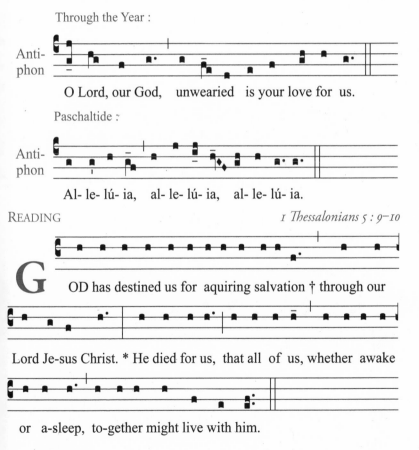

Anti-
phon

O Lord, our God,   unwearied   is your love for us.

Paschaltide :

Anti-
phon

Al- le- lú- ia,   al- le- lú- ia,   al- le- lú- ia.

READING   *1 Thessalonians 5 : 9–10*

GOD has destined us for aquiring salvation † through our

Lord Je-sus Christ. * He died for us, that all of us, whether awake

or a-sleep, to-gether might live with him.

Ordinary, **9**.

Oratio

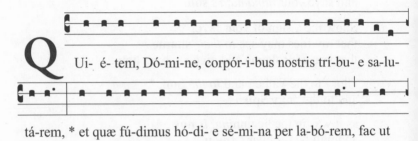

Q Ui- é- tem, Dó-mi-ne, corpór-i-bus nostris trí-bu- e sa-lu-

tá-rem, * et quæ fú-dimus hó-di- e sé-mi-na per la-bó-rem, fac ut

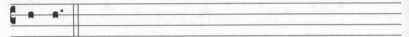

messem gérmi-nent sempi- térnam. Per Christum Dóminum nostrum.

℟. A-men.

Conclusio Horæ et antiphona ad B. M. V., ut in Ordinario, 16.

FERIA TERTIA

Omnia ut in Ordinario, 2, praeter sequentia :

Psalmodia

Per annum :

Ant.
8 G.

N ON abscóndas * fáci- em tu-am a me, qui- a in te sperá-vi.

Tempore paschali :

Ant.
8 G.

A L- le- lú- ia, * al- le- lú- ia, al- le- lú- ia.

Prayer

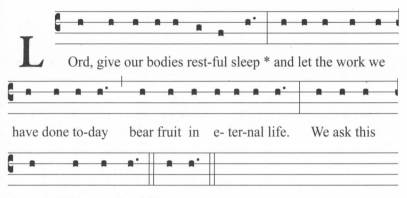

LOrd, give our bodies rest-ful sleep * and let the work we have done to-day bear fruit in e-ter-nal life. We ask this through Christ our Lord. ℟. A-men.

Conclusion of the Hour and antiphon to the B. V. M., as in the Ordinary, 17.

TUESDAY

All as in the Ordinary, 3, except the following :

PSALMODY

Through the Year :

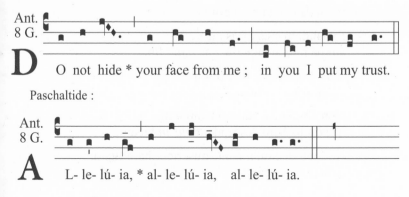

Ant. 8 G.

DO not hide * your face from me ; in you I put my trust.

Paschaltide :

Ant. 8 G.

AL-le-lú-ia, * al-le-lú-ia, al-le-lú-ia.

Psalmus 142 (143) : 1–11

In angustiis oratio

Non iustificatur homo ex operibus legis nisi per fidem Iesu Christi (Gal 2 : 16)

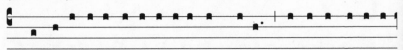

1. Dó-mi-ne, exáu-di o-ra- ti- ó-nem me- am, † áu-ri-bus pérci-pe

obsecra-ti- ó-nem me- am in ve-ri-tá-te **tu**- a ; * ex-áu-di me in

tu- *a iu***stí**- ti- a. *Flexa :* á- ni-mam **me**- am, †

2. Et non intres in iudícium cum servo **tu**o, *
   quia non iustificábitur in conspéctu tuo *omnis* **vi**vens.

3. Quia persecútus est inimícus ánimam **me**am, †
   contrívit in terra vitam **me**am, *
   collocávit me in obscúris sicut mórtu*os a* **sǽ**culo.

4. Et anxiátus est in me spíritus **me**us, *
   in médio mei obrígu*it cor* **me**um.

5. Memor fui diérum anti**quó**rum, †
   meditátus sum in ómnibus opéribus **tu**is, *
   in factis mánuum tuárum re*cogi***tá**bam.

6. Expándi manus meas **ad** te, *
   ánima mea sicut terra sine *aqua* **ti**bi.

7. Velóciter exáudi me, **Dó**mine ; *
   defécit sp*íritus* **me**us.

8. Non abscóndas fáciem tuam **a** me, *
   ne símilis fiam descendénti*bus in* **la**cum.

9. Audítam fac mihi mane misericórdiam **tu**am, *
   quia in *te* sp*e***rá**vi.

Psalm 142 (143) : 1–11

Prayer in distress

Only by faith in Jesus Christ is a man made holy in God's sight. No observance of the law can achieve this (Galations 2 : 16).

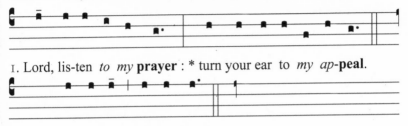

1. Lord, lis-ten *to my* **prayer** : * turn your ear to *my ap*-**peal**.

Pause : you are just ; give an-swer. †

2. You are faithful, you are just ; give answer. †
   Do not call your ser*vant to* **judg**ment *
   for no one is just *in your* **sight**.

3. The enemy pur*sues my* **soul** ; *
   he has crushed my life *to the* **ground** ;

4. he has made me *dwell in* **dark**ness *
   like the dead, *long for*gotten.

5. Therefore my *spirit* **fails** ; *
   my heart is *numb with*in me.

6. I remember the days *that are* **past** : *
   I ponder *all your* **works**.

7. I muse on what your hand has wrought †
   and to you I stretch *out my* **hands**. *
   Like a parched land my soul *thirsts for* **you**.

8. Lord, make *haste and* **an**swer ; *
   for my spirit *fails with*in me.

9. Do not *hide your* **face** *
   lest I become like those *in the* **grave**.

10. In the morning let me *know your* **love** *
    for I put my *trust in* **you**.

10. Notam fac mihi viam, in qua **ám**bulem, *
quia ad te levávi á*nimam* **me**am.

11. Eripe me de inímicis **me**is, *
Dómine, ad *te con*fu*gi.

12. Doce me fácere voluntátem **tu**am, *
quia Deus *meus* **es** tu.

13. Spíritus tuus bonus dedúcet me in terram **rec**tam ; *
propter nomen tuum, Dómine, vi*vifi***cá**bis me.

14. In iustítia **tua** *
edúces me de tribulatióne á*nimam* **me**am.

15. Glória Patri, et **Fí**lio, *
et Spirí*tui* **San**cto.

16. Sicut erat in princípio, et nunc et **sem**per, *
et in sæcula sæcu*lórum*. **A**men.

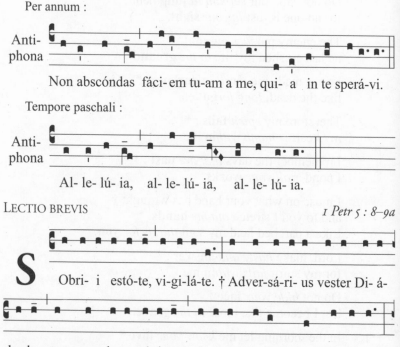

Per annum :

Anti-
phona

Non abscóndas fáci- em tu-am a me, qui- a in te sperá-vi.

Tempore paschali :

Anti-
phona

Al- le- lú- ia, al- le- lú- ia, al- le- lú- ia.

LECTIO BREVIS   *1 Petr 5 : 8–9a*

S

Obri- i estó-te, vi-gi-lá-te. † Adver-sá-ri- us vester Di- á-

bo-lus tamquam le- o rúgi- ens círcu- it quærens quem dé-vo-ret. *

11. Make me know the way *I should* **walk** : *
    to you I lift *up my* **soul**.

12. Rescue me, Lord, *from my* **en**emies ; *
    I have fled to *you for* **re**fuge.

13. Teach me to *do your* **will** *
    for you, O Lord, *are my* **God**.

14. Let your good *spirit* **guide** me *
    in ways that are lev*el and* **smooth**.

15. For your name's sake, Lord, *save my* **life** ; *
    in your justice save my soul *from dis***tress**.

16. Glory to the Father, and *to the* **Son**, *
    and to the *Holy* **Spir**it :

17. as it was in the beginn*ing, is* **now**, *
    and will be for ev*er. A***men**.

Through the Year :

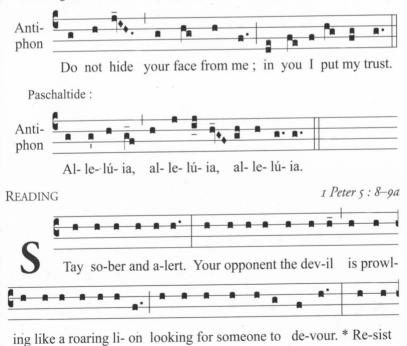

Do not hide your face from me ; in you I put my trust.

Paschaltide :

Anti-
phon

Al- le- lú- ia, al- le- lú- ia, al- le- lú- ia.

READING   *1 Peter 5 : 8–9a*

S Tay so-ber and a-lert. Your opponent the dev-il is prowl-

ing like a roaring li- on looking for someone to de-vour. * Re-sist

Cu- i re-sí-sti- te fortes in fi- de.

Ordinarium, 8.

Oratio

Noctem i-stam, quǽ-sumus, Dó-mi-ne, be-ní-gnus il- lú-mi-na, † et i- ta fac in pa-ce nos tu- os fámu-los obdormí-re, * ut læ-ti ad no-vi di- é- i cla-ri-tá-tem in tu- o nómi-ne susci-témur.

Per Christum Dómi-num nostrum. ℞. A-men.

Conclusio Horæ et antiphona ad B. M. V., ut in Ordinario, 16.

FERIA QUARTA

Omnia ut in Ordinario, 2, praeter sequentia :

P**SALMODIA**

Per annum :

1 Ant.
1 g.

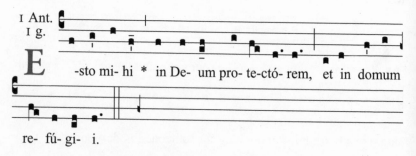

E-sto mi- hi * in De- um pro- te-ctó- rem, et in domum re- fú- gi- i.

him, sol- id in your faith.

Ordinary, 9.

Prayer

Lord, fill this night with your ra-di-ance. † May we sleep

in peace and rise with joy * to welcome the light of a new day in

your name. We ask this through Christ our Lord. ℟ A-men.

Conclusion of the Hour and antiphon to the B. V. M., as in the Ordinary, 17.

WEDNESDAY

All as in the Ordinary, 3, except the following :

PSALMODY

Through the Year :

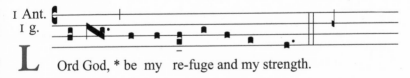

I Ant.
I g.

Lord God, * be my re-fuge and my strength.

Psalmus 30 (31) : 2–6

Afflicti supplicatio cum fiducia

Pater, in manus tuas commendo spiritum meum (Lc 23 : 46).

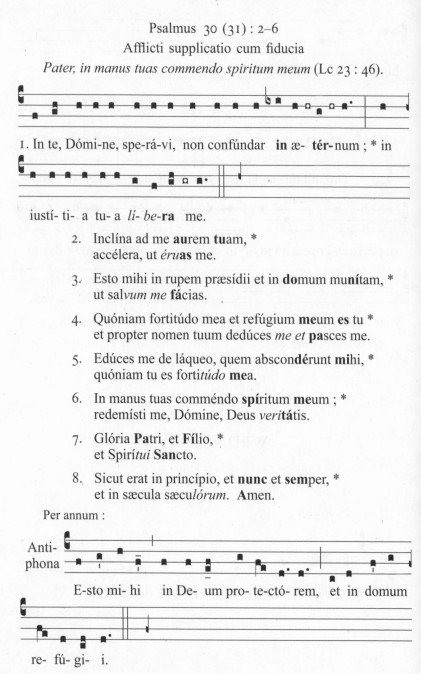

1. In te, Dómi-ne, spe-rá-vi, non confúndar in æ- tér-num ; * in

iustí- ti- a tu- a *lí- be-ra* me.

2. Inclína ad me **au**rem **tu**am, *
accélera, ut *éru***as** me.

3. Esto mihi in rupem præsídii et in **do**mum mu**ní**tam, *
ut sal*vum me* **fá**cias.

4. Quóniam fortitúdo mea et refúgium **meum es** tu *
et propter nomen tuum dedúces *me et* **pa**sces me.

5. Edúces me de láqueo, quem abscon**dé**runt **mi**hi, *
quóniam tu es forti*túdo* **me**a.

6. In manus tuas comméndo **spí**ritum **me**um ; *
redemísti me, Dómine, Deus *veri***tá**tis.

7. Glória **Pa**tri, et **Fí**lio, *
et Spirí*tui* **San**cto.

8. Sicut erat in princípio, et **nunc** et **sem**per, *
et in sæcula sæcu*lórum*. **A**men.

Per annum :

Anti-
phona

E-sto mi- hi   in De- um pro- te-ctó- rem,   et in domum

re- fú- gi- i.

Psalm 30 (31) : 2–6

Trustful prayer in adversity

Father, into your hands I commend my spirit (Luke 23 : 46).

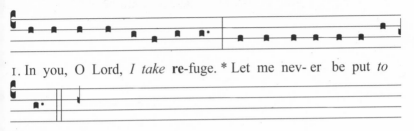

1. In you, O Lord, *I take* **re**-fuge. * Let me nev- er be put *to*

shame.

2. In your justice, *set me* **free**, *
   hear me and speedi*ly* **res**cue me.

3. Be a rock of re*fuge for* **me**, *
   a mighty stronghold *to* **save** me,

4. for you are my *rock, my* **strong**hold. *
   For your name's sake, lead me *and* **guide** me.

5. Release me from the snares *they have* **hid**den *
   for you are my re*fuge*, **Lord**.

6. Into your hands I com*mend my* **spir**it. *
   It is you who will redeem *me*, **Lord**.

7. Glory to the Father, and *to the* **Son**, *
   and to the Ho*ly* **Spir**it :

8. as it was in the beginn*ing, is* **now**, *
   and will be for ever. *A*men.

Through the Year :

Anti-
phon

Lord God, be my re-fuge and my strength.

2 Ant.
8 c.

DE pro-fúndis * cla-má- vi　ad te, Dómi-ne. †

Psalmus 129 (130)

De profundis clamavi

Ipse salvum faciet populum suum a peccatis eorum (Mt 1 : 21).

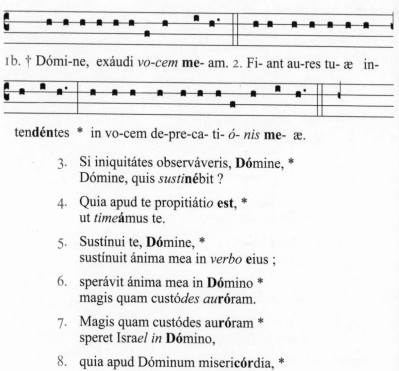

1b. † Dómi-ne,　exáudi *vo-cem* **me**- am. 2. Fi- ant au-res tu- æ　in-

tendéntes　*　in vo-cem de-pre-ca- ti- ó- *nis* **me**- æ.

3. Si iniquitátes observáveris, **Dó**mine, *
   Dómine, quis *sustin*ébit ?

4. Quia apud te propitiáti*o* **est**, *
   ut *time*ámus te.

5. Sustínui te, **Dó**mine, *
   sustínuit ánima mea in *verbo* **e**ius ;

6. sperávit ánima mea in **Dó**mino *
   magis quam custó*des au***ró**ram.

7. Magis quam custódes au**ró**ram *
   speret Isra*el in* **Dó**mino,

8. quia apud Dóminum miseri**cór**dia, *
   et copiósa apud e*um re***démp**tio.

9. Et ipse rédimet **Is**rael *
   ex ómnibus iniquitá*tibus* **e**ius.

10. Glória Patri, et **Fí**lio, *
    et Spirí*tui* **San**cto.

11. Sicut erat in princípio, et nunc et **sem**per, *
    et in sæcula sæcu*lórum*. **A**men.

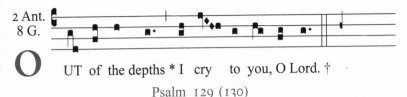

O UT of the depths * I cry to you, O Lord. †

Psalm 129 (130)

A cry from the depths

He will save his people from their sins (Matthew 1 : 21).

1b. †Lord, hear my voice! 2. O let your ears be at-**ten**-tive * to the

voice *of my* **plead**ing.

3. If you, O Lord, should *mark our* **guilt**, *
   Lord, who *would sur***vive** ?

4. But with you is *found for***give**ness : *
   for this *we re***vere** you.

5. My soul is waiting *for the* **Lord**, *
   I count *on his* **word**.

6. My soul is longing *for the* **Lord** *
   more than watch*man for* **day**break.

7. Let the watchman *count on* **day**break *
   and Israel *on the* **Lord**.

8. Because with the Lord *there is* **mer**cy *
   and fullness *of re***demp**tion,

9. Israel indeed he *will re***deem** *
   from all *its i*niquity.

10. Glory to the Father, and *to the* **Son**, *
    and to the *Holy* **Spir**it :

11. as it was in the beginn*ing, is* **now**, *
    and will be for ev*er.* **A**men.

Per annum :

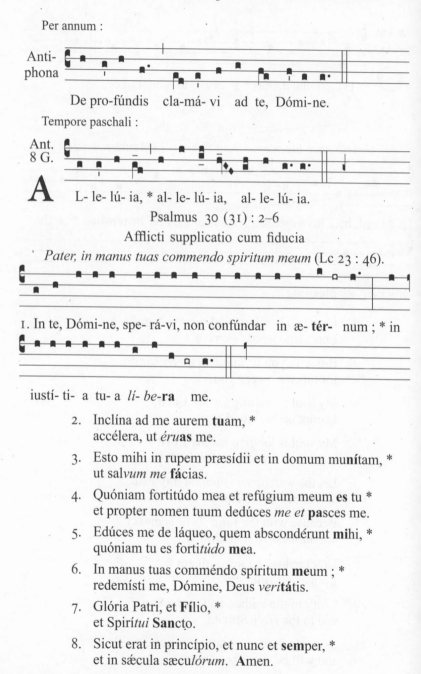

De pro-fúndis cla-má- vi ad te, Dómi-ne.

Tempore paschali :

Ant.
8 G.

A L- le- lú- ia, * al- le- lú- ia, al- le- lú- ia.

Psalmus 30 (31) : 2–6

Afflicti supplicatio cum fiducia

Pater, in manus tuas commendo spiritum meum (Lc 23 : 46).

1. In te, Dómi-ne, spe- rá-vi, non confúndar in æ- **tér**- num ; * in

iustí- ti- a tu- a *lí- be-***ra** me.

2. Inclína ad me aurem **tu**am, *
    accélera, ut *éru***as** me.

3. Esto mihi in rupem præsídii et in domum mu**ní**tam, *
    ut sal*vum me* **fá**cias.

4. Quóniam fortitúdo mea et refúgium meum **es tu** *
    et propter nomen tuum dedúces *me et* **pa**sces me.

5. Edúces me de láqueo, quem abscondérunt **mi**hi, *
    quóniam tu es forti*túdo* **me**a.

6. In manus tuas comméndo spíritum **meum** ; *
    redemísti me, Dómine, Deus *veri***tá**tis.

7. Glória Patri, et **Fí**lio, *
    et Spirí*tui* **Sanc**to.

8. Sicut erat in princípio, et nunc et **sem**per, *
    et in sǽcula sæcu*lórum*. **A**men.

Through the Year :

Anti-
phon

Out of the depths I cry   to you, O Lord.

Paschaltide :

Ant.
8 G.

AL- le- lú- ia, * al- le- lú- ia,   al- le- lú- ia.

Psalm 30 (31) : 2–6

Trustful prayer in adversity

Father, into your hands I commend my spirit (Luke 23 : 46).

1. In you, O Lord, *I take* **re**-fuge. * Let me nev- er be *put to*

shame.

2. In your justice, *set me* **free**, *
   hear me and spee*dily* **res**cue me.

3. Be a rock of re*fuge for* **me**, *
   a mighty strong*hold to* **save** me,

4. for you are my *rock, my* **strong**hold. *
   For your name's sake, lead *me and* **guide** me.

5. Release me from the snares *they have* **hid**den *
   for you are my *refuge*, **Lord**.

6. Into your hands I com*mend my* **spir**it. *
   It is you who will re*deem me*, **Lord**.

7. Glory to the Father, and *to the* **Son**, *
   and to the *Holy* **Spir**it :

8. as it was in the begin*ning, is* **now**, *
   and will be for eve*r. A*men.

Psalmus 129 (130)
De profundis clamavi

Ipse salvum faciet populum suum a peccatis eorum (Mt 1 : 21).

1. De profúndis clamávi ad te, **Dó**mine ; *
   Dómine, exáudi *vocem* **me**am.

2. Fiant aures tuæ intendéntes *
   in vocem deprecatiónis meæ.

3. Si iniquitátes observáveris, **Dó**mine, *
   Dómine, quis *susti***né**bit ?

4. Quia apud te propitiáti*o* **est**, *
   ut *time***á**mus te.

5. Sustínui te, **Dó**mine, *
   sustínuit ánima mea in *verbo* eius ;

6. sperávit ánima mea in **Dó**mino *
   magis quam custó*des au***ró**ram.

7. Magis quam custódes au**ró**ram *
   speret Isra*el in* **Dó**mino,

8. quia apud Dóminum miseri**cór**dia, *
   et copiósa apud e*um re***démp**tio.

9. Et ipse rédimet **Is**rael *
   ex ómnibus iniquitá*tibus* eius.

10. Glória Patri, et **Fí**lio, *
    et Spir*ítui* **San**cto.

11. Sicut erat in princípio, et nunc et **sem**per, *
    et in sæcula sæcu*lórum*. **Amen**.

Anti-
phona

Al- le- lú- ia,   al- le- lú- ia,   al- le- lú- ia.

LECTIO BREVIS   *Eph 4 : 26–27*

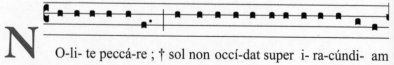

O-li- te peccá-re ; † sol non occí-dat super i- ra-cúndi- am

Psalm 129 (130)

A cry from the depths

He will save his people from their sins (Matthew 1 : 21).

1. Out of the depths I cry to *you, O* **Lord**, *
   Lord, *hear my* **voice** !

2. O let your ears *be at*tentive *
   to the voice *of my* **plead**ing.

3. If you, O Lord, should *mark our* **guilt**, *
   Lord, who *would sur***vive** ?

4. But with you is *found for***give**ness : *
   for this *we re***vere** you.

5. My soul is waiting *for the* **Lord**, *
   I count *on his* **word**.

6. My soul is longing *for the* **Lord** *
   more than watch*man for* **day**break.

7. Let the watchman *count on* **day**break *
   and Israel *on the* **Lord**.

8. Because with the Lord *there is* **mer**cy *
   and fullness *of re***demp**tion,

9. Israel indeed he *will re***deem** *
   from all *its i*niquity.

10. Glory to the Father, and *to the* **Son**, *
    and to the *Holy* **Spir**it :

11. as it was in the beginn*ing, is* **now**, *
    and will be for ev*er. A*men.

Anti-
phon

Al- le- lú- ia, al- le- lú- ia, al- le- lú- ia.

READING   *Ephesians 4 : 26–27*

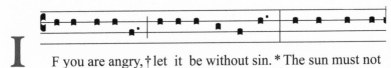

IF you are angry, † let it be without sin. * The sun must not

vestram, * et no- lí- te lo-cum da- re Di- á- bo- lo.

Ordinarium, 8.

Oratio

DOmi-ne Ie- su Chri-ste, qui iu-gum su- á- ve te sequén-

ti- bus o-núsque le-ve pér-hi-bes mi- tis et húmi- lis, † digná-re

hu-ius di- é- i vo-ta et ó-pe-ra nostra su-scí-pe-re, * et qui- é-tem

tri-bú- e- re, qua tu- o nos fá-ci- as serví- ti- o prompti- ó- res.

Qui vi-vis et regnas in sæcula sæcu-ló-rum. ℟ A-men.

Conclusio Horæ et antiphona ad B. M. V., ut in Ordinario, 16.

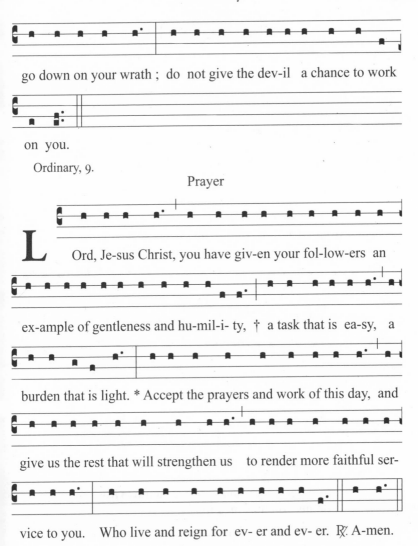

go down on your wrath ; do not give the dev-il a chance to work

on you.

Ordinary, 9.

Prayer

Lord, Je-sus Christ, you have giv-en your fol-low-ers an

ex-ample of gentleness and hu-mil-i- ty, † a task that is ea-sy, a

burden that is light. * Accept the prayers and work of this day, and

give us the rest that will strengthen us to render more faithful ser-

vice to you. Who live and reign for ev- er and ev- er. ℟. A-men.

Conclusion of the Hour and antiphon to the B. V. M., as in the Ordi-nary, 17.

FERIA QUINTA

Omnia ut in Ordinario, 2, praeter sequentia :

PSALMODIA

Per annum :

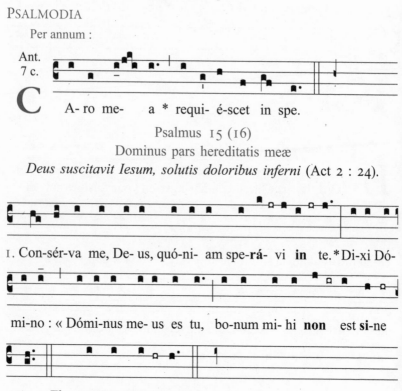

Ant.
7 c.

C A- ro me-   a * requi- é-scet in spe.

Psalmus 15 (16)
Dominus pars hereditatis meæ
Deus suscitavit Iesum, solutis doloribus inferni (Act 2 : 24).

1. Con-sér-va me, De- us, quó-ni- am spe-rá- vi in te.*Di-xi Dó-

mi-no : « Dómi-nus me- us es tu,   bo-num mi- hi **non**   est **si**-ne

te. » *Flex :* est cor **me-**   um, †

2. In sanctos, qui sunt in terra, ínclitos **viros**,
   omnis volúntas **me**a in **e**os.

3. Multiplicántur dolóres eórum, *
   qui post deos aliénos acceleravérunt.

4. Non effúndam libatiónes eórum **de** sanguínibus, *
   neque assúmam nómina eórum in **lá**biis **me**is.

5. Dóminus pars hereditátis meæ et **cá**licis **me**i : *
   tu es qui détines **sor**tem **me**am.

6. Funes cecidérunt mihi in præ**clá**ris ; *
   ínsuper et heréditas mea speci**ó**sa est **mi**hi.

THURSDAY

All as in the Ordinary, 3, except the following :

P<small>SALMODY</small>

Through the Year :

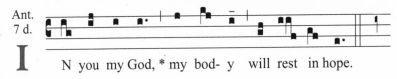

Ant.
7 d.

IN you my God, * my bod- y will rest in hope.

Psalm 15 (16)
God is my portion, my inheritance

The Father raised up Jesus from the dead and broke the bonds of death (Acts 2 : 24).

1. Preserve me, God,   I take re-fuge in you. † I say to the

Lord : " You *are my* **God**. * My hap-pi-ness lies in you *a-***lone**. "

Pause : the path of life, †

2.   He has put into my heart a mar*vellous* **love** *
   for the faithful ones who dwell in *his* **land**.

3.   Those who choose *other* **gods** *
   increase *their* **sor**rows.

4.   Never will I offer their offer*ings of* **blood**. *
   Never will I take their name upon *my* **lips**.

5.   O Lord, it is you who are my por*tion and* **cup** ; *
   it is you yourself who are *my* **prize**.

6.   The lot marked out for me is *my de***light** : *
   welcome indeed the heritage that falls *to* **me** !

7. Benedícam Dóminum qui tríbuit mihi **int**elléctum ; *
   ínsuper et in nóctibus erudiérunt me **renes mei**.

8. Proponébam Dóminum in conspéctu **meo sem**per ; *
   quóniam a dextris est mihi, non **com**movébor.

9. Propter hoc lætátum est cor **meum**, †
   et exsultavérunt præ**córd**ia **mea** ; *
   ínsuper et caro mea requiéscet **in** spe.

10. Quóniam non derelínques ánimam meam **in inférno**, *
    nec dabis sanctum tuum vidére cor**rupti**ónem.

11. Notas mihi fácies vias **vitæ**, †
    plenitúdinem lætítiæ cum **vultu tuo**, *
    delectatiónes in déxtera tua **us**que in **finem**.

12. Glória **Patri**, et **Fílio**, *
    et Spirítui **San**cto.

13. Sicut erat in princípio, et **nunc** et **sem**per, *
    et in sæcula sæcul**órum**. **Amen**.

Per annum :

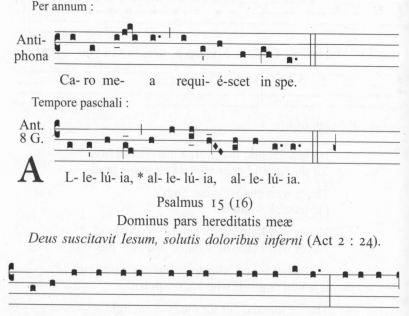

Ca- ro me-   a   requi- é-scet in spe.

Tempore paschali :

Ant.
8 G.

AL- le- lú- ia, * al- le- lú- ia,   al- le- lú- ia.

Psalmus 15 (16)

Dominus pars hereditatis meæ

Deus suscitavit Iesum, solutis doloribus inferni (Act 2 : 24).

1. Consér-va me, De- us, quó-ni- am spe-rá- vi **in** te. * Di-xi Dó-

7. I will bless the Lord who *gives me* **coun**sel, *
   who even at night directs *my* **heart**.

8. I keep the Lord ever *in my* **sight** : *
   since he is at my right hand, / I shall *stand* **firm**.

9. And so my heart rejoices, my *soul is* **glad** ; *
   even my body shall rest *in* **safe**ty.

10. For you will not leave my soul a*mong the* **dead**, *
    nor let your beloved know *de***cay**.

11. You will show me the path of life, †
    the fullness of joy *in your* **pres**ence, *
    at your right hand happiness *for* **ev**er.

12. Glory to the Father, and *to the* **Son**, *
    and to the Ho*ly* **Spir**it :

13. as it was in the begin*ning, is* **now**, *
    and will be for ever. *A***men**.

Through the Year :

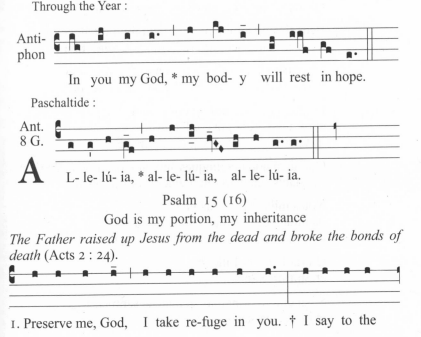

Anti-
phon

In you my God, * my bod- y will rest in hope.

Paschaltide :

Ant.
8 G.

A L- le- lú- ia, * al- le- lú- ia, al- le- lú- ia.

Psalm 15 (16)

God is my portion, my inheritance

The Father raised up Jesus from the dead and broke the bonds of death (Acts 2 : 24).

1. Preserve me, God, I take re-fuge in you. † I say to the

mi-no : « Dómi-nus me- us es tu, bo-num mi- hi *non est* si- ne

te. » *Flex :* est cor **me-** um, †

2. In sanctos, qui sunt in terra, ínclitos **vi**ros, *
   omnis volúntas me*a in* e**o**s.

3. Multiplicántur dolóres e**ó**rum, *
   qui post deos aliénos acce*lera*vé**r**unt.

4. Non effúndam libatiónes eórum de san**guí**nibus, *
   neque assúmam nómina eórum in lá*biis* **m**eis.

5. Dóminus pars hereditátis meæ et cálicis **me**i : *
   tu es qui détines *sortem* **me**am.

6. Funes cecidérunt mihi in præ**clá**ris ; *
   ínsuper et heréditas mea speció*sa est* **mi**hi.

7. Benedícam Dóminum qui tríbuit mihi intel**lé**ctum ; *
   ínsuper et in nóctibus erudiérunt me *renes* **me**i.

8. Proponébam Dóminum in conspéctu meo **sem**per ; *
   quóniam a dextris est mihi, non *commo*vé**b**or.

9. Propter hoc lætátum est cor **me**um, †
   et exsultavérunt præcórdia **me**a ; *
   ínsuper et caro mea requi*éscet* **in** spe.

10. Quóniam non derelínques ánimam meam in in**fér**no, *
    nec dabis sanctum tuum vidére cor*ruptió*nem.

11. Notas mihi fácies vias **vi**tæ, †
    plenitúdinem lætítiæ cum vultu **tu**o, *
    delectatiónes in déxtera tua us*que in* **fi**nem.

12. Glória Patri, et **Fí**lio, *
    et Spirí*tui* **San**cto.

13. Sicut erat in princípio, et nunc et **sem**per, *
    et in sæcula sæcu*lórum.* **A**men.

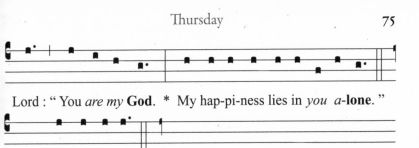

Lord : " You *are my* **God**. * My hap-pi-ness lies in *you* a-**lone**. "

Pause : the path of life, †

2.   He has put into my heart a mar*vellous* **love** *
   for the faithful ones who dwell *in his* **land**.

3.   Those who choose *other* **gods** *
   in*crease their* **sor**rows.

4.   Never will I offer their offer*ings of* **blood**. *
   Never will I take their name up*on my* **lips**.

5.   O Lord, it is you who are my por*tion and* **cup** ; *
   it is you yourself who *are my* **prize**.

6.   The lot marked out for me is *my de*light : *
   welcome indeed the heritage that *falls to* **me** !

7.   I will bless the Lord who *gives me* **coun**sel, *
   who even at night di*rects my* **heart**.

8.   I keep the Lord ever *in my* **sight** : *
   since he is at my right hand, / I *shall stand* **firm**.

9.   And so my heart rejoices, my *soul is* **glad** ; *
   even my body shall *rest in* **safe**ty.

10.   For you will not leave my soul a*mong the* **dead**, *
    nor let your beloved *know de*cay.

11.   You will show me the path of life, †
    the fullness of joy *in your* **pres**ence, *
    at your right hand happi*ness for* **ev**er.

12.   Glory to the Father, and *to the* **Son**, *
    and to the *Holy* **Spir**it :

13.   as it was in the beginn*ing, is* **now**, *
    and will be for ev*er.* *A***men**.

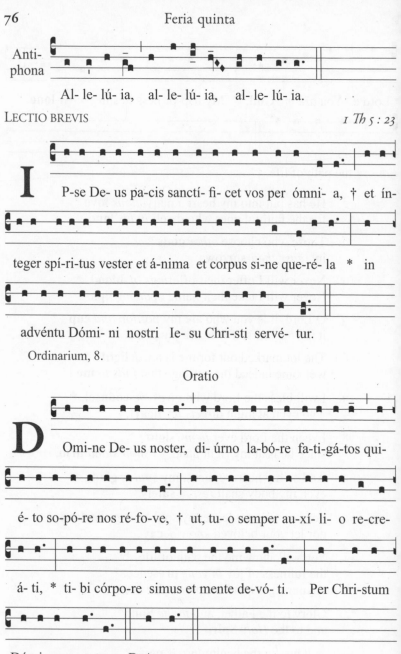

Anti-
phona

Al- le- lú- ia,   al- le- lú- ia,   al- le- lú- ia.

LECTIO BREVIS   *1 Th* 5 : 23

I

P-se De- us pa-cis sanctí- fi- cet vos per ómni- a, † et ín-

teger spí-ri-tus vester et á-nima et corpus si-ne que-ré- la   *   in

advéntu Dómi- ni nostri Ie- su Chri-sti servé- tur.

Ordinarium, 8.

Oratio

D

Omi-ne De- us noster, di- úrno la-bó-re fa-ti-gá-tos qui-

é- to so-pó-re nos ré-fo-ve, † ut, tu- o semper au-xí- li- o re-cre-

á- ti, * ti- bi córpo-re simus et mente de-vó- ti.   Per Chri-stum

Dómi-num nostrum. ℟. A-men.

Conclusio Horæ et antiphona ad B. M. V., ut in Ordinario, 16.

Anti-
phon

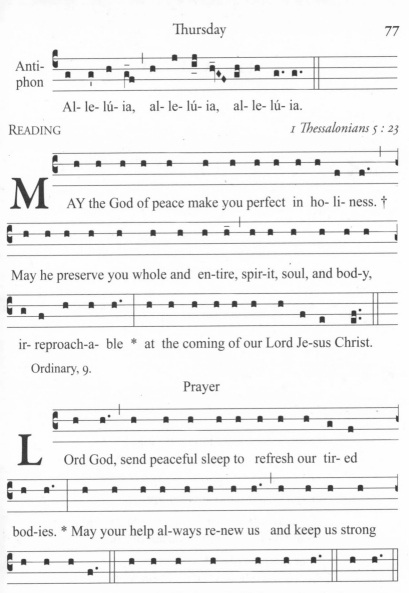

Al- le- lú- ia, al- le- lú- ia, al- le- lú- ia.

READING *1 Thessalonians 5 : 23*

M AY the God of peace make you perfect in ho- li- ness. †

May he preserve you whole and en-tire, spir-it, soul, and bod-y,

ir- reproach-a- ble * at the coming of our Lord Je-sus Christ.

Ordinary, 9.

Prayer

L Ord God, send peaceful sleep to refresh our tir- ed

bod-ies. * May your help al-ways re-new us and keep us strong

in your service. We ask this through Christ our Lord. A-men.

Conclusion of the Hour and antiphon to the B. V. M., as in the Ordinary, 17.

FERIA SEXTA

Omnia ut in Ordinario, 2, praeter sequentia :

PSALMODIA

Per annum :

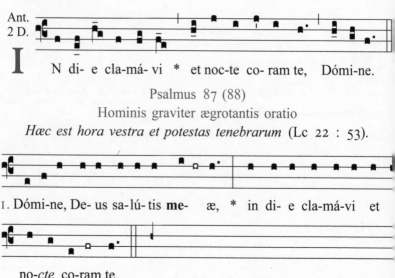

Ant.
2 D.

I N di- e cla-má- vi   *   et noc-te co- ram te,   Dómi-ne.

Psalmus 87 (88)

Hominis graviter ægrotantis oratio

Hæc est hora vestra et potestas tenebrarum (Lc 22 : 53).

1. Dómi-ne, De- us sa-lú- tis **me-** æ,   *   in di- e cla-má-vi   et

no-*cte* co-ram te.

2. Intret in conspéctu tuo orátio **me**a ; *
   inclína aurem tuam ad pre*cem* **me**am.

3. Quia repléta est malis ánima **me**a, *
   et vita mea inférno appro*pinquá*vit.

4. Æstimátus sum cum descendéntibus in la**cum**, *
   factus sum sicut homo sine ad*iu*tório.

5. Inter mórtuos **liber**, *
   sicut vulneráti dormiéntes in *se***púl**cris ;

6. quorum non es memor **ám**plius, *
   et ipsi de manu tua *ab***scí**ssi sunt.

7. Posuísti me in lacu inferióri, *
   in tenebrósis et in um*bra* **mort**is.

8. Super me gravátus est furor **tu**us, *
   et omnes fluctus tuos induxí*sti* **su**per me.

FRIDAY

All as in the Ordinary, 3, except the following :

PSALMODY

Through the Year :

Ant.
2 D.

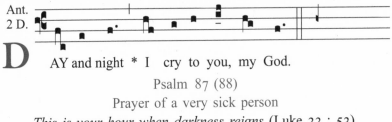

D AY and night * I cry to you, my God.

Psalm 87 (88)

Prayer of a very sick person

This is your hour when darkness reigns (Luke 22 : 53).

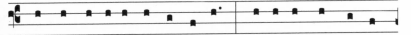

1. Lord my God, I call for *help by* **day** ; * I cry at night *be-***fore**

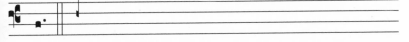

you.

2. Let my prayer come in*to your* **pres**ence. *
   O turn your ear to *my* **cry**.

3. For my soul is *filled with* **e**vils ; *
   my life is on the brink of *the* **grave**.

4. I am reckoned as one *in the* **tomb** : *
   I have reached the end of *my* **strength**,

5. like one alone a*mong the* **dead** ; *
   like the slain lying in *their* **graves** ;

6. like those you remem*ber no* **more**, *
   cut off, as they are, from *your* **hand**.

7. You have laid me in the depths *of the* **tomb**, *
   in places that are dark, in *the* **depths**.

8. Your anger weighs *down up***on** me : *
   I am drowned beneath *your* **waves**.

9. Longe fecísti notos meos **a** me, *
   posuísti me abominati*ónem* **e**is ;

10. conclúsus sum et non e**gré**diar. *
    Oculi mei languérunt præ affli*ctió*ne.

11. Clamávi ad te, Dómine, tota **die**, *
    expándi ad te ma*nus* **me**as.

12. Numquid mórtuis fácies mirabília, *
    aut surgent umbræ et confitebún*tur* tibi ?

13. Numquid narrábit áliquis in sepúlcro misericórdiam **tu**am *
    et veritátem tuam in loco perdi*tió*nis ?

14. Numquid cognoscéntur in ténebris mirabília **tu**a *
    et iustítia tua in terra obli*vió*nis ?

15. Et ego ad te, Dómine, cla**má**vi, *
    et mane orátio mea prævé*nie*t te.

16. Ut quid, Dómine, repéllis ánimam **me**am, *
    abscóndis fáciem tu*am* **a** me ?

17. Pauper sum ego et móriens a iuventúte **me**a ; *
    portávi pavóres tuos et con*tur***bá**tus sum.

18. Super me transiérunt iræ **tu**æ, *
    et terróres tui ex*ci***dé**runt me.

19. Circuiérunt me sicut aqua tota **die**, *
    circumdedérunt *me* **si**mul.

20. Elongásti a me amícum et **pró**ximum, *
    et noti mei *sunt* **té**nebræ.

21. Glória Patri, et **Fí**lio, *
    et Spirítu*i* **San**cto.

22. Sicut erat in princípio, et nunc et **sem**per, *
    et in sæcula sæcul*órum*. **A**men.

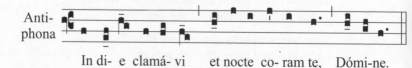

Anti-
phona
    In di- e clamá- vi   et nocte co- ram te,   Dómi-ne.

9. You have taken a*way my* **friends** *
   and made me hateful in *their* **sight**.

10. Imprisoned, I can*not es***cape** ; *
    my eyes are sunken *with* **grief**.

11. I call to you, Lord, all *the day* **long** : *
    to you I stretch out *my* **hands**.

12. Will you work your wonders *for the* **dead** ? *
    Will the shades stand *and* **praise** you ?

13. Will your love be told *in the* **grave** *
    or your faithfulness among *the* **dead** ?

14. Will your wonders be known *in the* **dark** *
    or your justice in the land of *o*bli*v*ion ?

15. As for me, Lord, I call to *you for* **help** : *
    in the morning my prayer comes *be***fore** you.

16. Lord, why do *you re***ject** me ? *
    Why do you hide *your* **face** ?

17. Wretched, close to death *from my* **youth**, *
    I have borne your trials ; I *am* **numb**.

18. Your fury has swept *down up***on** me ; *
    your terrors have utterly *de***stroyed** me.

19. They surround me all the day *like a* **flood**, *
    they assail me all *to***geth**er.

20. Friend and neighbor you have tak*en a***way** : *
    my one companion *is* **dark**ness.

21. Glory to the Father, and *to the* **Son**, *
    and to the Ho*ly* **Spir**it :

22. as it was in the beginn*ing, is* **now**, *
    and will be for ever. *A***men**.

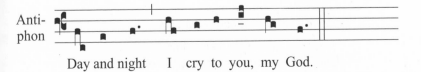

Anti-
phon

Day and night   I   cry to you, my God.

Tempore paschali :

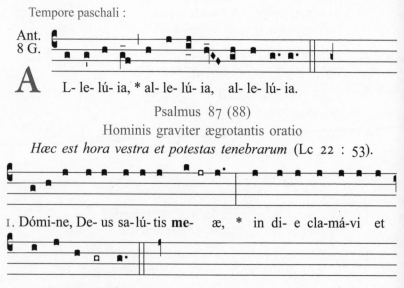

Ant.
8 G.

A L- le- lú- ia, * al- le- lú- ia,   al- le- lú- ia.

Psalmus 87 (88)
Hominis graviter ægrotantis oratio
Hæc est hora vestra et potestas tenebrarum (Lc 22 : 53).

1. Dómi-ne, De- us sa-lú- tis **me**-   æ, * in di- e cla-má-vi   et

no-cte **co**- ram te.

2. Intret in conspéctu tuo orátio **me**a ; *
   inclína aurem tuam ad *precem* **me**a'm.

3. Quia repléta est malis ánima **me**a, *
   et vita mea inférno ap*propin***quá**vit.

4. Æstimátus sum cum descendéntibus in **la**cum, *
   factus sum sicut homo sine *adiu***tó**rio.

5. Inter mórtuos **li**ber, *
   sicut vulneráti dormiéntes *in se***púl**cris ;

6. quorum non es memor **ám**plius, *
   et ipsi de manu tu*a ab***scí**ssi sunt.

7. Posuísti me in lacu inferió**ri**, *
   in tenebrósis et in *umbra* **mor**tis.

8. Super me gravátus est furor **tu**us, *
   et omnes fluctus tuos indu*xísti* **su**per me.

9. Longe fecísti notos meos **a** me, *
   posuísti me abominatió*nem* eis ;

10. conclúsus sum et non e**gré**diar. *
    Oculi mei languérunt præ affli*cti***ó**ne.

Paschaltide :

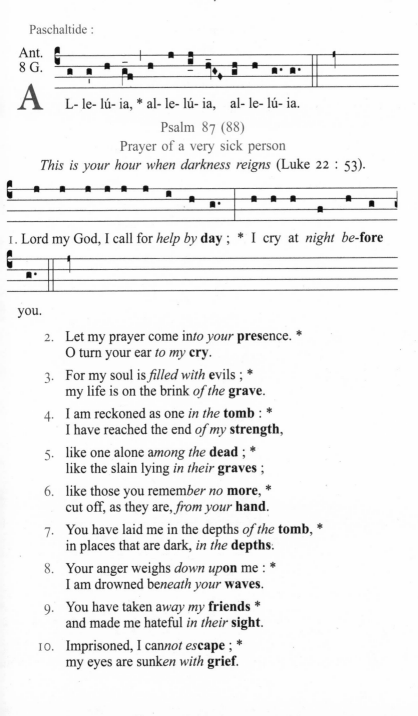

Ant.
8 G.

AL- le- lú- ia, * al- le- lú- ia,   al- le- lú- ia.

Psalm 87 (88)
Prayer of a very sick person
This is your hour when darkness reigns (Luke 22 : 53).

1. Lord my God, I call for *help by* **day** ; * I cry at *night be-***fore**
you.

2. Let my prayer come in*to your* **pres**ence. *
   O turn your ear *to my* **cry**.

3. For my soul is *filled with* **e**vils ; *
   my life is on the brink *of the* **grave**.

4. I am reckoned as one *in the* **tomb** : *
   I have reached the end *of my* **strength**,

5. like one alone a*mong the* **dead** ; *
   like the slain lying *in their* **graves** ;

6. like those you remem*ber no* **more**, *
   cut off, as they are, *from your* **hand**.

7. You have laid me in the depths *of the* **tomb**, *
   in places that are dark, *in the* **depths**.

8. Your anger weighs *down up***on** me : *
   I am drowned be*neath your* **waves**.

9. You have taken a*way my* **friends** *
   and made me hateful *in their* **sight**.

10. Imprisoned, I can*not es***cape** ; *
    my eyes are sunk*en with* **grief**.

11. Clamávi ad te, Dómine, tota **die**, *
    expándi ad te *manus* **me**as.

12. Numquid mórtuis fácies mirabília, *
    aut surgent umbræ et confite*búntur* **ti**bi ?

13. Numquid narrábit áliquis in sepúlcro misericórdiam **tu**am *
    et veritátem tuam in loco per*ditió*nis ?

14. Numquid cognoscéntur in ténebris mirabília **tu**a *
    et iustítia tua in terra ob*livió*nis ?

15. Et ego ad te, Dómine, clam**á**vi, *
    et mane orátio mea præ*véni*et te.

16. Ut quid, Dómine, repéllis ánimam **me**am, *
    abscóndis fáciem *tuam* **a** me ?

17. Pauper sum ego et móriens a iuventúte **me**a ; *
    portávi pavóres tuos et *contur***bá**tus sum.

18. Super me transiérunt iræ **tu**æ, *
    et terróres tui *exci***dé**runt me.

19. Circuiérunt me sicut aqua tota **die**, *
    circumdedé*runt me* **si**mul.

20. Elongásti a me amícum et **pró**ximum, *
    et noti me*i sunt* **té**nebræ.

21. Glória Patri, et **Fí**lio, *
    et Spirí*tui* **San**cto.

22. Sicut erat in princípio, et nunc et **sem**per, *
    et in sǽcula sæcu*lórum*. **A**men.

Tempore paschali :

Anti-phona   Al- le- lú- ia,   al- le- lú- ia,   al- le- lú- ia.

LECTIO BREVIS   *Jer 14 : 9*

TU autem in mé-di- o nostri es, Dómi-ne, † et nomen tu- um

11. I call to you, Lord, all *the day* **long** : *
to you I stretch *out my* **hands**.

12. Will you work your wonders *for the* **dead** ? *
Will the shades *stand and* **praise** you ?

13. Will your love be told *in the* **grave** *
or your faithfulness a*mong the* **dead** ?

14. Will your wonders be known *in the* **dark** *
or your justice in the land *of o*bli**vion** ?

15. As for me, Lord, I call to *you for* **help** : *
in the morning my prayer *comes be*fore you.

16. Lord, why do *you re*ject me ? *
Why do you *hide your* **face** ?

17. Wretched, close to death *from my* **youth**, *
I have borne your trials ; *I am* **numb**.

18. Your fury has swept *down up*on me ; *
your terrors have utter*ly de*stroyed me.

19. They surround me all the day *like a* **flood**, *
they assail me *all to*geth er.

20. Friend and neighbor you have tak*en a*way : *
my one compan*ion is* **dark**ness.

21. Glory to the Father, and *to the* **Son**, *
and to the *Holy* **Spir**it :

22. as it was in the beginn*ing, is* **now**, *
and will be for ev*er. A*men.

Paschaltide :

Anti-
phon

Al- le- lú- ia, al- le- lú- ia, al- le- lú- ia.

READING *Jeremiah 14 : 9*

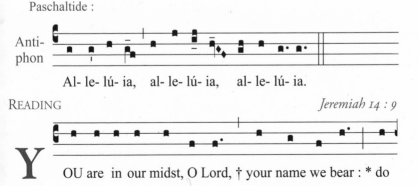

Y OU are in our midst, O Lord, † your name we bear : * do

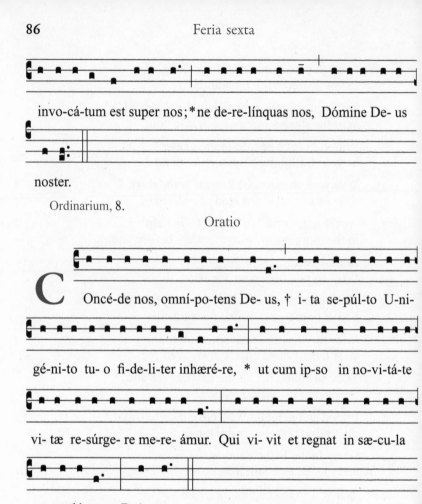

invo-cá-tum est super nos;*ne de-re-línquas nos, Dómine De- us

noster.

Ordinarium, 8.

Oratio

Oncé-de nos, omní-po-tens De- us, † i- ta se-púl-to U-ni-

gé-ni-to tu- o fi-de-li-ter inhæré-re, * ut cum ip-so in no-vi-tá-te

vi- tæ re-súrge- re me-re- ámur. Qui vi- vit et regnat in sæ-cu-la

sæ-cu-ló-rum. ℟. A-men.

Conclusio Horæ et antiphona ad B. M. V., ut in Ordinario, 16.

87

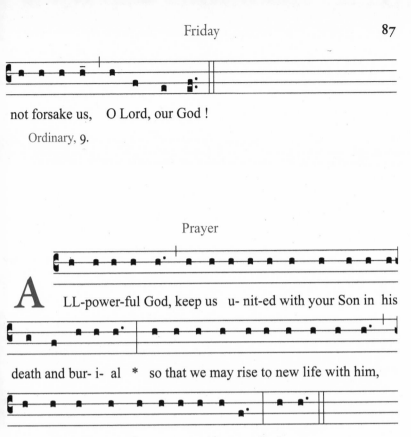

not forsake us,   O Lord, our God !

Ordinary, 9.

Prayer

ALL-power-ful God, keep us   u- nit-ed with your Son in his

death and bur- i- al   *   so that we may rise to new life with him,

who lives and reigns for ev- er and ev- er. ℟ A-men.

Conclusion of the Hour and antiphon to the B. V. M., as in the Ordinary, 17.

III

Hymnarium / Hymnal

1. In Feriis per Annum

Mode 8

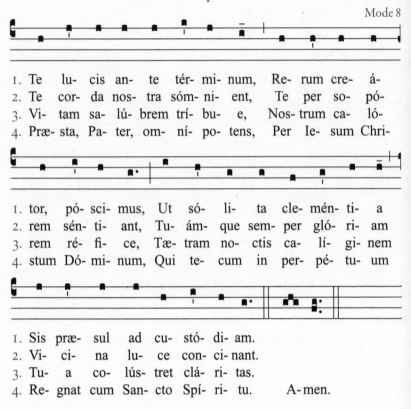

1. Te lu- cis an- te tér- mi- num, Re- rum cre- á-
2. Te cor- da nos- tra sóm- ni- ent, Te per so- pó-
3. Vi- tam sa- lú- brem trí- bu- e, Nos- trum ca- ló-
4. Præ- sta, Pa- ter, om- ní- po- tens, Per Ie- sum Chri-

1. tor, pó- sci- mus, Ut só- li- ta cle- mén- ti- a
2. rem sén- ti- ant, Tu- ám- que sem- per gló- ri- am
3. rem ré- fi- ce, Tæ- tram no- ctis ca- lí- gi- nem
4. stum Dó- mi- num, Qui te- cum in per- pé- tu- um

1. Sis præ- sul ad cu- stó- di- am.
2. Vi- ci- na lu- ce con- ci- nant.
3. Tu- a co- lús- tret clá- ri- tas.
4. Re- gnat cum San- cto Spí- ri- tu.   A- men.

2. On Ferial Days of the Year

Mode 8

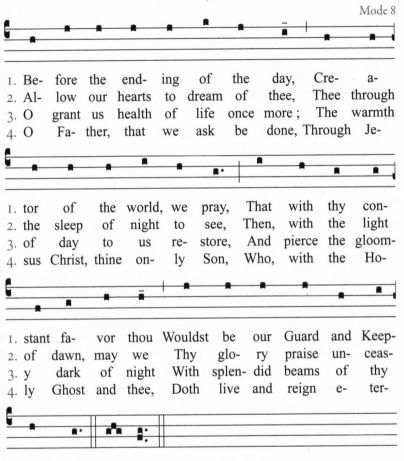

1. Be- fore the end- ing of the day, Cre- a-
2. Al- low our hearts to dream of thee, Thee through
3. O grant us health of life once more; The warmth
4. O Fa- ther, that we ask be done, Through Je-

1. tor of the world, we pray, That with thy con-
2. the sleep of night to see, Then, with the light
3. of day to us re- store, And pierce the gloom-
4. sus Christ, thine on- ly Son, Who, with the Ho-

1. stant fa- vor thou Wouldst be our Guard and Keep-
2. of dawn, may we Thy glo- ry praise un- ceas-
3. y dark of night With splen- did beams of thy
4. ly Ghost and thee, Doth live and reign e- ter-

1. er now.
2. ing- ly.
3. pure light.
4. nal- ly. A- men.

3. In Feriis per Annum

Mode 8

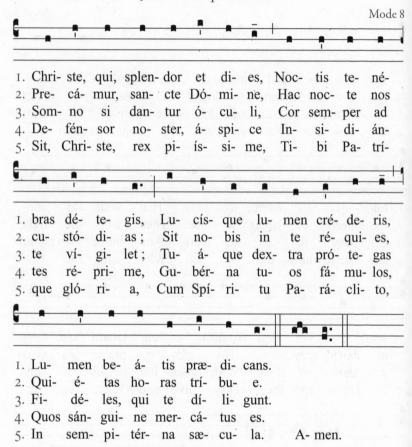

1. Chri- ste, qui, splen- dor et di- es, Noc- tis te- né-
2. Pre- cá- mur, san- cte Dó- mi- ne, Hac noc- te nos
3. Som- no si dan- tur ó- cu- li, Cor sem- per ad
4. De- fén- sor no- ster, á- spi- ce In- si- di- án-
5. Sit, Chri- ste, rex pi- ís- si- me, Ti- bi Pa- trí-

1. bras dé- te- gis, Lu- cís- que lu- men cré- de- ris,
2. cu- stó- di- as ; Sit no- bis in te ré- qui- es,
3. te ví- gi- let ; Tu- á- que dex- tra pró- te- gas
4. tes ré- pri- me, Gu- bér- na tu- os fá- mu- los,
5. que gló- ri- a, Cum Spí- ri- tu Pa- rá- cli- to,

1. Lu- men be- á- tis præ- di- cans.
2. Qui- é- tas ho- ras trí- bu- e.
3. Fi- dé- les, qui te dí- li- gunt.
4. Quos sán- gui- ne mer- cá- tus es.
5. In sem- pi- tér- na sæ- cu- la. A- men.

4. On Ferial Days of the Year

Mode 8

1. O   Christ, who art the Light and Day, Thou driv- est
2. All- ho- ly Lord, we pray to thee, Keep us to-
3. And while the eyes soft slum- ber take, Still be the
4. Yea, our De- fen- der, be thou nigh To bid the
5. To God the Fa- ther let us sing, To God the

1. dark- some night a- way! We know thee as the Light
2. night from dan- ger free; Grant us, dear Lord, in thee
3. heart to thee a- wake; Be thy right hand up- held
4. pow'rs of dark- ness fly; Keep us from sin, and guide
5. Son, most lov- ing King, And e- qual- ly let us

1. of Light, il- lu- mi- nat- ing mor- tal sight.
2. to rest, So be our sleep in qui- et blest.
3. a- bove Thy ser- vants rest- ing in thy love.
4. for good Thy ser- vants pur-chased by thy Blood.
5. a- dore The Spir- it, God for- ev- er- more. A- men.

5. In Dominicis et Memoriis per Annum

Mode 8

1. Te   lu- cis an- te tér- mi- num, Re- rum cre- á-
2. Te   cor- da nos- tra sóm- ni- ent, Te   per so- pó-
3. Vi- tam sa- lú- brem trí- bu- e, Nos- trum ca- ló-
4. Præ- sta, Pa- ter, om- ní- po- tens, Per Ie- sum Chri-

1. tor,   pó- sci- mus, Ut só- li-   ta cle- mén- ti- a
2. rem   sén- ti- ant, Tu- ám- que sem- per gló- ri- am
3. rem   ré- fi- ce, Tæ- tram no- ctis ca- lí- gi- nem
4. stum Dó- mi- num, Qui te- cum in per- pé- tu- um

1. Sis præ- sul ad cu- stó- di- am.
2. Vi- ci- na lu- ce con- ci- nant.
3. Tu- a co- lús- tret clá- ri- tas.
4. Re- gnat cum San- cto Spí- ri- tu.　　A- men.

6. On Sundays and Memorials of the Year

Mode 8

1. Be- fore the end- ing of the day, Cre- a-
2. Al- low our hearts to dream of thee, Thee through
3. O grant us health of life once more ; The warmth
4. O Fa- ther, that we ask be done, Through Je-

1. tor of the world, we pray, That with thy con-
2. the sleep of night to see, Then, with the light
3. of day to us re- store, And pierce the gloom-
4. sus Christ, thine on- ly Son, Who, with the Ho-

1. stant fa- vor thou Wouldst be our Guard and Keep-
2. of dawn, may we Thy glo- ry praise un- ceas-
3. y dark of night With splen- did beams of thy
4. ly Ghost and thee, Doth live and reign e- ter-

1. er now.
2. ing- ly.
3. pure light.
4. nal- ly.   A- men.

7. In Dominicis et Memoriis per Annum

Mode 8

1. Chri- ste, qui, splen- dor et di- es, Noc- tis te- né-
2. Pre- cá- mur, san- cte Dó- mi- ne, Hac noc- te nos
3. Som- no si dan- tur ó- cu- li, Cor sem- per ad
4. De- fén- sor no- ster, á- spi- ce In- si- di- án-
5. Sit, Chri- ste, rex pi- ís- si- me, Ti- bi Pa- trí-

1. bras dé- te- gis, Lu- cís- que lu- men cré- de- ris,
2. cu- stó- di- as ; Sit no- bis in te ré- qui- es,
3. te ví- gi- let ; Tu- á- que dex- tra pró- te- gas
4. tes ré- pri- me, Gu- bér- na tu- os fá- mu- los,
5. que gló- ri- a, Cum Spí- ri- tu Pa- rá- cli- to,

1. Lu- men be- á- tis præ- di- cans.
2. Qui- é- tas ho- ras trí- bu- e.
3. Fi- dé- les, qui te dí- li- gunt.
4. Quos sán- gui- ne mer- cá- tus es.
5. In sem- pi- tér- na sæ- cu- la.   A- men.

8. On Sundays and Memorials of the Year

Mode 8

1. O   Christ, who   art   the   Light and   Day,   Thou   driv- est
2. All-   ho-   ly   Lord,   we   pray   to   thee,   Keep   us   to-
3. And   while   the   eyes   soft   slum- ber   take,   Still   be   the
4. Yea,   our   De-   fen- der,   be   thou   nigh   To   bid   the
5. To   God   the   Fa-   ther   let   us   sing,   To   God   the

1. dark- some night   a-   way !   We   know thee   as   the   Light
2. night   from   dan-   ger   free ;   Grant   us,   dear Lord,   in   thee
3. heart   to   thee   a-   wake ;   Be   thy   right hand   up- held
4. pow'rs   of   dark-   ness   fly ;   Keep   us   from   sin,   and   guide
5. Son,   most   lov-   ing   King,   And   e-   qual-   ly   let   us

1. of   Light,   il-   lu-   mi-   nat-   ing   mor- tal   sight.
2. to   rest,   So   be   our   sleep   in   qui-   et   blest.
3. a-   bove Thy   ser- vants   rest- ing   in   thy   love.
4. for   good Thy   ser- vants   pur- chased   by   thy   Blood.
5. a-   dore The   Spir-   it,   God   for-   ev-   er-   more.   A- men.

9. In Festis per Annum

Mode 4

1. Te lu- cis an- te tér- mi- num, Re- rum cre- á-
2. Te cor- da nos- tra sóm- ni- ent, Te per so- pó-
3. Vi- tam sa- lú- brem trí- bu- e, Nos- trum ca- ló-
4. Præ- sta, Pa- ter, om- ní- po- tens, Per Ie- sum Chri-

1. tor, pó- sci- mus, Ut só- li- ta cle- mén- ti- a
2. rem sén- ti- ant, Tu- ám- que sem- per gló- ri- am
3. rem ré- fi- ce, Tæ- tram no- ctis ca- lí- gi- nem
4. stum Dó- mi- num, Qui te- cum in per- pé- tu- um

1. Sis præ- sul ad cu- stó- di- am.
2. Vi- ci- na lu- ce con- ci- nant.
3. Tu- a co- lús- tret clá- ri- tas.
4. Re- gnat cum San- cto Spí- ri- tu.   A- men.

10. On Feasts of the Year

Mode 2

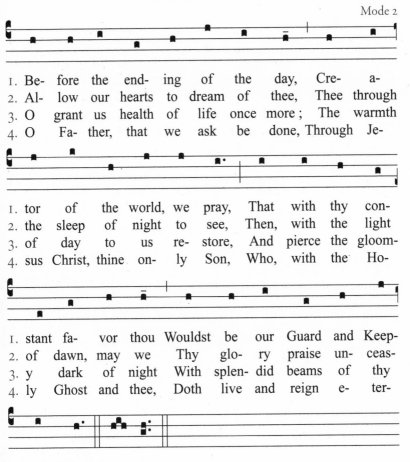

1. Be- fore the end- ing of the day, Cre- a-
2. Al- low our hearts to dream of thee, Thee through
3. O grant us health of life once more; The warmth
4. O Fa- ther, that we ask be done, Through Je-

1. tor of the world, we pray, That with thy con-
2. the sleep of night to see, Then, with the light
3. of day to us re- store, And pierce the gloom-
4. sus Christ, thine on- ly Son, Who, with the Ho-

1. stant fa- vor thou Wouldst be our Guard and Keep-
2. of dawn, may we Thy glo- ry praise un- ceas-
3. y dark of night With splen- did beams of thy
4. ly Ghost and thee, Doth live and reign e- ter-

1. er now.
2. ing- ly.
3. pure light.
4. nal- ly.   A- men.

11. In Festis per Annum

Mode 4

1. Chri- ste, qui, splen- dor et di- es, Noc- tis te- né-
2. Pre- cá- mur, san- cte Dó- mi- ne, Hac noc- te nos
3. Som- no si dan- tur ó- cu- li, Cor sem- per ad
4. De- fén- sor no- ster, á- spi- ce In- si- di- án-
5. Sit, Chri- ste, rex pi- ís- si- me, Ti- bi Pa- trí-

1. bras dé- te- gis, Lu- cís- que lu- men cré- de- ris,
2. cu- stó- di- as; Sit no- bis in te ré- qui- es,
3. te ví- gi- let; Tu- á- que dex- tra pró- te- gas
4. tes ré- pri- me, Gu- bér- na tu- os fá- mu- los,
5. que gló- ri- a, Cum Spí- ri- tu Pa- rá- cli- to,

1. Lu- men be- á- tis præ- di- cans.
2. Qui- é- tas ho- ras trí- bu- e.
3. Fi- dé- les, qui te dí- li- gunt.
4. Quos sán- gui- ne mer- cá- tus es.
5. In sem- pi- tér- na sæ- cu- la. A- men.

12. On Feasts of the Year

Mode 2

1. O   Christ, who   art   the Light and Day,   Thou   driv- est
2. All- ho-   ly Lord, we pray to thee,   Keep   us   to-
3. And while   the eyes soft slum- ber take,   Still   be   the
4. Yea,   our   De- fen- der,   be thou nigh   To   bid the
5. To   God   the Fa- ther let   us   sing,   To   God the

1. dark- some night a- way ! We know thee   as   the Light
2. night from dan- ger free ; Grant us,   dear Lord, in   thee
3. heart   to   thee   a- wake ; Be   thy right hand up- held
4. pow'rs of dark- ness fly ; Keep   us   from sin, and guide
5. Son, most lov- ing King, And   e- qual- ly let   us

1. of Light, il- lu- mi- nat- ing mor- tal   sight.
2. to   rest, So   be   our sleep in   qui- et   blest.
3. a- bove Thy ser- vants rest- ing   in   thy love.
4. for good Thy ser- vants pur-chased by   thy Blood.
5. a- dore The Spir- it, God for- ev- er- more. A-men.

13. Tempore Paschale, in Dominicis et in Festis
(exceptis Festis B. M. V.)

Mode 8

1. Te lu- cis an- te tér- mi- num, Re- rum cre- á-
2. Te cor- da nos- tra sóm- ni- ent, Te per so- pó-
3. Vi- tam sa- lú- brem trí- bu- e, Nos- trum ca- ló-
4. Præ- sta, Pa- ter, om- ní- po- tens, Per Ie- sum Chri-

1. tor, pó- sci- mus, Ut só- li- ta cle- mén- ti-
2. rem sén- ti- ant, Tu- ám- que sem- per gló- ri-
3. rem ré- fi- ce, Tæ- tram no- ctis ca- lí- gi-
4. stum Dó- mi- num, Qui te- cum in per- pé- tu-

1. a Sis præ- sul ad cu- stó- di- am.
2. am Vi- ci- na lu- ce con- ci- nant.
3. nem Tu- a co- lús- tret clá- ri- tas.
4. um Re- gnat cum San- cto Spí- ri- tu. A- men.

14. In Paschaltide, on Sundays and Feasts
(Feasts of the B. V. M. excepted)

Mode 8

1. Be- fore the end- ing of the day, Cre- a-
2. Al- low our hearts to dream of thee, Thee through
3. O grant us health of life once more; The warmth
4. O Fa- ther, that we ask be done, Through Je-

1. tor of the world, we pray, That with thy con-
2. the sleep of night to see, Then, with the light
3. of day to us re- store, And pierce the gloom-
4. sus Christ, thine on- ly Son, Who, with the Ho-

1. stant fa- vor thou Wouldst be our Guard and Keep-
2. of dawn, may we Thy glo- ry praise un- ceas-
3. y dark of night With splen- did beams of thy
4. ly Ghost and thee, Doth live and reign e- ter-

1. er now.
2. ing- ly.
3. pure light.
4. nal- ly.   A- men.

15. Tempore Paschale, in Dominicis et in Festis
(exceptis Festis B. M. V.)

Mode 8

1. Chri- ste, qui, splen- dor et di- es, Noc- tis te- né-
2. Pre- cá- mur, san- cte Dó- mi- ne, Hac noc- te nos
3. Som- no si dan- tur ó- cu- li, Cor sem- per ad
4. De- fén- sor no- ster, á- spi- ce In- si- di- án-
5. Sit, Chri- ste, rex pi- ís- si- me, Ti- bi Pa- trí-

1. bras dé- te- gis, Lu- cís- que lu- men cré- de-
2. cu- stó- di- as; Sit no- bis in te ré- qui-
3. te ví- gi- let; Tu- á- que dex- tra pró- te-
4. tes ré- pri- me, Gu- bér- na tu- os fá- mu-
5. que gló- ri- a, Cum Spí- ri- tu Pa- rá- cli-

1. ris, Lu- men be- á- tis præ- di- cans.
2. es, Qui- é- tas ho- ras trí- bu- e.
3. gas Fi- dé- les, qui te dí- li- gunt.
4. los, Quos sán- gui- ne mer- cá- tus es.
5. to, In sem- pi- tér- na sæ- cu- la. A- men.

16. In Paschaltide. On Sundays and Feasts.
   (Feasts of B. V. M. excepted)

Mode 8

1. O Christ, who art the Light and Day, Thou driv- est
2. All- ho- ly Lord, we pray to thee, Keep us to-
3. And while the eyes soft slum- ber take, Still be the
4. Yea, our De- fen- der, be thou nigh To bid the
5. To God the Fa- ther let us sing, To God the

1. dark- some night a- way ! We know thee as the Light
2. night from dan- ger free ; Grant us, dear Lord, in thee
3. heart to thee a- wake ; Be thy right hand up- held
4. pow'rs of dark- ness fly ; Keep us from sin, and guide
5. Son, most lov- ing King, And e- qual- ly let us

1. of Light, il- lu- mi- nat- ing mor- tal sight.
2. to rest, So be our sleep in qui- et blest.
3. a- bove Thy ser- vants rest- ing in thy love.
4. for good Thy ser- vants pur-chased by thy Blood.
5. a- dore The Spir- it, God for- ev- er- more. A-men.

17. In Festis B. Mariae Virginis
(etiam Tempore Paschale)

Mode 2

1. Te lu- cis an- te tér- mi- num, Re- rum cre- á-
2. Te cor- da nos- tra sóm- ni- ent, Te per so- pó-
3. Vi- tam sa- lú- brem trí- bu- e, Nos- trum ca- ló-
4. Præ- sta, Pa- ter, om- ní- po- tens, Per Ie- sum Chri-

1. tor, pó- sci- mus, Ut só- li- ta cle- mén- ti-
2. rem sén- ti- ant, Tu- ám- que sem- per gló- ri-
3. rem ré- fi- ce, Tæ- tram no- ctis ca- lí- gi-
4. stum Dó- mi- num, Qui te- cum in per- pé- tu-

1. a   Sis præ- sul ad cu- stó- di- am.
2. am   Vi- ci- na lu- ce con- ci- nant.
3. nem Tu- a co- lús- tret clá- ri- tas.
4. um   Re- gnat cum San- cto Spí- ri- tu.   A- men.

Die 15 Septembris. Beatæ Mariæ Virginis Perdolentis, 29.

18. On Feasts of the Blessed Virgin Mary
(even in Paschaltide)

Mode 2

1. Be- fore the end- ing of the day, Cre- a-
2. Al- low our hearts to dream of thee, Thee through
3. O grant us health of life once more ; The warmth
4. O Fa- ther, that we ask be done, Through Je-

1. tor of the world, we pray, That with thy con-
2. the sleep of night to see, Then, with the light
3. of day to us re- store, And pierce the gloom-
4. sus Christ, thine on- ly Son, Who, with the Ho-

1. stant fa- vor thou Wouldst be our Guard and Keep-
2. of dawn, may we Thy glo- ry praise un- ceas-
3. y dark of night With splen- did beams of thy
4. ly Ghost and thee, Doth live and reign e- ter-

1. er now.
2. ing- ly.
3. pure light.
4. nal- ly. A- men.

September 15. Feast of Our Lady of Sorrows, 30.

19. In Festis B. Mariae Virginis
(etiam Tempore Paschale)

Mode 2

1. Chri- ste, qui, splen- dor et di- es, Noc- tis te- né-
2. Pre- cá- mur, san- cte Dó- mi- ne, Hac noc- te nos
3. Som- no si dan- tur ó- cu- li, Cor sem- per ad
4. De- fén- sor no- ster, á- spi- ce In- si- di- án-
5. Sit, Chri- ste, rex pi- ís- si- me, Ti- bi Pa- trí-

1. bras dé- te- gis, Lu- cís- que lu- men cré- de-
2. cu- stó- di- as ; Sit no- bis in te ré- qui-
3. te ví- gi- let ; Tu- á- que dex- tra pró- te-
4. tes ré- pri- me, Gu- bér- na tu- os fá- mu-
5. que gló- ri- a, Cum Spí- ri- tu Pa- rá- cli-

1. ris, Lu- men be- á- tis præ- di- cans.
2. es, Qui é- tas ho- ras trí- bu- e.
3. gas Fi- dé- les, qui te dí- li- gunt.
4. los, Quos sán- gui- ne mer- cá- tus es.
5. to, In sem- pi- tér- na sæ- cu- la. A- men.

Die 15 Septembris. Beatæ Mariæ Virginis Perdolentis, 31.

20. On Feasts of the Blessed Virgin Mary
(even in Paschaltide)

Mode 2

1. O   Christ, who art   the Light and Day,   Thou   driv- est
2. All- ho-   ly Lord, we pray to thee,   Keep   us to-
3. And while   the eyes soft slum- ber take,   Still   be the
4. Yea, our   De- fen- der, be thou nigh   To   bid the
5. To   God   the Fa- ther let us sing,   To   God the

1. dark- some night a-   way ! We know thee   as   the Light
2. night from dan- ger free ; Grant us, dear Lord, in   thee
3. heart to   thee a-   wake ; Be   thy right hand up- held
4. pow'rs of dark- ness fly ; Keep us from sin, and guide
5. Son, most lov- ing King, And e- qual- ly let   us

1. of Light, il- lu- mi- nat- ing mor- tal sight.
2. to   rest, So   be our sleep in   qui- et blest.
3. a- bove Thy ser- vants rest- ing   in   thy love.
4. for good Thy ser- vants pur-chased by   thy Blood.
5. a- dore The Spir- it, God for- ev- er- more. A- men.

September 15. Feast of Our Lady of Sorrows, 32.

21. Tempus Adventus I. Usque ad diem 16 Decembris

Mode 2

1. Te   lu- cis an- te   tér- mi- num, Re- rum cre- á-
2. Te   cor- da nos- tra sóm- ni- ent,   Te   per so- pó-
3. Vi- tam sa- lú- brem trí- bu- e,   Nos- trum ca- ló-
4. Præ- sta, Pa- ter, om- ní- po- tens, Per Ie- sum Chri-

1. tor,   pó- sci- mus, Ut   só-   li-   ta   cle- mén- ti- a
2. rem sén- ti- ant, Tu- ám- que sem- per gló- ri- am
3. rem ré-   fi-   ce,   Tæ- tram no- ctis ca- lí- gi- nem
4. stum Dó- mi- num, Qui te-   cum in   per- pé- tu- um

1. Sis præ- sul   ad   cu- stó- di- am.
2. Vi- ci-   na   lu- ce con- ci- nant.
3. Tu- a   co- lús- tret clá- ri- tas.
4. Re- gnat cum San- cto Spí- ri- tu.　　 A- men.

22. Advent I. Until 16 December

Mode 4

1. Be- fore the end- ing of the day, Cre- a-
2. Al- low our hearts to dream of thee, Thee through
3. O grant us health of life once more ; The warmth
4. O Fa- ther, that we ask be done, Through Je-

1. tor of the world, we pray, That with thy con-
2. the sleep of night to see, Then, with the light
3. of day to us re- store, And pierce the gloom-
4. sus Christ, thine on- ly Son, Who, with the Ho-

1. stant fa- vor thou Wouldst be our Guard and Keep-
2. of dawn, may we Thy glo- ry praise un- ceas-
3. y dark of night With splen- did beams of thy
4. ly Ghost and thee, Doth live and reign e- ter-

1. er now.
2. ing- ly.
3. pure light.
4. nal- ly.   A- men.

23. Tempus Adventus II. Post diem 16 Decembris

Mode 2

1. Chri- ste, qui, splen- dor et di- es, Noc- tis te- né-
2. Pre- cá- mur, san- cte Dó- mi- ne, Hac noc- te nos
3. Som- no si dan- tur ó- cu- li, Cor sem- per ad
4. De- fén- sor no- ster, á- spi- ce In- si- di- án-
5. Sit, Chri- ste, rex pi- ís- si- me, Ti- bi Pa- trí-

1. bras dé- te- gis, Lu- cís- que lu- men cré- de-
2. cu- stó- di- as ; Sit no- bis in te ré- qui-
3. te ví- gi- let ; Tu- á- que dex- tra pró- te-
4. tes ré- pri- me, Gu- bér- na tu- os fá- mu-
5. que gló- ri- a, Cum Spí- ri- tu Pa- rá- cli-

1. ris, Lu- men be- á- tis præ- di- cans.
2. es, Qui é- tas ho- ras trí- bu- e.
3. gas Fi- dé- les, qui te dí- li- gunt.
4. los, Quos sán- gui- ne mer- cá- tus es.
5. to, In sem- pi- tér- na sæ- cu- la. A- men.

24. Advent II. After 16 December

Mode 4

1. O Christ, who art the Light and Day, Thou driv- est
2. All- ho- ly Lord, we pray to thee, Keep us to-
3. And while the eyes soft slum- ber take, Still be the
4. Yea, our De- fen- der, be thou nigh To bid the
5. To God the Fa- ther let us sing, To God the

1. dark- some night a- way ! We know thee as the Light
2. night from dan- ger free ; Grant us, dear Lord, in thee
3. heart to thee a- wake ; Be thy right hand up- held
4. pow'rs of dark- ness fly ; Keep us from sin, and guide
5. Son, most lov- ing King, And e- qual- ly let us

1. of Light, il- lu- mi- nat- ing mor- tal sight.
2. to rest, So be our sleep in qui- et blest.
3. a- bove Thy ser- vants rest- ing in thy love.
4. for good Thy ser- vants pur-chased by thy Blood.
5. a- dore The Spir- it, God for- ev- er- more. A- men.

25. Tempus Nativitatis I. Usque ad Solemnitatem Epiphaniæ

Mode 8

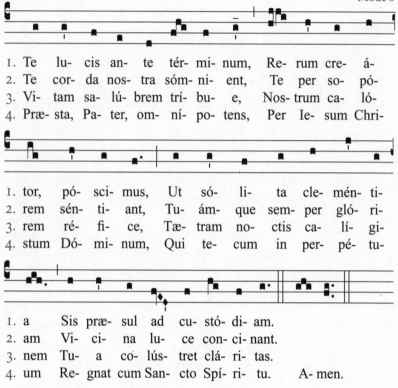

1. Te   lu-   cis an- te tér- mi- num, Re- rum cre- á-
2. Te   cor- da nos- tra sóm- ni- ent, Te   per so-   pó-
3. Vi-   tam   sa- lú- brem trí- bu- e,   Nos- trum ca-   ló-
4. Præ- sta, Pa- ter, om- ní- po- tens, Per Ie- sum Chri-

1. tor,   pó- sci- mus, Ut   só- li- ta cle- mén- ti-
2. rem   sén- ti- ant, Tu- ám- que sem- per gló- ri-
3. rem   ré-   fi- ce,   Tæ- tram no- ctis ca- lí-   gi-
4. stum Dó-   mi- num, Qui te- cum in   per- pé-   tu-

1. a   Sis præ- sul ad   cu- stó- di- am.
2. am   Vi- ci- na   lu- ce con- ci- nant.
3. nem   Tu- a   co- lús- tret clá- ri- tas.
4. um   Re- gnat cum San- cto Spí- ri- tu.   A- men.

Etiam in Festo Corporis Christi.

26. Christmas I. Until the Solemnity of the Epiphany

Mode 8

1. Be- fore the end- ing of the day, Cre- a-
2. Al- low our hearts to dream of thee, Thee through
3. O grant us health of life once more ; The warmth
4. O Fa- ther, that we ask be done, Through Je-

1. tor of the world, we pray, That with thy con-
2. the sleep of night to see, Then, with the light
3. of day to us re- store, And pierce the gloom-
4. sus Christ, thine on- ly Son, Who, with the Ho-

1. stant fa- vor thou Wouldst be our Guard and Keep-
2. of dawn, may we Thy glo- ry praise un- ceas-
3. y dark of night With splen- did beams of thy
4. ly Ghost and thee, Doth live and reign e- ter-

1. er now.
2. ing- ly.
3. pure light.
4. nal- ly.   A- men.

Also on the Feast of Corpus Christi.

27. Tempus Nativitatis II. A Solemnitate Epiphaniæ

Mode 8

1. Chri- ste, qui, splen- dor et di- es, Noc- tis te- né-
2. Pre- cá- mur, san- cte Dó- mi- ne, Hac noc- te nos
3. Som- no si dan- tur ó- cu- li, Cor sem- per ad
4. De- fén- sor no- ster, á- spi- ce In- si- di- án-
5. Sit, Chri- ste, rex pi- ís- si- me, Ti- bi Pa- trí-

1. bras dé- te- gis, Lu- cís- que lu- men cré- de-
2. cu- stó- di- as; Sit no- bis in te ré- qui-
3. te ví- gi- let; Tu- á- que dex- tra pró- te-
4. tes ré- pri- me, Gu- bér- na tu- os fá- mu-
5. que gló- ri- a, Cum Spí- ri- tu Pa- rá- cli-

1. ris, Lu- men be- á- tis præ- di- cans.
2. es, Qui- é- tas ho- ras trí- bu- e.
3. gas Fi- dé- les, qui te dí- li- gunt.
4. los, Quos sán- gui- ne mer- cá- tus es.
5. to, In sem- pi- tér- na sæ- cu- la. A- men.

28. Christmas II. From the Solemnity of the Epiphany

Mode 8

1. O Christ, who art the Light and Day, Thou driv- est
2. All- ho- ly Lord, we pray to thee, Keep us to-
3. And while the eyes soft slum- ber take, Still be the
4. Yea, our De- fen- der, be thou nigh To bid the
5. To God the Fa- ther let us sing, To God the

1. dark- some night a- way! We know thee as the Light
2. night from dan- ger free; Grant us, dear Lord, in thee
3. heart to thee a- wake; Be thy right hand up- held
4. pow'rs of dark- ness fly; Keep us from sin, and guide
5. Son, most lov- ing King, And e- qual- ly let us

1. of Light, il- lu- mi- nat- ing mor- tal sight.
2. to rest, So be our sleep in qui- et blest.
3. a- bove Thy ser- vants rest- ing in thy love.
4. for good Thy ser- vants pur-chased by thy Blood.
5. a- dore The Spir- it, God for- ev- er- more. A-men.

29. Tempus Quadragesimæ
I. Usque ad Sabbatum Hebdomadae Quintæ
Per hebdomadas I, III, et V

Mode 2

1. Te lu- cis an- te tér- mi- num, Re- rum cre- á-
2. Te cor- da nos- tra sóm- ni- ent, Te per so- pó-
3. Vi- tam sa- lú- brem trí- bu- e, Nos- trum ca- ló-
4. Præ- sta, Pa- ter, om- ní- po- tens, Per Ie- sum Chri-

1. tor, pó- sci- mus, Ut só- li- ta cle- mén- ti-
2. rem sén- ti- ant, Tu- ám- que sem- per gló- ri-
3. rem ré- fi- ce, Tæ- tram no- ctis ca- lí- gi-
4. stum Dó- mi- num, Qui te- cum in per- pé- tu-

1. a   Sis præ- sul ad cu- stó- di- am.
2. am Vi- ci- na lu- ce con- ci- nant.
3. nem Tu- a co- lús- tret clá- ri- tas.
4. um Re- gnat cum San- cto Spí- ri- tu.   A- men.

30. Lent

I. Until Saturday of the Fifth Week of Lent
During weeks I, III, and V

Mode 2

1. Be- fore the end- ing of the day, Cre- a-
2. Al- low our hearts to dream of thee, Thee through
3. O grant us health of life once more; The warmth
4. O Fa- ther, that we ask be done, Through Je-

1. tor of the world, we pray, That with thy con-
2. the sleep of night to see, Then, with the light
3. of day to us re- store, And pierce the gloom-
4. sus Christ, thine on- ly Son, Who, with the Ho-

1. stant fa- vor thou Wouldst be our Guard and Keep-
2. of dawn, may we Thy glo- ry praise un- ceas-
3. y dark of night With splen- did beams of thy
4. ly Ghost and thee, Doth live and reign e- ter-

1. er now.
2. ing- ly.
3. pure light.
4. nal- ly. A- men.

31. Tempus Quadragesimæ

I. Usque ad Sabbatum Hebdomadae Quintæ
Per hebdomadas II et IV

Mode 2

1. Chri- ste, qui, splen- dor et di- es, Noc- tis te- né-
2. Pre- cá- mur, san- cte Dó- mi- ne, Hac noc- te nos
3. Som- no si dan- tur ó- cu- li, Cor sem- per ad
4. De- fén- sor no- ster, á- spi- ce In- si- di- án-
5. Sit, Chri- ste, rex pi- ís- si- me, Ti- bi Pa- trí-

1. bras dé- te- gis, Lu- cís- que lu- men cré- de-
2. cu- stó- di- as; Sit no- bis in te ré- qui-
3. te ví- gi- let; Tu- á- que dex- tra pró- te-
4. tes ré- pri- me, Gu- bér- na tu- os fá- mu-
5. que gló- ri- a, Cum Spí- ri- tu Pa- rá- cli-

1. ris, Lu- men be- á- tis præ- di- cans.
2. es, Qui- é- tas ho- ras trí- bu- e.
3. gas Fi- dé- les, qui te dí- li- gunt.
4. los, Quos sán- gui- ne mer- cá- tus es.
5. to, In sem- pi- tér- na sæ- cu- la. A- men.

32. Lent

I. Until Saturday of the Fifth Week of Lent
During weeks II and IV

Mode 2

1. O   Christ, who art the Light and Day,   Thou   driv- est
2. All- ho-   ly Lord, we pray to thee,   Keep   us to-
3. And while the eyes soft slum- ber take,   Still   be the
4. Yea, our De- fen- der, be thou nigh   To   bid the
5. To   God the Fa- ther let us sing,   To   God the

1. dark- some night a-   way ! We know thee   as   the Light
2. night from dan- ger free ; Grant us, dear Lord, in   thee
3. heart to   thee a- wake ; Be   thy right hand up- held
4. pow'rs of   dark- ness fly ; Keep us from sin, and guide
5. Son, most lov- ing King, And e- qual- ly let us

1. of Light, il- lu- mi- nat- ing mor- tal sight.
2. to   rest, So   be   our sleep in   qui- et blest.
3. a- bove Thy ser- vants rest- ing   in   thy love.
4. for good Thy ser- vants pur-chased by   thy Blood.
5. a- dore The Spir- it, God for- ev- er- more. A- men.

33. Tempus Quadragesimæ
II. Hebdomada Sancta

Mode 2

1. Chri- ste, qui, splen- dor et di- es, Noc- tis te- né-
2. Pre- cá- mur, san- cte Dó- mi- ne, Hac noc- te nos
3. Som- no si dan- tur ó- cu- li, Cor sem- per ad
4. De- fén- sor no- ster, á- spi- ce In- si- di- án-
5. Sit, Chri- ste, rex pi- ís- si- me, Ti- bi Pa- trí-

1. bras dé- te- gis, Lu- cís- que lu- men cré- de-
2. cu- stó- di- as ; Sit no- bis in te ré- qui-
3. te ví- gi- let ; Tu- á- que dex- tra pró- te-
4. tes ré- pri- me, Gu- bér- na tu- os fá- mu-
5. que gló- ri- a, Cum Spí- ri- tu Pa- rá- cli-

1. ris, Lu- men be- á- tis præ- di- cans.
2. es, Qui- é- tas ho- ras trí- bu- e.
3. gas Fi- dé- les, qui te dí- li- gunt.
4. los, Quos sán- gui- ne mer- cá- tus es.
5. to, In sem- pi- tér- na sæ- cu- la. A- men.

34. Lent
II. Holy Week

Mode 2

1. O Christ, who art the Light and Day, Thou driv- est
2. All- ho- ly Lord, we pray to thee, Keep us to-
3. And while the eyes soft slum- ber take, Still be the
4. Yea, our De- fen- der, be thou nigh To bid the
5. To God the Fa- ther let us sing, To God the

1. dark- some night a- way ! We know thee as the Light
2. night from dan- ger free ; Grant us, dear Lord, in thee
3. heart to thee a- wake ; Be thy right hand up- held
4. pow'rs of dark- ness fly ; Keep us from sin, and guide
5. Son, most lov- ing King, And e- qual- ly let us

1. of Light, il- lu- mi- nat- ing mor- tal sight.
2. to rest, So be our sleep in qui- et blest.
3. a- bove Thy ser- vants rest- ing in thy love.
4. for good Thy ser- vants pur-chased by thy Blood.
5. a- dore The Spir- it, God for- ev- er- more. A- men.

35. Tempore Paschale
I. Usque ad Ascensionem Domini

Mode 8

1. Ie- su, re- démp- tor sǽ- cu- li, Ver- bum Pa- tris
2. Tu fa- bri- cá- tor óm- ni- um Dis- cré- tor at-
3. Qui fran- gis i- ma tár- ta- ra, Tu nos ab ho-
4. Ut, dum gra- vá- ti cór- po- re Bre- vi ma- né-
5. Ie- su, ti- bi sit gló- ri- a, Qui mor- te vic-

1. al- tís- si- mi, Lux lu- cis in- vi- sí- bi-
2. que tém- po- rum, Fes- sa la- bó- re cór- po-
3. ste lí- be- ra, Ne vá- le- at se- dú- ce-
4. mus tém- po- re, Sic ca- ro no- stra dór- mi-
5. ta prǽ- ni- tes, Cum Pa- tre et al- mo Spí- ri-

1. lis, Cu- stos tu- ó- rum pér- vi- gil.
2. ra No- ctis qui- é- te ré- cre- a.
3. re Tu- o re- démp- tos sán- gui- ne,
4. at Ut mens so- pó- rem né- sci- at.
5. tu, In sem- pi- tér- na sǽ- cu- la.   A- men.

36. In Paschaltide
I. Until the Ascension of the Lord

Mode 8

1. Je-   sus, Re- deem- er   of   the   earth,   The
2. O   Mak- er   blest, thou Lord sub- lime,   Who
3. Thou break- est Hell's fierce pow'rs be- low ; Make
4. Though mor- tal bod- ies tire and strain,   How
5. O   Je-   sus, be   all glo- ry thine,   Who

1. Fa-   ther's Word of heav'n- ly birth, Bright splen-
2. judg- est wise- ly space and time, Though dail-
3. haste to   free us from the foe   Lest by
4. brief- ly   do   we thus re- main ! And while
5. o-   ver death in tri- umph shine, Whom with

1. dor   of   the un- seen Light, Pro- tect thine
2. y   toil hath worn us through, Our wea- ry
3. his   craf- ty lures be caught Those whom thy
4. these bod- ies lie a-   sleep, Grant that our
5. the   Fa- ther we a-   dore And Ho-   ly

1. own   through- out this night.
2. frame this   night re- new.
3. Pre- cious Blood hath bought.
4. minds their watch may keep.
5. Ghost for   ev- er- more.   A- men.

37. Tempore Paschale
II. Post Ascensionem Domini

Mode 4

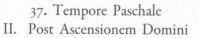

1. Ie- su, re- démp- tor sǽ- cu- li, Ver- bum Pa- tris
2. Tu fa- bri- cá- tor óm- ni- um Dis- cré- tor at-
3. Qui fran- gis i- ma tár- ta- ra, Tu nos ab ho-
4. Ut, dum gra- vá- ti cór- po- re Bre- vi ma- né-
5. Ie- su, ti- bi sit gló- ri- a, Qui mor- te vic-

1. al- tís- si- mi, Lux lu- cis in- vi- sí- bi-
2. que tém- po- rum, Fes- sa la- bó- re cór- po-
3. ste lí- be- ra, Ne vá- le- at se- dú- ce-
4. mus tém- po- re, Sic ca- ro no- stra dór- mi-
5. ta prǽ- ni- tes, Cum Pa- tre et al- mo Spí- ri-

1. lis, Cu- stos tu- ó- rum pér- vi- gil.
2. ra No- ctis qui- é- te ré- cre- a.
3. re Tu- o re- démp- tos sán- gui- ne,
4. at Ut mens so- pó- rem né- sci- at.
5. tu, In sem- pi- tér- na sǽ- cu- la.   A- men.

38. In Paschaltide
II. After the Ascension of the Lord

Mode 4

1. Je- sus, Re- deem- er of the earth, The
2. O Mak- er blest, Thou Lord sub- lime, Who
3. Thou break- est Hell's fierce pow'rs be- low; Make
4. Though mor- tal bod- ies tire and strain, How
5. O Je- sus, be all glo- ry thine, Who

1. Fa- ther's Word of heav'n- ly birth, Bright splen-
2. judg- est wise- ly space and time, Though dail-
3. haste to free us from the foe Lest by
4. brief- ly do we thus re- main! And while
5. o- ver death in tri- umph shine, Whom with

1. dor of the un- seen Light, Pro- tect thine
2. y toil hath worn us through, Our wea- ry
3. his craf- ty lures be caught Those whom thy
4. these bod- ies lie a- sleep, Grant that our
5. the Fa- ther we a- dore And Ho- ly

1. own through- out this night.
2. frame this night re- new.
3. Pre- cious Blood hath bought.
4. minds their watch may keep.
5. Ghost for ev- er- more. A- men.

39. Dominica Pentecostes

Mode 1

1. Ie-   su,   re- démp- tor sǽ- cu- li,   Ver- bum Pa-   tris
2. Tu   fa- bri- cá-   tor óm- ni- um   Dis- cré- tor at-
3. Qui fran- gis i-   ma tár- ta- ra,   Tu nos ab ho-
4. Ut, dum gra- vá- ti cór- po- re   Bre- vi ma- né-
5. Ie-   su,   ti- bi sit gló- ri- a,   Qui mor- te vic-

1. al- tís- si- mi, Lux lu- cis in- vi- sí- bi-
2. que tém- po- rum, Fes- sa la- bó- re cór- po-
3. ste lí- be- ra, Ne vá- le- at se- dú- ce-
4. mus tém- po- re, Sic ca- ro no- stra dór- mi-
5. ta prǽ- ni- tes, Cum Pa- tre͜ et al- mo Spí- ri-

1. lis, Cu- stos tu- ó- rum pér- vi- gil.
2. ra No- ctis qui- é- te ré- cre- a.
3. re Tu- o re- démp- tos sán- gui- ne,
4. at Ut mens so- pó- rem né- sci- at.
5. tu, In sem- pi- tér- na sǽ- cu- la.   A- men.

Vel : Te lucis ante terminum, 43.

40. Pentecost Sunday

Mode 1

1. Je- sus, Re- deem- er of the earth, The
2. O Mak- er blest, Thou Lord sub- lime, Who
3. Thou break- est Hell's fierce pow'rs be- low; Make
4. Though mor- tal bod- ies tire and strain, How
5. O Je- sus, be all glo- ry thine, Who

1. Fa- ther's Word of heav'n- ly birth, Bright splen-
2. judg- est wise- ly space and time, Though dail-
3. haste to free us from the foe Lest by
4. brief- ly do we thus re- main! And while
5. o- ver death in tri- umph shine, Whom with

1. dor of the un- seen Light, Pro- tect thine
2. y toil hath worn us through, Our weak- ened
3. his craf- ty lures be caught Those whom thy
4. these bod- ies lie a- sleep, Grant that our
5. the Fa- ther we a- dore And Ho- ly

1. own through- out this night.
2. frame this night re- new.
3. Pre- cious Blood hath bought.
4. minds their watch may keep.
5. Ghost for ev- er- more. A- men.

Or : Before the ending of the day, 44.

41. Feria VI post dominicam II post Pentecosten
Sacratissimi Cordis Iesu

Mode 3

1. Te lu- cis an- te tér- mi- num, Re- rum cre- á-
2. Te cor- da nos- tra sóm- ni- ent, Te per so- pó-
3. Vi- tam sa- lú- brem trí- bu- e, Nos- trum ca- ló-
4. Præ- sta, Pa- ter, om- ní- po- tens, Per Ie- sum Chri-

1. tor, pó- sci- mus, Ut só- li- ta cle- mén- ti-
2. rem sén- ti- ant, Tu- ám- que sem- per gló- ri-
3. rem ré- fi- ce, Tæ- tram no- ctis ca- lí- gi-
4. stum Dó- mi- num, Qui te- cum in per- pé- tu-

1. a Sis præ- sul ad cu- stó- di- am.
2. am Vi- ci- na lu- ce con- ci- nant.
3. nem Tu- a co- lús- tret clá- ri- tas.
4. um Re- gnat cum San- cto Spí- ri- tu. A- men.

42. Friday after the Second Sunday after Pentecost
Most Sacred Heart of Jesus

Mode 3

1. Be- fore the end- ing of the day, Cre- a-
2. Al- low our hearts to dream of thee, Thee through
3. O grant us health of life once more ; The warmth
4. O Fa- ther, that we ask be done, Through Je-

1. tor of the world, we pray, That with thy con-
2. the sleep of night to see, Then, with the light
3. of day to us re- store, And pierce the gloom-
4. sus Christ, thine on- ly Son, Who, with the Ho-

1. stant fa- vor thou Wouldst be our Guard and Keep-
2. of dawn, may we Thy glo- ry praise un- ceas-
3. y dark of night With splen- did beams of thy
4. ly Ghost and thee, Doth live and reign e- ter-

1. er now.
2. ing- ly.
3. pure light.
4. nal- ly.   A- men.

43. Dominica XXXIV per annum
Domini Nostri Iesu Christi Universorum Regis

Mode 1

1. Te lu- cis an- te tér- mi- num, Re- rum cre- á-
2. Te cor- da nos- tra sóm- ni- ent, Te per so- pó-
3. Vi- tam sa- lú- brem trí- bu- e, Nos- trum ca- ló-
4. Præ- sta, Pa- ter, om- ní- po- tens, Per Ie- sum Chri-

1. tor, pó- sci- mus, Ut só- li- ta cle- mén- ti-
2. rem sén- ti- ant, Tu- ám- que sem- per gló- ri-
3. rem ré- fi- ce, Tæ- tram no- ctis ca- lí- gi-
4. stum Dó- mi- num, Qui te- cum in per- pé- tu-

1. a Sis præ- sul ad cu- stó- di- am.
2. am Vi- ci- na lu- ce con- ci- nant.
3. nem Tu- a co- lús- tret clá- ri- tas.
4. um Re- gnat cum San- cto Spí- ri- tu.   A- men.

44. Thirty-fourth Sunday of the Year
Our Lord Jesus Christ King

Mode 1

[musical notation]

1. Be- fore the end- ing of the day, Cre- a-
2. Al- low our hearts to dream of thee, Thee through
3. O grant us health of life once more ; The warmth
4. O Fa- ther, that we ask be done, Through Je-

[musical notation]

1. tor of the world, we pray, That with thy con-
2. the sleep of night to see, Then, with the light
3. of day to us re- store, And pierce the gloom-
4. sus Christ, thine on- ly Son, Who, with the Ho-

[musical notation]

1. stant fa- vor thou Wouldst be our Guard and Keep-
2. of dawn, may we Thy glo- ry praise un- ceas-
3. y dark of night With splen- did beams of thy
4. ly Ghost and thee, Doth live and reign e- ter-

[musical notation]

1. er now.
2. ing- ly.
3. pure light.
4. nal- ly.   A- men.